Ruth Shirl...
(otherwise Ruthie)

A momento of your
first trip Colby, Jr. College
Dad
Apr. 19. 1939.

THE POEMS AND PLAYS OF
JOHN MASEFIELD
———
POEMS

THE MACMILLAN COMPANY
NEW YORK · BOSTON · CHICAGO · DALLAS
ATLANTA · SAN FRANCISCO

MACMILLAN & CO., Limited
LONDON · BOMBAY · CALCUTTA
MELBOURNE

THE MACMILLAN CO. OF CANADA, Ltd.
TORONTO

John Masefield.

THE
POEMS AND PLAYS OF
JOHN MASEFIELD

VOLUME ONE

POEMS

New York

THE MACMILLAN COMPANY

1918

PREFACE

I do not remember writing verses in my childhood; I made many but did not write them down. I remember writing two poems when I was nine years and nine months old, one about a pony called Gypsy, the other about a Red Indian. Two or three years later I wrote a few more poems, a birthday poem to one of my brothers, a poem about a horse, a satire on a clergyman, and some fragments in imitation of Sir Walter Scott.

Early verses are nearly always reflections from early reading. I remember my early reading fairly clearly. The first poems which moved me were these:

1. A poem about An Old White Horse, in some way connected with the 10th Hussars in the Soudan Campaign. This poem appeared in a daily paper, perhaps *The Standard*, perhaps *The Daily Telegraph*, during or just after, the Soudan Campaign.

2. A poem in *Good Words* —— ——, *A Friend*, by Adeline Sargent. I liked this poem quite as much for its little engraved illustrations as for its words.

3. The poems of Longfellow, especially *Hiawatha*.

4. *The Ingoldsby Legends*.

5. *The Wild Swan* by Tennyson, "*I remember, I remember,*" by Thomas Hood. I had to learn these by heart for my Mother. I thought them beautiful at the time and think so still.

6. Du Maurier's *Ballad of Camelot*, in *Punch* for (I think) 1864. I did not understand the words of this poem, but the pre-Raphaelite engravings which illustrated it, moved me deeply.

I do not remember any other poems which gave me pleasure

during my childhood, except one or two of the lyrics of William Allingham.

When I was ten years old, I began to read Sir Walter Scott's poems, Percy's *Reliques of Ancient Poetry*, and a little red *Anthology of English Poetry* which contained some good poems. I read most of these poems many times with enjoyment. At the age of 14, I began to read Macaulay's *Lays of Ancient Rome*, which put an end to my liking for Scott, as they were more modern and more direct. I wrote some imitations of the Lays, they were then my favourite poems, but I had a very great fondness for two other poems, *The Braes of Yarrow*, by Wm. Hamilton of Blairgowrie, and *The Voyage of Maeldune*, by Tennyson. At this time I had read none of the great poems of the English tongue, except two or three lyrics by Shakespeare "When Dick the Shepherd, etc.," and Milton's *L'Allegro* and *Il Penseroso*. As I was then being trained for a sea life I had little opportunity for reading poetry.

When I was 16, I wrote some poems about life at sea. Two of these were short poems, one describing a man falling from a loft, and one, the miseries of what was then (nearly thirty years ago) a harsh profession. I remember writing one long poem, describing the incidents of a voyage, but this was never finished. I read little and wrote little between the ages of 14 and 18.

I did not begin to read poetry with passion and system until 1896. I was living then in Yonkers, N. Y. (at 8 Maple Street), Chaucer was the poet, and the *Parliament of Fowls* the poem, of my conversion. I read the *Parliament* all through one Sunday afternoon, with the feeling that I had been kept out of my inheritance and had then suddenly entered upon it, and had found it a new world of wonder and delight. I had never realized, until then, what poetry could be. After that Sunday afternoon, I read many poets (Chaucer, Keats, Shelley, Milton and Shakespeare, more than others) and wrote many imitations of them. About a year later, when I was living in London, I wrote two or three of the verses now printed in *Salt Water Ballads*.

For the next few years I wrote little. I wrote the rest of the verses in *Salt Water Ballads* in about six weeks, at Christmas time, 1901, in a London lodging. A few poems and ballads were printed in 1903–4. After these, I published no more verses for eight years, except some choruses in a play and perhaps half a dozen contributions to magazines and journals.

In May and June, 1911, I wrote the narrative, *The Everlasting Mercy*, at Great Hampden, where I was then staying. I wished to write of conversion, of a turbulent man suddenly made gentle. The scene of the poem is laid at a place called Ledbury, in Herefordshire, in the Western Midlands. When I had finished the story, I felt that I ought to write something unlike it, that as I had shewn one thing, which often happens in life, the seemingly unworthy man made happy, for no apparent reason, so I ought to write the opposite, the seemingly worthy woman made heartbroken, for no apparent reason. I began the second tale, *The Widow in the Bye Street*, at Capel Curig in North Wales, in June, and finished it at Great Hampden in July, 1911. Each of these two tales was written in three weeks and three days. The other poems, *Ships*, and *Biography* were written later in the same Summer in the North of Ireland.

In 1912, I wrote the stories *Dauber* and *The Daffodil Fields*, mostly at Great Hampden. The character of Dauber was partly suggested by a man once known to me, who fell from the lower topgallant yard of a ship, called (if I remember rightly) the *Westlands*, and was killed. This was many years ago. He would not have become a good painter, but he had courage and the will to succeed, and these things are in themselves a kind of genius. I found the plot of *The Daffodil Fields* story in a footnote to Sir W. Mackenzie's *Travels in Iceland*. It is there stated that the events described in the tale happened in Iceland in the Eleventh Century.

Early in 1913, I wrote the poem, *The Wanderer*, about a very beautiful but unlucky ship which I had seen years before in the Mersey. *The Wanderer* stays in my mind as one of the loveliest things ever made by men. She is still freshly remembered in Liverpool, and many men who sailed in her must be still alive. She was run down and sunk (I believe in daylight) in the Elbe near Hamburg about 1897. After *The Wanderer* (in 1913) I wrote *The River*, a tale current among sailors as having happened in the Hugli River, not far from Calcutta, at some unknown time, not very long ago. I have had versions of the tale from three or four sailors, all agreeing, that the ship struck, had her fo'csle jammed, and was held on the quicksand for some time, but at last sank, with all her forward hands except one man who dived through a manhole into the hold, as I have described, and by luck or Fate reached the fore hatch and escaped. In this year I wrote a draft of the story of Juan Manuel Rosas, the dictator of the Argentine.

In 1914, before the war began, I wrote two plays in verse. When the war began, I wrote some verses, called *August, 1914*, which at the time I thought of calling *Lollingdon Hill*, from the little chalk hill on which they were written. Some other verses were written in the first months of the war, including some of the sonnets; but that was the end of my verse-writing. Perhaps, when the war is over and the mess of the war is cleaned up and the world is at some sort of peace, there may be leisure and feeling for verse-making. One may go back to that life in the mind, in which the eyes of the mind see butterflies and petals of blossoms blowing from the unseen world of beauty into this world. In that life, if it comes again, one may not be too old to look towards that world of beauty, and to see it and tell of it.

> There is continuall Spring, and harvest there
> Continuall, both meeting at one time . . .

And though, before this war, when I was writing, I saw little enough of that land, life is kind and wise and generous, and perhaps, in that new time, I may see more, and be able to tell more, and know in fuller measure what the poets of my race have known, about that world and those people existing forever over in England, the images of what England and the English may become, or spiritually are. Chaucer and Shakespeare, some lines of Gray, of Keats, of Wordsworth and of William Morris, the depth, force, beauty and tenderness of the English mind, are inspiration enough, and school enough and star enough to urge and guide in any night of the soul, however wayless from our blindness or black from our passions and our follies.

JOHN MASEFIELD.

CONTENTS

SALT-WATER BALLADS

CONTENTS

MISCELLANEOUS POEMS

(From "The Story of a Round House")

CONTENTS

CONTENTS

SALT–WATER BALLADS

Some of this book was written in my boyhood, all of it in my youth; it is now re-issued, much as it was when first published nearly eleven years ago.   J. M.
9*th June*, 1913

A CONSECRATION

Not of the princes and prelates with periwigged charioteers
Riding triumphantly laurelled to lap the fat of the years,—
Rather the scorned—the rejected—the men hemmed in with the
    spears;

The men of the tattered battalion which fights till it dies,
Dazed with the dust of the battle, the din and the cries,
The men with the broken heads and the blood running into their eyes.

Not the be-medalled Commander, beloved of the throne,
Riding cock-horse to parade when the bugles are blown,
But the lads who carried the koppie and cannot be known.

Not the ruler for me, but the ranker, the tramp of the road,
The slave with the sack on his shoulders pricked on with the goad,
The man with too weighty a burden, too weary a load.

The sailor, the stoker of steamers, the man with the clout,
The chantyman bent at the halliards putting a tune to the shout,
The drowsy man at the wheel and the tired lookout.

Others may sing of the wine and the wealth and the mirth,
The portly presence of potentates goodly in girth;—
Mine be the dirt and the dross, the dust and scum of the earth!

THEIRS be the music, the colour, the glory, the gold;
Mine be a handful of ashes, a mouthful of mould.
Of the maimed, of the halt and the blind in the rain and the cold—
Of these shall my songs be fashioned, my tales be told.   AMEN.

[3]

THE YARN OF THE "LOCH ACHRAY"

The "Loch Achray" was a clipper tall
With seven-and-twenty hands in all.
Twenty to hand and reef and haul,
A skipper to sail and mates to bawl
" Tally on to the tackle-fall,
Heave now 'n' start her, heave 'n' pawl!'
     Hear the yarn of a sailor,
     An old yarn learned at sea.

Her crew were shipped and they said "Farewell,
So-long, my Tottie, my lovely gell;
We sail to-day if we fetch to hell,
It's time we tackled the wheel a spell."
     Hear the yarn of sailor,
     An old yarn learned at sea.

The dockside loafers talked on the quay
The day that she towed down to sea:
" Lord, what a handsome ship she be!
Cheer her, sonny boys, three times three!"
And the dockside loafers gave her a shout
As the red-funnelled tug-boat towed her out;
They gave her a cheer as the custom is,
And the crew yelled "Take our loves to Liz—
Three cheers, bullies, for old Pier Head
'N' the bloody stay-at-homes!" they said.
     Hear the yarn of a sailor,
     An old yarn learned at sea.

THE YARN OF THE "LOCH ACHRAY"

In the grey of the coming on of night
She dropped the tug at the Tuskar Light,
'N' the topsails went to the topmast head
To a chorus that fairly awoke the dead.
She trimmed her yards and slanted South
With her royals set and a bone in her mouth.
      Hear the yarn of a sailor,
      An old yarn learned at sea.

She crossed the Line and all went well,
They ate, they slept, and they struck the bell
And I give you a gospel truth when I state
The crowd didn't find any fault with the Mate,
But one night off the River Plate.
      Hear the yarn of a sailor,
      An old yarn learned at sea.

It freshened up till it blew like thunder
And burrowed her deep lee-scuppers under.
The old man said, "I mean to hang on
Till her canvas busts or her sticks are gone"—
Which the blushing looney did, till at last
Overboard went her mizzen-mast.
      Hear the yarn of a sailor,
      An old yarn learned at sea.

Then a fierce squall struck the "Loch Achray"
And bowed her down to her water-way;
Her main-shrouds gave and her forestay,
And a green sea carried her wheel away;

Ere the watch below had time to dress.
She was cluttered up in a blushing mess
    Hear the yarn of a sailor,
      An old yarn learned at sea.

She couldn't lay-to nor yet pay-off,
And she got swept clean in the bloody trough;
Her masts were gone, and afore you knowed
She filled by the head and down she goed.
Her crew made seven-and-twenty dishes
For the big jack-sharks and the little fishes,
And over their bones the water swishes.
    Hear the yarn of a sailor,
      An old yarn learned at sea.

The wives and girls they watch in the rain
For a ship as won't come home again.
"I reckon it's them head-winds," they say,
"She'll be home to-morrow, if not to-day.
I'll just nip home 'n' I'll air the sheets
'N' buy the fixins 'n' cook the meats
As my man likes 'n' as my man eats."

So home they goes by the windy streets,
Thinking their men are homeward bound
With anchors hungry for English ground,
And the bloody fun of it is, they're drowned!
    Hear the yarn of a sailor,
      An old yarn learned at sea.

SING A SONG O' SHIPWRECK

He lolled on a bollard, a sun-burned son of the sea,
With ear-rings of brass and a jumper of dungaree,
"'N' many a queer lash-up have I seen," says he.

" But the toughest hooray o' the racket," he says, " I'll be sworn,
'N' the roughest traverse I worked since the day I was born,
Was a packet o' Sailor's Delight as I scoffed in the seas o' the
        Horn.

" All day long in the calm she had rolled to the swell,
Rolling through fifty degrees till she clattered her bell:
'N' then came snow, 'n' a squall, 'n' a wind was colder 'n hell.

"It blew like the Bull of Barney, a beast of a breeze,
'N' over the rail come the cold green lollopin' seas,
'N' she went ashore at the dawn on the Ramirez.

"She was settlin' down by the stern when I got to the deck,
Her waist was a smother o' sea as was up to your neck,
'N' her masts were gone, 'n' her rails, 'n' she was a wreck.

"We rigged up a tackle, a purchase, a sort of a shift,
To hoist the boats off o' the deck-house and get them adrift,
When her stern gives a sickenin' settle, her bows give a lift,

"'N' comes a crash of green water as sets me afloat
With freezing fingers clutching the keel of a boat—
The bottom-up whaler—'n' that was the juice of a note.

[7]

"Well, I clambers acrost o' the keel 'n' I gets me secured,
When I sees a face in the white o' the smother to looard,
So I gives 'im a 'and, 'n' be shot if it wasn't the stooard!

"So he climbs up forrard o' me, 'n' 'thanky,' a' says,
'N' we sits 'n' shivers 'n' freeze to the bone wi' the sprays,
'N' *I* sings 'Abel Brown,' 'n' the stooard he prays.

"Wi' never a dollop to sup nor a morsel to bite,
The lips of us blue with the cold 'n' the heads of us light,
Adrift in a Cape Horn sea for a day 'n' a night.

"'N' then the stooard goes dotty 'n' puts a tune to his lip,
'N' moans about Love like a dern old hen wi' the pip—
(I sets no store upon stooards—they ain't no use on a ship).

"'N' 'mother,' the looney cackles, 'come 'n' put Willy to bed!'
So I says 'Dry up, or I'll fetch you a crack o' the head ';
'The kettle's a-bilin',' he answers, ' 'n' I'll go butter the bread.'

"'N' he falls to singin' some slush about clinkin' a can,
'N' at last he dies, so he does, 'n' I tells you, Jan,
I was glad when he did, for he weren't no fun for a man.

"So he falls forrard, he does, 'n' he closes his eye,
'N' quiet he lays 'n' quiet I leaves him lie,
'N' I was alone with his corp, 'n' the cold green sea and the sky.

"'N' then I dithers, I guess, for the next as I knew
Was the voice of a mate as was sayin' to one of the crew,
'Easy, my son, wi' the brandy, be shot if he ain't comin'-to!'"

BURIAL PARTY

"He's deader 'n nails," the fo'c's'le said, "'n' gone to his long
  sleep;"
"'N' about his corp," said Tom to Dan, "d'ye think his corp'll
  keep
Till the day's done, 'n' the work's through, 'n' the ebb's upon
  the neap?"

"He's deader 'n nails," said Dan to Tom, "'n' I wish his
  sperrit j'y;
He spat straight 'n' he steered true, but listen to me, say I,
Take 'n' cover 'n' bury him now, 'n' I'll take 'n' tell you why.

"It's a rummy rig of a guffy's yarn, 'n' the juice of a rummy
  note,
But if you buries a corp at night, it takes 'n' keeps afloat,
For its bloody soul's afraid o' the dark 'n' sticks within the
  throat.

"'N' all the night till the grey o' the dawn the dead 'un has
  to swim
With a blue 'n' beastly Will o' the Wisp a-burnin' over him,
With a herring, maybe, a-scoffin' a toe or a shark a-chewin'
  a limb.

"'N' all the night the shiverin' corp it has to swim the sea,
With its shudderin' soul inside the throat (where a soul's no
  right to be),
Till the sky's grey 'n' the dawn's clear, 'n' then the sperrit's
  free.

"Now Joe was a man was right as rain. I'm sort of sore for
Joe.
'N' if we bury him durin' the day, his soul can take 'n' go;
So we'll dump his corp when the bell strikes 'n' we can get below.

"I'd fairly hate for him to swim in a blue 'n' beastly light,
With his shudderin' soul inside of him a-feelin' the fishes bite,
So over he goes at noon, say I, 'n' he shall sleep to-night."

BILL

He lay dead on the cluttered deck and stared at the cold skies,
With never a friend to mourn for him nor a hand to close his
eyes:
"Bill, he's dead," was all they said; "he's dead, 'n' there he
lies."

The mate came forrard at seven bells and spat across the rail:
"Just lash him up wi' some holystone in a clout o' rotten sail,
'N', rot ye, get a gait on ye, ye're slower'n a bloody snail!"

When the rising moon was a copper disc and the sea was a
strip of steel,
We dumped him down to the swaying weeds ten fathom beneath the keel.
"It's rough about Bill," the fo'c's'le said, "we'll have to stand
his wheel."

FEVER SHIP

There'll be no weepin' gells ashore when *our* ship sails,
Nor no crews cherrin' us, standin' at the rails,
'N' no Blue Peter a-foul the royal stay,
For we've the Yellow Fever—Harry died to-day.—
    It's cruel when a fo'c's'le gets the fever!

'N' Dick has got the fever-shakes, 'n' look what I was told
(I went to get a sack for him to keep from the cold):
"Sir, can I have a sack?" I says, "for Dick 'e's fit to die."
"Oh, sack be shot!" the skipper says, "jest let the rotter lie!"—
    It's cruel when a fo'c's'le gets the fever!

It's a cruel port is Santos, and a hungry land,
With rows o' graves already dug in yonder strip of sand,
'N' Dick is hollerin' up the hatch, 'e says e's' goin' blue,
His pore teeth are chattering, 'n' what's a man to do?—
    It's cruel when a fo'c's'le gets the fever!

FEVER–CHILLS

He tottered out of the alleyway with cheeks the colour of paste,
And shivered a spell and mopped his brow with a clout of cotton
    waste:
"I've a lick of fever-chills," he said, "'n' my inside it's green,
But I'd be as right as rain," he said, "if I had some quinine,—
    But there ain't no quinine for us poor sailor-men.

"But them there passengers," he said, "if they gets fever-chills,
There's brimmin' buckets o' quinine for them, 'n' bulgin'
    crates o' pills,
'N' a doctor with Latin 'n' drugs 'n' all—enough to sink a town,
'N' they lies quiet in their blushin' bunks 'n' mops their gruel
    down,—
    But their ain't none o' them fine ways for us poor sailor-
    men.

"But the Chief comes forrard 'n' he says, says he, "I gives you
    a straight tip:
Come none o' your Cape Horn fever lays aboard o' this yer ship.
On wi' your rags o' duds, my son, 'n' aft, 'n' down the hole:
The best cure known for fever-chills is shovelling bloody coal."
    It's *hard*, my son, that's what it is, for us poor sailor-men."

ONE OF THE BO'SUN'S YARNS

Loafin' around in Sailor Town, a-bluin' o' my advance,
I met a derelict donkeyman who led me a merry dance,
Till he landed me 'n' bleached me fair in the bar of a rum-
    saloon,
'N' there he spun me a juice of a yarn to this-yer brand of tune.

"It's a solemn gospel, mate," he says, "but a man as ships
    aboard
A steamer-tramp, he gets his whack of the wonders of the Lord—
Such as roaches crawlin' over his bunk, 'n' snakes inside his
    bread,
And work by night and work by day enough to strike him dead.

"But that there's by the way," says he; "the yarn I'm goin'
to spin
Is about myself 'n' the life I led in the last ship I was in,
The 'Esmeralda,' casual tramp, from Hull towards the Hook,
Wi' one o' the brand o' Cain for mate 'n' a human mistake for
cook.

"We'd a week or so of dippin' around in a wind from outer hell,
With a fathom or more of broken sea at large in the forrard well,
Till our boats were bashed and bust and broke and gone to
Davy Jones,
'N' then come white Atlantic fog as chilled us to the bones.

"We slowed her down and started the horn and watch and
watch about,
We froze the marrow in all our bones a-keepin' a good look-out,
'N' the ninth night out, in the middle watch, I woke from a
pleasant dream,
With the smash of a steamer ramming our plates a point abaft
the beam.

"'Twas cold and dark when I fetched the deck, dirty 'n' cold
'n' thick,
'N' there was a feel in the way she rode as fairly turned me
sick;—
She was settlin', listin' quickly down, 'n' I heard the mates
a-cursin,'
'N' I heard the wash 'n' the grumble-grunt of a steamer's
screws reversin'.

"She was leavin' us, mate, to sink or swim, 'n' the words we
took 'n' said
They turned the port-light grassy-green 'n' the starboard
rosy-red,

We give her a hot perpetual taste of the singeing curse of Cain,
As we heard her back 'n' clear the wreck 'n' off to her course
    again.

"Then the mate came dancin' on to the scene, 'n' he says,
    "Now quit yer chin,
Or I'll smash yer skulls, so help me James, 'n' let some wisdom in.
Ye dodderin' scum o' the slums," he says, "are ye drunk or
    blazin' daft?
If ye wish to save yer sickly hides, ye'd best contrive a raft."

"So he spoke us fair and turned us to, 'n' we wrought wi' tooth
    and nail
Wi' scantling, casks, 'n' coops 'n' ropes, 'n' boiler-plates 'n'
    sail,
'N' all the while it were dark 'n' cold 'n' dirty as it could be,
'N' she was soggy 'n' settlin' down to a berth beneath the sea.

"Soggy she grew, 'n' she didn't lift, 'n' she listed more 'n' more,
Till her bell struck 'n' her boiler-pipes began to wheeze 'n' snore;
She settled, settled, listed, heeled, 'n' then may I be cust,
If her sneezin', wheezin' boiler-pipes did not begin to bust!

"'N' then the stars began to shine, 'n' the birds began to sing,
'N' the next I knowed I was bandaged up 'n' my arm were in
    a sling,
'N' a swab in uniform were there, 'n' 'Well,' says he, ' 'n' how
Are yer arms, 'n' legs, 'n' liver, 'n' lungs, 'n' bones a-feelin'
    now?'

" 'Where am I?' says I, 'n' he says, says he, a-cantin' to the roll,
'You're aboard the R. M. S. "Marie" in the after Glory-Hole,

'N' you've had a shave, if you wish to know, from the port o'
    Kingdom Come.
Drink this,' he says, 'n' I takes 'n' drinks, 'n' s'elp me, it was
    rum!

"Seven survivors seen 'n' saved of the 'Esmeralda's' crowd,
Taken aboard the sweet 'Marie' 'n' bunked 'n' treated proud,
'N' D. B. S.'d to Mersey Docks ('n' a joyful trip we made),
'N' there the skipper were given a purse by a grateful Board
    of Trade.

"That's the end o' the yarn," he says, 'n' he takes 'n' wipes
    his lips,
"Them's the works o' the Lord you sees in steam 'n' sailin'
    ships,—
Rocks 'n' fogs 'n' shatterin' seas 'n' breakers right ahead,
'N' work o' nights 'n' work o' days enough to strike you dead."

HELL'S PAVEMENT

"When I'm discharged in Liverpool 'n' draws my bit o' pay,
    I won't come to sea no more.
I'll court a pretty little lass 'n' have a weddin' day,
    'N' settle somewhere down ashore.
I'll never fare to sea again a-temptin' Davy Jones,
A-hearkening to the cruel sharks a-hungerin' for my bones;
I'll run a blushin' dairy-farm or go a-crackin' stones,
    Or buy 'n' keep a little liquor-store,"—
                       So he said.

They towed her in to Liverpool, we made the hooker fast,
  And the copper-bound officials paid the crew,
And Billy drew his money, but the money didn't last,
  For he painted the alongshore blue,—

It was rum for Poll, and rum for Nan, and gin for Jolly Jack.
He shipped a week later in the clothes upon his back,
He had to pinch a little straw, he had to beg a sack
  To sleep on, when his watch was through,—
                              So he did.

SEA–CHANGE

"Goneys and gullies an' all o' the birds o' the sea,
  They ain't no birds, not really," said Billy the Dane.
"Not mollies, nor gullies, nor goneys at all," said he,
  "But simply the sperrits of mariners livin' again.

"Them birds goin' fishin' is nothin' but souls o' the drowned,
  Souls o' the drowned an' the kicked as are never no more;
An' that there haughty old albatross cruisin' around,
  Belike he's Admiral Nelson or Admiral Noah.

"An' merry's the life they are living. They settle and dip,
  They fishes, they never stands watches, they waggle their
    wings;
When a ship comes by, they fly to look at the ship
  To see how the nowaday mariners manages things.

"When freezing aloft in a snorter, I tell you I wish—
  (Though maybe it ain't like a Christian)—I wish I could be
A haughty old copper-bound albatross dipping for fish
  And coming the proud over all o' the birds o' the sea."

HARBOUR-BAR

All in the feathered palm-tree tops the bright green parrots
    screech,
The white line of the running surf goes booming down the beach,
But I shall never see them, though the land lies close aboard,
I've shaped the last long silent tack as takes one to the Lord.

Give me the Scripters, Jakey, 'n' my pipe atween my lips,
I'm bound for somewhere south and far beyond the track of
    ships;
I've run my rags of colours up and clinched them to the stay,
And God the pilot's come aboard to bring me up the bay.

You'll mainsail-haul my bits o' things when Christ has took
    my soul,
'N' you'll lay me quiet somewhere at the landward end the
    Mole,
Where I shall hear the steamers' sterns a-squattering from the
    heave,
And the topsail blocks a-piping when a rope-yarn fouls the
    sheave.

Give me a sup of lime-juice; Lord, I'm drifting in to port,
The landfall lies to windward and the wind comes light and
    short,
And I'm for signing off and out to take my watch below,
And—prop a fellow, Jakey—Lord, it's time for me to go!

THE TURN OF THE TIDE

An' Bill can have my sea-boots, Nigger Jim can have my knife,
   You can divvy up the dungarees an' bed,
An' the ship can have my blessing, an' the Lord can have my life,
   An' sails an' fish my body when I'm dead.

An' dreaming down below there in the tangled greens an' blues,
   Where the sunlight shudders golden round about,
I shall hear the ships complainin' an' the cursin' of the crews,
   An' be sorry when the watch is tumbled out.

I shall hear them hilly-hollying the weather crojick brace,
   And the sucking of the wash about the hull;
When they chanty up the topsail I'll be hauling in my place,
   For my soul will follow seawards like a gull.

I shall hear the blocks a-grunting in the bumpkins over-side,
   An' the slatting of the storm-sails on the stay,
An' the rippling of the catspaw at the making of the tide,
   An' the swirl and splash of porpoises at play.

An' Bill can have my sea-boots, Nigger Jim can have my knife,
   You can divvy up the whack I haven't scofft,
An' the ship can have my blessing and the Lord can have my life,
   For it's time I quit the deck and went aloft.

ONE OF WALLY'S YARNS

The watch was up on the topsail-yard a-making fast the sail,
'N' Joe was swiggin' his gasket taut, 'n' I felt the stirrup *give*,
'N' he dropped sheer from the tops'l-yard 'n' barely cleared the
    rail,
'N' o' course, we bein' aloft, *we* couldn't do nothin'—
We couldn't lower a boat and go a-lookin' for him,
For it blew hard 'n' there was sech a sea runnin'
        That no boat wouldn't live.

I seed him rise in the white o' the wake, I seed him lift a hand
('N' him in his oilskin suit 'n' all), I heard him lift a cry;
'N' there was his place on the yard 'n' all, 'n' the stirrup's
    busted strand.
'N' the old man said there's a cruel old sea runnin',
A cold green Barney's Bull of a sea runnin';
It's hard, but I ain't agoin' to let a boat be lowered:
        So we left him there to die.

He couldn't have kept afloat for long an' him lashed up 'n' all,
'N' we couldn't see him for long, for the sea was blurred with
    the sleet 'n' snow,
'N' we couldn't think of him much because o' the snortin',
    screamin' squall.
There was a hand less at the halliards 'n' the braces,
'N' a name less when the watch spoke to the muster-roll,
'N' a empty bunk 'n' a pannikin as wasn't wanted
        When the watch went below.

A VALEDICTION (LIVERPOOL DOCKS)

A CRIMP.   A DRUNKEN SAILOR.

Is there anything as I can do ashore for you
When you've dropped down the tide?—

You can take 'n' tell Nan I'm goin' about the world agen,
        'N' that the world's wide.
'N' tell her that there ain't no postal service
        Not down on the blue sea.
'N' tell her that she'd best not keep her fires alight
        Nor set up late for me.
'N' tell her I'll have forgotten all about her
        Afore we cross the Line.
'N' tell her that the dollars of any other sailor-man
        Is as good red gold as mine.

Is there anything as I can do aboard for you
Afore the tow-rope's taut?

I'm new to this packet and all the ways of her,
        'N' I don't know of aught;
But I knows as I'm goin' down to the seas agen
        'N' the seas are salt 'n' drear;
But I knows as all the doin' as you're man enough for
        Won't make them lager-beer.

'N' ain't there nothin' *as I can do ashore for you*
When you've got fair afloat?—

You can buy a farm with the dollars as you've done me of
'N' cash my advance-note.

Is there anythin' you'd fancy for your breakfastin'
When you're home across Mersey Bar?—

I wants a red herrin' 'n' a prairie oyster
'N' a bucket of Three Star,
'N' a gell with redder lips than Polly has got,
'N' prettier ways than Nan——

Well, so-long, Billy, 'n' a spankin' heavy pay-day to you!

So-long, my fancy man!

A NIGHT AT DAGO TOM'S

Oh yesterday, I t'ink it was, while cruisin' down the street,
I met with Bill.—"Hullo," he says, "let's give the girls a treat."
We'd red bandanas round our necks 'n' our shrouds new rattled
down,
So we filled a couple of Santy Cruz and cleared for Sailor Town.

We scooted south with a press of sail till we fetched to a caboose,
The "Sailor's Rest," by Dago Tom, alongside "Paddy's Goose."
Red curtains to the windies, ay, 'n' white sand to the floor,
And an old blind fiddler liltin' the tune of "Lowlands no more."

He played the "Shaking of the Sheets" 'n' the couples did
advance,
Bowing, stamping, curtsying, in the shuffling of the dance;
The old floor rocked and quivered, so it struck beholders dumb,
'N' arterwards there was sweet songs 'n' good Jamaikey rum.

'N' there was many a merry yarn of many a merry spree
Aboard the ships with royals set a-sailing on the sea,
Yarns of the hooker "Spindrift," her as had the clipper-bow—
"There ain't no ships," says Bill to me, "like that there hooker
  now."

When the old blind fiddler played the tune of "Pipe the Watch
  Below,"
The skew-eyed landlord dowsed the glim and bade us "stamp
  'n' go,"
'N' we linked it home, did Bill 'n' I, adown the scattered streets,
Until we fetched to Land o' Nod atween the linen sheets.

PORT OF MANY SHIPS

"It's a sunny pleasant anchorage, is Kingdom Come,
Where crews is always layin' aft for double-tots o' rum,
'N' there's dancin' 'n' fiddlin' of ev'ry kind o' sort,
It's a fine place for sailor-men is that there port.
        'N' I wish—
        I wish as I was there.

"The winds is never nothin' more than jest light airs,
'N' no-one gets belayin'-pinned, 'n' no-one never swears,
Yer free to loaf an' laze around, yer pipe atween yer lips,
Lollin' on the fo'c's'le, sonny, lookin' at the ships.
        'N' I wish—
        I wish as I was there.

"For ridin' in the anchorage the ships of all the world
Have got one anchor down 'n' all sails furled.
All the sunken hookers 'n' the crews as took 'n' died
They lays there merry, sonny, swingin' to the tide.
    'N' I wish—
    I wish as I was there.

"Drowned old wooden hookers green wi' drippin' wrack,
Ships as never fetched to port, as never came back,
Swingin' to the blushin' tide, dippin' to the swell,
'N' the crews all singin', sonny, beatin' on the bell.
    'N' I wish—
    I wish as I was there."

CAPE HORN GOSPEL—I

"I was in a hooker once," said Karlssen,
"And Bill, as was a seaman, died,
So we lashed him in an old tarpaulin
And tumbled him across the side;
And the fun of it was that all his gear was
Divided up among the crew
Before that blushing human error,
Our crawling little captain, knew.

"On the passage home one morning
(As certain as I prays for grace)
There was old Bill's shadder a-hauling
At the weather mizzen-topsail brace.
He was all grown green with sea-weed,

[23]

He was all lashed up and shored;
So I says to him, I says, 'Why, Billy!
What's a-bringin' of you back aboard?'

"'I'm a-weary of them there mermaids,'
Says old Bill's ghost to me;
'It ain't no place for a Christian
Below there—under sea.
For it's all blown sand and shipwrecks,
And old bones eaten bare,
And them cold fishy females
With long green weeds for hair.

"'And there ain't no dances shuffled,
And no old yarns is spun,
And there ain't no stars but starfish,
And never any moon or sun.
I heard your keel a-passing
And the running rattle of the brace,'
And he says, 'Stand by,' says William,
'For a shift towards a better place.'

"Well, he sogered about decks till sunrise,
When a rooster in the hen-coop crowed,
And as so much smoke he faded
And as so much smoke he goed;
And I've often wondered since, Jan,
How his old ghost stands to fare
Long o' them cold fishy females
With long green weeds for hair."

CAPE HORN GOSPEL—II

Jake was a dirty Dago lad, an' he gave the skipper chin,
An' the skipper up an' took him a crack with an iron belaying-
pin
Which stiffened him out a rusty corp, as pretty as you could
wish,
An' then we shovelled him up in a sack an' dumped him to
the fish.
      That was jest arter we'd got sail on her.

Josey slipped from the tops'l-yard an' bust his bloody back
(Which comed from playing the giddy goat an' leavin' go the
jack);
We lashed his chips in clouts of sail an' ballasted him with stones,
"The Lord hath taken away," we says, an' we give him to
Davy Jones.
      An' that was afore we were up with the Line.

Joe were chippin' a rusty plate a-squattin' upon the deck,
An' all the watch he had the sun a-singein' him on the neck,
An' forrard he falls at last, he does, an' he lets his mallet go,
Dead as a nail with a calenture, an' that was the end of Joe.
      An' that was just afore we made the Plate.

All o' the rest were sailor-men, an' it come to rain an' squall,
An' then it was halliards, sheets, an 'tacks "clue up, an' let
go all."
We snugged her down an' hove her to, an' the old contrairy
cuss
Started a plate, an' settled an' sank, an' that was the end of us.

We slopped around on coops an' planks in the cold an' in the
    dark,
An' Bill were drowned, an' Tom were ate by a swine of a cruel
    shark,
An' a mail-boat reskied Harry an' I (which comed of pious
    prayers),
Which brings me here a-kickin' my heels in the port of Buenos
    Ayres.

I'm bound for home in the "Oronook," in a suit of looted duds,
A D. B. S. a-earnin' a stake by helpin' peelin' spuds,
An' if ever I fetch to Prince's Stage an' sets my feet ashore,
You bet your hide that there I stay, an' follers the sea no more.

MOTHER CAREY

(AS TOLD ME BY THE BO'SUN)

Mother Carey? She's the mother o' the witches
    'N' all *them* sort o' rips;
She's a fine gell to look at, but the hitch is,
    She's a sight too fond of ships.
She lives upon a iceberg to the norred,
    'N' her man he's Davy Jones,
'N' she combs the weeds upon her forred
    With pore drowned sailor's bones.

    She's the mother o' the wrecks, 'n' the mother
        Of all big winds as blows;
    She's up to some devilry or other
        When it storms, or sleets, or snows.

The noise of the wind's her screamin',
  "I'm arter a plump, young, fine,
Brass-buttoned, beefy-ribbed young seam'n
  So as me 'n' my mate kin dine."

She's a hungry old rip 'n' a cruel
  For sailor-men like we,
She's give a many mariners the gruel
  'N' a long sleep under sea.
She's the blood o' many a crew upon her
  'N' the bones of many a wreck,
'N' she's barnacles a-growin' on her
  'N' shark's teeth round her neck.

I ain't never had no schoolin'
  Nor read no books like you,
But I knows 't ain't healthy to be foolin'
  With that there gristly two.
You're young, you thinks, 'n' you're lairy,
  But if you're to make old bones,
Steer clear, I says, o' Mother Carey,
  'N' that there Davy Jones.

EVENING—REGATTA DAY

Your nose is a red jelly, your mouth's a toothless wreck,
And I'm atop of you, banging your head upon the dirty deck;
And both your eyes are bunged and blind like those of a mewl-
    ing pup,
For you're the juggins who caught the crab and lost the ship
    the Cup.

He caught a crab in the spurt home, this blushing cherub did,
And the "Craigie's" whaler slipped ahead like a cart-wheel
    on the skid,
And beat us fair by a boat's nose though we sweated fit to
    start her,
So we are playing at Nero now, and *he's* the Christian martyr.

And Stroke is lashing a bunch of keys to the buckle-end a belt,
And we're going to lay you over a chest and baste you till you
    melt.
The "Craigie" boys are beating the bell and cheering down
    the tier,
D'ye hear, you Port Mahone baboon, I ask you, do you *hear?*

A VALEDICTION

We're bound for blue water where the great winds blow,
It's time to get the tacks aboard, time for us to go;
The crowd's at the capstan and the tune's in the shout,
"A long pull, a strong pull, *and warp the hooker out.*"

The bow-wash is eddying, spreading from the bows,
Aloft and loose the topsails and some one give a rouse;
A salt Atlantic chanty shall be music to the dead,
"A long pull, a strong pull, *and the yard to the masthead.*"

Green and merry run the seas, the wind comes cold,
Salt and strong and pleasant, and worth a mint of gold;
And she's staggering, swooping, as she feels her feet,
"A long pull, a strong pull, *and aft the main-sheet.*"

[28]

A PIER–HEAD CHORUS

Shrilly squeal the running sheaves, the weather-gear strains,
Such a clatter of chain-sheets, the devil's in the chains;
Over us the bright stars, under us the drowned,
"A long pull, a strong pull, *and we're outward bound!*"

Yonder, round and ruddy, is the mellow old moon,
The red-funnelled tug has gone, and now, sonny, soon
We'll be clear of the Channel, so watch how you steer,
"Ease her when she pitches, *and so-long, my dear!*"

A PIER–HEAD CHORUS

Oh I'll be chewing salted horse and biting flinty bread,
And dancing with the stars to watch, upon the fo'c's'le head,
Hearkening to the bow-wash and the welter of the tread
    Of a thousand tons of clipper running free.

For the tug has got the tow-rope and will take us to the Downs,
Her paddles churn the river-wrack to muddy greens and browns,
And I have given river-wrack and all the filth of towns
    For the rolling, combing cresters of the sea.

We'll sheet the mizzen-royals home and shimmer down the Bay,
The sea-line blue with billows, the land-line blurred and grey;
The bow-wash will be piling high and thrashing into spray,
    As the hooker's fore-foot tramples down the swell.

She'll log a giddy seventeen and rattle out the reel,
The weight of all the run-out line will be a thing to feel,
As the bacca-quidding shell-back shambles aft to take the wheel,
    And the sea-sick little middy strikes the bell.

THE GOLDEN CITY OF ST. MARY

Out beyond the sunset, could I but find the way,
Is a sleepy blue laguna which widens to a bay,
And there's the Blessed City—so the sailors say—
   The Golden City of St. Mary.

It's built of fair marble—white—without a stain,
And in the cool twilight when the sea-winds wane
The bells chime faintly, like a soft, warm rain,
   In the Golden City of St. Mary.

Among the green palm-trees where the fire-flies shine,
Are the white tavern tables where the gallants dine,
Singing slow Spanish songs like old mulled wine,
   In the Golden City of St. Mary.

Oh I'll be shipping sunset-wards and westward-ho
Through the green toppling combers a-shattering into snow,
Till I come to quiet moorings and a watch below,
   In the Golden City of St. Mary.

TRADE WINDS

In the harbour, in the island, in the Spanish Seas,
Are the tiny white houses and the orange-trees,
And day-long, night long, the cool and pleasant breeze
   Of the steady Trade Winds blowing.

SEA–FEVER

There is the red wine, the nutty Spanish ale,
The shuffle of the dancers, the old salt's tale,
The squeaking fiddle, and the soughing in the sail
  Of the steady Trade Winds blowing.

And o' nights there's fire-flies and the yellow moon,
And in the ghostly palm-trees the sleepy tune
Of the quiet voice calling me, the long low croon
  Of the steady Trade Winds blowing.

SEA–FEVER

I must go down to the seas again, to the lonely sea and the sky,
And all I ask is a tall ship and a star to steer her by,
And the wheel's kick and the wind's song and the white sail's
    shaking,
And a grey mist on the sea's face and a grey dawn breaking.

I must go down to the seas again, for the call of the running tide
Is a wild call and a clear call that may not be denied;
And all I ask is a windy day with the white clouds flying,
And the flung spray and the blown spume, and the sea-gulls
    crying.

I must go down to the seas again to the vagrant gypsy life,
To the gull's way and the whale's way where the wind's like
    a whetted knife;
And all I ask is a merry yarn from a laughing fellow-rover,
And quiet sleep and a sweet dream when the long trick's over.

A WANDERER'S SONG

A wind's in the heart of me, a fire's in my heels,
I am tired of brick and stone and rumbling wagon-wheels;
I hunger for the sea's edge, the limits of the land,
Where the wild old Atlantic is shouting on the sand.

Oh I'll be going, leaving the noises of the street,
To where a lifting foresail-foot is yanking at the sheet;
To a windy, tossing anchorage where yawls and ketches ride,
Oh I'll be going, going, until I meet the tide.

And first I'll hear the sea-wind, the mewing of the gulls,
The clucking, sucking of the sea about the rusty hulls,
The songs at the capstan in the hooker warping out,
And then the heart of me'll know I'm there or thereabout.

Oh I am tired of brick and stone, the heart of me is sick,
For windy green, unquiet sea, the realm of Moby Dick;
And I'll be going, going, from the roaring of the wheels,
For a wind's in the heart of me, a fire's in my heels.

CARDIGAN BAY

Clean, green, windy billows notching out the sky,
Grey clouds tattered into rags, sea-winds blowing high,
And the ships under topsails, beating, thrashing by,
And the mewing of the herring gulls.

CHRISTMAS EVE AT SEA

Dancing, flashing green seas shaking white locks,
Boiling in blind eddies over hidden rocks,
And the wind in the rigging, the creaking of the blocks,
   And the straining of the timber hulls.

Delicate, cool sea-weeds, green and amber-brown,
   beds where shaken sunlight slowly filters down
On many a drowned seventy-four, and many a sunken town,
   And the whitening of the dead men's skulls.

CHRISTMAS EVE AT SEA

A wind is rustling "south and soft,"
   Cooing a quiet country tune,
The calm sea sighs, and far aloft
   The sails are ghostly in the moon.

Unquiet ripples lisp and purr,
   A block there pipes and chirps i' the sheave,
The wheel-ropes jar, the reef-points stir
   Faintly—and it is Christmas Eve.

The hushed sea seems to hold her breath,
   And o'er the giddy, swaying spars,
Silent and excellent as Death,
   The dim blue skies are bright with stars.

Dear God—they shone in Palestine
   Like this, and yon pale moon serene
Looked down among the lowing kine
   On Mary and the Nazarene.

[33]

The angels called from deep to deep,
   The burning heavens felt the thrill,
Startling the flocks of silly sheep
   And lonely shepherds on the hill.

To-night beneath the dripping bows
   Where flashing bubbles burst and throng,
The bow-wash murmurs and sighs and soughs
   A message from the angels' song.

The moon goes nodding down the west,
   The drowsy helmsman strikes the bell;
Rex Judæorum natus est,
   I charge you, brothers, sing *Nowell, Nowell,*
Rex Judæorum natus est.

A BALLAD OF CAPE ST. VINCENT

Now, Bill, ain't it prime to be a-sailin',
   Slippin' easy, splashin' up the sea,
Dossin' snug aneath the weather-railin',
   Quiddin' bonded Jacky out a-lee?
English sea astern us and afore us,
   Reaching out three thousand miles ahead,
God's own stars a-risin' solemn o'er us,
   And—yonder's Cape St. Vincent and the Dead.

There they lie, Bill, man and mate together,
   Dreamin' out the dog-watch down below,
Anchored in the Port of Pleasant Weather,
   Waiting for the Bo'sun's call to blow.

THE TARRY BUCCANEER

Over them the tide goes lappin',' swayin',
  Under them's the wide bay's muddy bed,
And it's pleasant dreams—to them—to hear us sayin',
  Yonder's Cape St. Vincent and the Dead.

Hear that P. and O. boat's engines dronin',
  Beating out of time and out of tune,
Ripping past with every plate a-groanin',
  Spitting smoke and cinders at the moon?
Ports a-lit like little stars a-settin',
  See 'em glintin' yaller, green, and red,
Loggin' twenty knots, Bill,—but forgettin',
  Yonder's Cape St. Vincent and the Dead.

They're "discharged" now, Billy, "left the service,"
  Rough an' bitter was the watch they stood,
Drake an' Blake, an' Collingwood an' Jervis,
  Nelson, Rodney, Hawke, an' Howe an' Hood.
They'd a hard time, haulin' an' directin',
  There's the flag they left us, Billy—tread
Straight an' keep it flyin'—recollectin',
  Yonder's Cape St. Vincent and the Dead.

THE TARRY BUCCANEER

I'm going to be a pirate with a bright brass pivot-gun,
And an island in the Spanish Main beyond the setting sun,
And a silver flagon full of red wine to drink when work is done,
  Like a fine old salt-sea scavenger, like a tarry Buccaneer.

With a sandy creek to careen in, and a pig-tailed Spanish mate,
And under my main-hatches a sparkling merry freight
Of doubloons and double moidores and pieces of eight,
    Like a fine old salt-sea scavenger, like a tarry Buccaneer.

With a taste for Spanish wine-shops and for spending my
    doubloons,
And a crew of swart mulattoes and black-eyed octoroons,
And a thoughtful way with mutineers of making them maroons,
    Like a fine old salt-sea scavenger, like a tarry Buccaneer.

With a sash of crimson velvet and a diamond-hilted sword,
And a silver whistle about my neck secured to a golden cord,
And a habit of taking captives and walking them along a board,
    Like a fine old salt-sea scavenger, like a tarry Buccaneer.

With a spy-glass tucked beneath my arm and a cocked hat
    cocked askew,
And a long low rakish schooner a-cutting of the waves in two,
And a flag of skull and cross-bones the wickedest that ever flew,
    Like a fine old salt-sea scavenger, like a tarry Buccaneer.

A BALLAD OF JOHN SILVER

We were schooner-rigged and rakish, with a long and lissome
    hull,
And we flew the pretty colours of the cross-bones and the skull;
We'd a big black Jolly Roger flapping grimly at the fore,
And we sailed the Spanish Water in the happy days of yore.

A BALLAD OF JOHN SILVER

We'd a long brass gun amidship, like a well-conducted ship,
We had each a brace of pistols and a cutlass at the hip;
It's a point which tells against us, and a fact to be deplored,
But we chased the goodly merchant-men and laid their ships
  aboard.

Then the dead men fouled the scuppers and the wounded filled
  the chains,
And the paint-work all was spatter-dashed with other people's
  brains,
She was boarded, she was looted, she was scuttled till she sank,
And the pale survivors left us by the medium of the plank.

O! then it was (while standing by the taffrail on the poop)
We could hear the drowning folk lament the absent chicken-
  coop;
Then, having washed the blood away, we'd little else to do
Than to dance a quiet hornpipe as the old salts taught us to.

O! the fiddle on the fo'c's'le, and the slapping naked soles,
And the genial "Down the middle, Jake, and curtsey when she
  rolls!"
With the silver seas around us and the pale moon overhead,
And the look-out not a-looking and his pipe-bowl glowing red.

Ah! the pig-tailed, quidding pirates and the pretty pranks we
  played,
All have since been put a stop-to by the naughty Board of
  Trade;
The schooners and the merry crews are laid away to rest,
A little south the sunset in the Islands of the Blest.

LYRICS FROM "THE BUCCANEER"

I

We are far from sight of the harbour lights,
    Of the sea-ports whence we came,
But the old sea calls and the cold wind bites,
    And our hearts are turned to flame.

And merry and rich is the goodly gear
    We'll win upon the tossing sea,
A silken gown for my dainty dear,
    And a gold doubloon for me.

It's the old old road and the old old quest
    Of the cut-throat sons of Cain,
South by west and a quarter west,
    And hey for the Spanish Main.

II

There's a sea-way somewhere where all day long
    Is the hushed susurrus of the sea,
The mewing of the skuas, and the sailor's song,
    And the wind's cry calling me.

There's a haven somewhere where the quiet of the bay
    Is troubled with the shifting tide,
Where the gulls are flying, crying in the bright white spray,
    And the tan-sailed schooners ride.

III

The toppling rollers at the harbour mouth
  Are spattering the bows with foam,
And the anchor's catted, and she's heading for the south
  With her topsails sheeted home.

And a merry measure is the dance she'll tread
  (To the clanking of the staysail's hanks)
When the guns are growling and the blood runs red,
  And the prisoners are walking of the planks.

D'AVALOS' PRAYER

When the last sea is sailed and the last shallow charted,
  When the last field is reaped and the last harvest stored,
When the last fire is out and the last guest departed,
  Grant the last prayer that I shall pray, Be good to me, O
  Lord!

And let me pass in a night at sea, a night of storm and thunder,
  In the loud crying of the wind through sail and rope and
  spar;
Send me a ninth great peaceful wave to drown and roll me
  under
  To the cold tunny-fishes' home where the drowned galleons
  are.

And in the dim green quiet place far out of sight and hearing,
  Grant I may hear at whiles the wash and thresh of the sea-
  foam
About the fine keen bows of the stately clippers steering
  Towards the lone northern star and the fair ports of home.

THE WEST WIND

It's a warm wind, the west wind, full of birds' cries;
I never hear the west wind but tears are in my eyes.
For it comes from the west lands, the old brown hills,
And April's in the west wind, and daffodils.

It's a fine land, the west land, for hearts as tired as mine,
Apple orchards blossom there, and the air's like wine.
There is cool green grass there, where men may lie at rest,
And the thrushes are in song there, fluting from the nest.

"Will you not come home, brother? you have been long away,
It's April, and blossom time, and white is the spray;
And bright is the sun, brother, and warm is the rain,—
Will you not come home, brother, home to us again?

The young corn is green, brother, where the rabbits run,
It's blue sky, and white clouds, and warm rain and sun.
It's song to a man's soul, brother, fire to a man's brain,
To hear the wild bees and see the merry spring again.

Larks are singing in the west, brother, above the green wheat,
So will ye not come home, brother, and rest your tired feet?
I've a balm for bruised hearts, brother, sleep for aching eyes,"
Says the warm wind, the west wind, full of birds' cries.

It's the white road westwards is the road I must tread
To the green grass, the cool grass, and rest for heart and head,
To the violets and the brown brooks and the thrushes' song,
In the fine land, the west land, the land where I belong.

[40]

THE GALLEY-ROWERS

Staggering over the running combers
 The long-ship heaves her dripping flanks,
Singing together, the sea-roamers
 Drive the oars grunting in the banks.
   A long pull,
   And a long long pull to Mydath.

"Where are ye bound, ye swart sea-farers,
 Vexing the grey wind-angered brine,
Bearers of home-spun cloth, and bearers
 Of goat-skins filled with country wine?"

"We are bound sunset-wards, not knowing,
 Over the whale's way miles and miles,
Going to Vine-Land, haply going
 To the Bright Beach of the Blessed Isles.

"In the wind's teeth and the spray's stinging
 Westward and outward forth we go,
Knowing not whither nor why, but singing
 An old old oar-song as we row.
   A long pull,
   And a long long pull to Mydath."

SORROW OF MYDATH

Weary the cry of the wind is, weary the sea,
Weary the heart and the mind and the body of me.
Would I were out of it, done with it, would I could be
  A white gull crying along the desolate sands!

Outcast, derelict soul in a body accurst,
Standing drenched with the spindrift standing athirst,
For the cool green waves of death to arise and burst
  In a tide of quiet for me on the desolate sands.

Would that the waves and the long white hair of the spray
Would gather in splendid terror and blot me away
To the sunless place of the wrecks where the waters sway
  Gently, dreamily quietly over desolate sands!

VAGABOND

Dunno a heap about the what an' why,
    Can't say's I ever knowed.
Heaven to me's a fair blue stretch of sky,
    Earth's jest a dusty road.

Dunno the names o' things, nor what they are,
    Can't say's I ever will.
Dunno about God—he's jest the noddin' star
    Atop the windy hill.

VISION

Dunno about Life—it's jest a tramp alone
    From wakin'-time to doss.
Dunno about Death—it's jest a quiet stone
    All over-grey wi' moss.

An' why I live, an' why the old world spins,
    Are things I never knowed;
My mark's the gypsy fires, the lonely inns,
    An' jest the dusty road.

VISION

I have drunken the red wine and flung the dice;
    Yet once in the noisy ale-house I have seen and heard
The dear pale lady with the mournful eyes,
    And a voice like that of a pure grey cooing bird.

With delicate white hands—white hands that I have kist
    (Oh frail white hands!)—she soothed my aching eyes;
And her hair fell about her in a dim clinging mist,
    Like smoke from a golden incense burned in Paradise.

With gentle loving words, like shredded balm and myrrh,
    She healed with sweet forgiveness my black bitter sins,
Then passed into the night, and I go seeking her
    Down the dark, silent streets, past the warm, lighted inns.

SPUNYARN

Spunyarn, spunyarn, with one to turn the crank,
And one to slather the spunyarn, and one to knot the hank;
It's an easy job for a summer watch, and a pleasant job enough,
To twist the tarry lengths of yarn to shapely sailor stuff.

Life is nothing but spunyarn on a winch in need of oil,
Little enough is twined and spun but fever-fret and moil.
I have travelled on land and sea, and all that I have found
Are these poor songs to brace the arms that help the winches
   round.

THE DEAD KNIGHT

The cleanly rush of the mountain air,
And the mumbling, grumbling humble-bees,
Are the only things that wander there,
The pitiful bones are laid at ease,
The grass has grown in his tangled hair,
And a rambling bramble binds his knees.

To shrieve his soul from the pangs of hell,
The only requiem-bells that rang
Were the hare-bell and the heather-bell.
Hushed he is with the holy spell
In the gentle hymn the wind sang,
And he lies quiet, and sleeps well.

PERSONAL

He is bleached and blanched with the summer sun;
The misty rain and the cold dew
Have altered him from the kingly one
(That his lady loved, and his men knew)
And dwindled him to a skeleton.

The vetches have twined about his bones,
The straggling ivy twists and creeps
In his eye-sockets; the nettle keeps
Vigil about him while he sleeps.
Over his body the wind moans
With a dreary tune throughout the day,
In a chorus wistful, eerie, thin
As the gull's cry—as the cry in the bay,
The mournful word the seas say
When tides are wandering out or in.

PERSONAL

Tramping at night in the cold and wet, I passed the lighted inn,
And an old tune, a sweet tune, was being played within.
It was full of the laugh of the leaves and the song the wind sings;
It brought the tears and the choked throat, and a catch to the
    heart-strings.

And it brought a bitter thought of the days that now were
    dead to me,
The merry days in the old home before I went to sea—
Days that were dead to me indeed. I bowed my head to the rain,
And I passed by the lighted inn to the lonely roads again.

ON MALVERN HILL

A wind is brushing down the clover,
  It sweeps the tossing branches bare,
Blowing the poising kestrel over
  The crumbling ramparts of the Caer.

It whirls the scattered leaves before us
  Along the dusty road to home,
Once it awakened into chorus
  The heart-strings in the ranks of Rome.

There by the gusty coppice border
  The shrilling trumpets broke the halt,
The Roman line, the Roman order,
  Swayed forwards to the blind assault.

Spearman and charioteer and bowman
  Charged and were scattered into spray,
Savage and taciturn the Roman
  Hewed upwards in the Roman way.

There—in the twilight—where the cattle
  Are lowing home across the fields,
The beaten warriors left the battle
  Dead on the clansmen's wicker shields.

The leaves whirl in the wind's riot
  Beneath the Beacon's jutting spur,
Quiet are clan and chief, and quiet
  Centurion and signifer.

TEWKESBURY ROAD

It is good to be out on the road, and going one knows not where,
  Going through meadow and village, one knows not whither
    nor why;
Through the grey light drift of the dust, in the keen cool rush
    of the air,
  Under the flying white clouds, and the broad blue lift of
    the sky;

And to halt at the chattering brook, in the tall green fern at
    the brink
  Where the harebell grows, and the gorse, and the fox-gloves
    purple and white;
Where the shy-eyed delicate deer troop down to the pools
    to drink,
  When the stars are mellow and large at the coming on of
    the night.

O! to feel the warmth of the rain, and the homely smell of the
    earth,
  Is a tune for the blood to jig to, a joy past power of words;
And the blessed green comely meadows seem all a-ripple with
    mirth
  At the lilt of the shifting feet, and the dear wild cry of the
    birds.

ON EASTNOR KNOLL

Silent are the woods, and the dim green boughs are
Hushed in the twilight: yonder, in the path through
The apple orchard, is a tired plough-boy
Calling the cows home.

A bright white star blinks, the pale moon rounds, but
Still the red, lurid wreckage of the sunset
Smoulders in smoky fire, and burns on
The misty hill-tops.

Ghostly it grows, and darker, the burning
Fades into smoke, and now the gusty oaks are
A silent army of phantoms thronging
A land of shadows.

"REST HER SOUL, SHE'S DEAD"

She has done with the sea's sorrow and all the world's way
   And the wind's grief;
Strew her with laurel, cover her with bay
   And ivy-leaf.
Let the slow mournful music sound before her,
Strew the white flowers about the bier, and o'er her
   The sleepy poppies red beyond belief.

On the black velvet covering her eyes
   Let the dull earth be thrown;
Hers is the mightier silence of the skies,
   And long, quiet rest alone.

"ALL YE THAT PASS BY"

Over the pure, dark, wistful eyes of her,
O'er all the human, all that dies of her,
   Gently let flowers be strown.

Lay her away in quiet old peaceful earth
   (This blossom of ours),
She has done with the world's anger and the world's mirth,
   Sunshine and rain-showers;
And over the poor, sad, tired face of her,
In the long grass above the place of her
(The grass which hides the glory and the grace of her),
   May the Spring bring the flowers.

"ALL YE THAT PASS BY"

On the long dusty ribbon of the long city street,
The pageant of life is passing me on multitudinous feet,
With a word here of the hills, and a song there of the sea,
And—the great movement changes—the pageant passes me.

Faces—passionate faces—of men I may not know,
They haunt me, burn me to the heart, as I turn aside to go:
The king's face and the cur's face, and the face of the stuffed
   swine,
They are passing, they are passing, their eyes look into mine.

I never can tire of the music of the noise of many feet,
The thrill of the blood pulsing, the tick of the heart's beat,
Of the men many as sands, of the squadrons ranked and massed
Who are passing, changing always, and never have changed
   or passed.

IN MEMORY OF A. P. R.

Once in the windy wintry weather,
  The road dust blowing in our eyes,
We starved or tramped or slept together
  Beneath the haystacks and the skies;

Until the tiring tramp was over,
  And then the call for him was blown,
He left his friend—his fellow-rover—
  To tramp the dusty roads alone.

The winds wail and the woods are yellow,
  The hills are blotted in the rain,
"And would he were with me," sighs his fellow,
  "With me upon the roads again!"

TO-MORROW

Oh yesterday the cutting edge drank thirstily and deep,
The upland outlaws ringed us in and herded us as sheep,
They drove us from the stricken field and bayed us into keep;
      But to-morrow
  By the living God, we'll try the game again!

Oh yesterday our little troop was ridden through and through,
Our swaying, tattered pennons fled, a broken, beaten few,
And all a summer afternoon they hunted us and slew;
      But to-morrow,
  By the living God, we'll try the game again!

[50]

CAVALIER

And here upon the turret-top the bale-fire glowers red,
The wake-lights burn and drip about our hacked, disfigured
    dead,
And many a broken heart is here and many a broken head;
      But to-morrow,
  By the living God, we'll try the game again!

CAVALIER

All the merry kettle-drums are thudding into rhyme,
  Dust is swimming dizzily down the village street,
The scabbards are clattering, the feathers nodding time,
  To a clink of many horses' shoes, a tramp of many feet.

Seven score of Cavaliers fighting for the King,
  Trolling lusty stirrup-songs, clamouring for wine,
Riding with a loose rein, marching with a swing,
  Beneath the blue bannerol of Rupert of the Rhine.

Hey the merry company;—the loud fifes playing—
  Blue scarves and bright steel and blossom of the may,
Roses in the feathered hats, the long plumes swaying,
  A king's son ahead of them showing them the way.

A SONG AT PARTING

The tick of the blood is settling slow, my heart will soon be
    still,
And ripe and ready am I for rest in the grave atop the hill;
So gather me up and lay me down, for ready and ripe am I,
For the weary vigil with sightless eyes that may not see the sky.

I have lived my life: I have spilt the wine that God the Maker
    gave,
So carry me up the lonely hill and lay me in the grave,
And cover me in with cleanly mould and old and lichened stones,
In a place where ever the cry of the wind shall thrill my sleepy
    bones.

Gather me up and lay me down with an old song and a prayer,
Cover me in with wholesome earth, and weep and leave me
    there;
And get you gone with a kindly thought and an old tune and a
    sigh,
And leave me alone, asleep, at rest, for ready and ripe am I.

GLOSSARY

Abaft the beam.—That half of a ship included between her amidship section and the taffrail. (For "taffrail," *see* below.)

Abel Brown.—An unquotable sea-song.

Advance-note.—A note for one month's wages issued to sailors on their signing a ship's articles.

Belaying-pins.—Bars of iron or hard wood to which running rigging may be secured or *belayed*.

Belaying-pins, from their handiness and peculiar club-shape, are sometimes used as bludgeons.

Bloody.—An intensive derived from the substantive "blood," a name applied to the Bucks, Scowrers, and Mohocks of the seventeenth and eighteenth centuries.

Blue Peter.—A blue and white flag hoisted at the fore-trucks of ships about to sail.

Bollard.—From *bōl* or *bole*, the round trunk of a tree. A phallic or "sparklet"-shaped ornament of the dock-side, of assistance to mariners in warping into or out of dock.

Bonded Jacky.—Negro-head tobacco or sweet cake.

Bull of Barney.—A beast mentioned in an unquotable sea-proverb.

Bumpkin.—An iron bar (projecting out-board from the ship's side) to which the lower and topsail brace blocks are sometimes hooked.

Cape Horn fever.—The illness proper to malingerers.

Catted.—Said of an anchor when weighed and secured to the "cat-head."

Chanty.—A song sung to lighten labour at the capstan sheets, and halliards. The soloist is known as the chanty-man, and is usually a person of some authority in the fo'c's'le. Many chanties are of great beauty and extreme antiquity.

Clipper-bow.—A bow of delicate curves and lines.

Clout.—A rag or cloth. Also a blow:—"I fetched him a clout i' the lug."

Crimp.—A sort of scoundrelly land-shark preying upon sailors.

D. B. S.—Distressed British Sailor. A term applied to those who are invalided home from foreign ports.

[53]

Dungaree.—A cheap, rough thin cloth (generally blue or brown), woven, I am told, of coco-nut fibre.

Forward or Forrard.—Towards the bows.

Fo'c's'le (Forecastle).—The deck-house or living-room of the crew. The word is often used to indicate the crew, or those members of it described by passengers as the "common sailors."

Fore-stay.—A powerful wire rope supporting the fore-mast forward.

Gaskets.—Ropes or plaited lines used to secure the sails in furling.

Goneys.—Albatrosses.

Guffy.—A marine or jolly.

Gullies.—Sea-gulls, Cape Horn pigeons, etc.

Heave and pawl.—A cry of encouragement at the capstan.

Hooker.—A periphrasis for ship, I suppose from a ship's carrying *hooks* or anchors.

Jack or Jackstay.—A slender iron rail running along the upper portions of the yards in some ships.

Leeward.—Pronounced "looard." That quarter to which the wind blows.

Mainsail haul.—An order in tacking ship bidding "swing the mainyards." To loot, steal, or "acquire."

Main-shrouds.—Ropes, usually wire, supporting lateral strains upon the main-mast.

Mollies.—Molly-hawks, or Fulmar petrels. Wide-winged dusky sea-fowls, common in high latitudes, oily to taste, gluttonous. Great fishers and garbage-eaters.

Port Mahon Baboon, or *Port Mahon Soger.*—I have been unable to discover either the origin of these insulting epithets or the reasons for the peculiar bitterness with which they sting the marine recipient. They are older than Dana (*circa* 1840).

An old merchant sailor, now dead, once told me that Port Mahon was that godless city from which the Ark set sail, in which case the name may have some traditional connection with that evil "Mahoun" or "Mahu," prince of darkness, mentioned by Shakespeare and some of our older poets.

GLOSSARY

The real Port Mahon, a fine harbour in Minorca, was taken by the French, from Admiral Byng, in the year 1756.

I think that the phrases originated at the time of Byng's consequent trial and execution.

Purchase.—*See* "Tackle."

Quidding.—Tobacco-chewing.

Sails.—The sail-maker.

Santa Cruz.—A brand of rum.

Scantling.—Planks.

Soger.—A laggard, malingerer, or hang-back. To loaf or skulk or work Tom Cox's Traverse.

Spunyarn.—A three-strand line spun out of old rope-yarns knotted together. Most sailing-ships carry a spunyarn winch, and the spinning of such yarn is a favourite occupation in fine weather.

Stirrup.—A short rope supporting the foot-rope on which the sailors stand when aloft on the yards.

Tack.—To stay or 'bout ship. A reach to windward. The weather lower corner of a course.

Tackle.—Pronounced *taykle*. A combination of pulleys for obtaining of artificial power.

Taffrail.—The rail or bulwark round the sternmost end of a ship's poop or after-deck.

Trick.—The ordinary two-hour spell at the wheel or on the look-out.

Windward or *Weather.*—That quarter from which the wind blows.

MISCELLANEOUS POEMS

(FROM "THE STORY OF A ROUND HOUSE")

BIOGRAPHY

When I am buried, all my thoughts and acts
Will be reduced to lists of dates and facts,
And long before this wandering flesh is rotten
The dates which made me will be all forgotten;
And none will know the gleam there used to be
About the feast days freshly kept by me,
But men will call the golden hour of bliss
"About this time," or "shortly after this."

Men do not heed the rungs by which men climb
Those glittering steps, those milestones upon Time,
Those tombstones of dead selves, those hours of birth,
Those moments of the soul in years of earth
They mark the height achieved, the main result,
The power of freedom in the perished cult,
The power of boredom in the dead man's deeds,
Not the bright moments of the sprinkled seeds.

By many waters and on many ways
I have known golden instants and bright days;
The day on which, beneath an arching sail,
I saw the Cordilleras and gave hail;
The summer day on which in heart's delight
I saw the Swansea Mumbles bursting white,
The glittering day when all the waves wore flags
And the ship *Wanderer* came with sails in rags;
That curlew-calling time in Irish dusk
When life became more splendid than its husk,

When the rent chapel on the brae at Slains
Shone with a doorway opening beyond brains;
The dawn when, with a brace-block's creaking cry,
Out of the mist a little barque slipped by,
Spilling the mist with changing gleams of red,
Then gone, with one raised hand and one turned head;
The howling evening when the spindrift's mists
Broke to display the four Evangelists,
Snow-capped, divinely granite, lashed by breakers,
Wind-beaten bones of long since buried acres;
The night alone near water when I heard
All the sea's spirit spoken by a bird;
The English dusk when I beheld once more
(With eyes so changed) the ship, the citied shore,
The lines of masts, the streets so cheerly trod
(In happier seasons) and gave thanks to God.
All had their beauty, their bright moments' gift,
Their something caught from Time, the ever-swift.

All of those gleams were golden; but life's hands
Have given more constant gifts in changing lands,
And when I count those gifts, I think them such
As no man's bounty could have bettered much:
The gift of country life, near hills and woods
Where happy waters sing in solitudes,
The gift of being near ships, of seeing each day
A city of ships with great ships under weigh,
The great street paved with water, filled with shipping,
And all the world's flags flying and seagulls dipping.

Yet when I am dust my penman may not know
Those water-trampling ships which made me glow,
But think my wonder mad and fail to find

[60]

BIOGRAPHY

Their glory, even dimly, from my mind,
And yet they made me:
                       not alone the ships
But men hard-palmed from tallying-on to whips,
The two close friends of nearly twenty years,
Sea-followers both, sea-wrestlers and sea-peers,
Whose feet with mine wore many a bolt-head bright
Treading the decks beneath the riding light.
Yet death will make that warmth of friendship cold
And who'll know what one said and what one told
Our hearts' communion and the broken spells
When the loud call blew at the strike of bells?
No one, I know, yet let me be believed
A soul entirely known is life achieved.

Years blank with hardship never speak a word
Live in the soul to make the being stirred,
Towns can be prisons where the spirit dulls
Away from mates and ocean-wandering hulls,
Away from all bright water and great hills
And sheep-walks where the curlews cry their fills,
Away in towns, where eyes have nought to see
But dead museums and miles of misery
And floating life unrooted from man's need
And miles of fish-hooks baited to catch greed
And life made wretched out of human ken
And miles of shopping women served by men.
So, if the penman sums my London days
Let him but say that there were holy ways,
Dull Bloomsbury streets of dull brick mansions old
With stinking doors where women stood to scold
And drunken waits at Christmas with their horn

[61]

Droning the news, in snow, that Christ was born;
And windy gas lamps and the wet roads shining
And that old carol of the midnight whining,
And that old room (above the noisy slum)
Where there was wine and fire and talk with some
Under strange pictures of the wakened soul
To whom this earth was but a burnt-out coal.

O Time, bring back those midnights and those friends,
Those glittering moments that a spirit lends
That all may be imagined from the flash
The cloud-hid god-game through the lightning gash
Those hours of stricken sparks from which men took
Light to send out to men in song or book.
Those friends who heard St. Pancras' bells strike two
Yet stayed until the barber's cockerel crew.
Talking of noble styles, the Frenchman's best,
The thought beyond great poets not expressed,
The glory of mood where human frailty failed,
The forts of human light not yet assailed,
Till the dim room had mind and seemed to brood
Binding our wills to mental brotherhood,
Till we became a college, and each night
Was discipline and manhood and delight,
Till our farewells and winding down the stairs
At each grey dawn had meaning that Time spares,
That we, so linked, should roam the whole world round
Teaching the ways our brooding minds had found
Making that room our Chapter, our one mind
Where all that this world soiled should be refined.

Often at night I tread those streets again
And see the alley glimmering in the rain,

BIOGRAPHY

Yet now I miss that sign of earlier tramps
A house with shadows of plane-boughs under lamps,
The secret house where once a beggar stood
Trembling and blind to show his woe for food.
And now I miss that friend who used to walk
Home to my lodgings with me, deep in talk,
Wearing the last of night out in still streets
Trodden by us and policemen on their beats
And cats, but else deserted; now I miss
That lively mind and guttural laugh of his
And that strange way he had of making gleam,
Like something real, the art we used to dream.
London has been my prison; but my books
Hills and great waters, labouring men and brooks,
Ships and deep friendships and remembered days
Which even now set all my mind ablaze
As that June day when, in the red bricks' chinks
I saw the old Roman ruins white with pinks
And felt the hillside haunted even then
By not dead memory of the Roman men.
And felt the hillside thronged by souls unseen
Who knew the interest in me and were keen
That man alive should understand man dead
So many centuries since the blood was shed.
And quickened with strange hush because this comer
Sensed a strange soul alive behind the summer.
That other day on Ercall when the stones
Were sunbleached white, like long unburied bones,
While the bees droned and all the air was sweet
From honey buried underneath my feet,
Honey of purple heather and white clover
Sealed in its gummy bags till summer's over.

Then other days by water, by bright sea,
Clear as clean glass and my bright friend with me,
The cove clean bottomed where we saw the brown
Red spotted plaice go skimming six feet down
And saw the long fronds waving, white with shells,
Waving, unfolding, drooping, to the swells;
That sadder day when we beheld the great
And terrible beauty of a Lammas spate
Roaring white-mouthed in all the great cliff's gaps
Headlong, tree-tumbling fury of collapse,
While drenching clouds drove by and every sense
Was water roaring or rushing or in offence,
And mountain sheep stood huddled and blown gaps gleamed
Where torn white hair of torrents shook and streamed.
That sadder day when we beheld again
A spate going down in sunshine after rain,
When the blue reach of water leaping bright
Was one long ripple and clatter, flecked with white.
And that far day, that never blotted page
When youth was bright like flowers about old age
Fair generations bringing thanks for life
To that old kindly man and trembling wife
After their sixty years: Time never made
A better beauty since the Earth was laid
Than that thanksgiving given to grey hair
For the great gift of life which brought them there.

Days of endeavour have been good: the days
Racing in cutters for the comrade's praise,
The day they led my cutter at the turn
Yet could not keep the lead and dropped astern,
The moment in the spurt when both boats' oars

BIOGRAPHY

Dipped in each other's wash and throats grew hoarse
And teeth ground into teeth and both strokes quickened
Lashing the sea, and gasps came, and hearts sickened
And coxswains damned us, dancing, banking stroke,
To put our weights on, though our hearts were broke
And both boats seemed to stick and sea seemed glue,
The tide a mill race we were struggling through
And every quick recover gave us squints
Of them still there, and oar tossed water-glints
And cheering came, our friends, our foemen cheering,
A long, wild, rallying murmur on the hearing—
"Port Fore!" and "Starboard Fore!" "Port Fore." "Port
    Fore!"
"Up with her, Starboard," and at that each oar
Lightened, though arms were bursting, and eyes shut
And the oak stretchers grunted in the strut
And the curse quickened from the cox, our bows
Crashed, and drove talking water, we made vows
Chastity vows and temperance; in our pain
We numbered things we'd never eat again
If we could only win; then came the yell
"Starboard," "Port Fore," and then a beaten bell
Rung as for fire to cheer us. "Now." Oars bent
Soul took the looms now body's bolt was spent,
"Damn it, come on now," "On now," "On now," "Starboard."
"Port Fore." "Up with her, Port"; each cutter harboured
Ten eye-shut painsick strugglers, "Heave, oh, heave,"
Catcalls waked echoes like a shrieking sheave.
"Heave," and I saw a back, then two. "Port Fore."
"Starboard." "Come on." I saw the midship oar
And knew we had done them. "Port Fore." "Starboard."
    "Now."

I saw bright water spurting at their bow
Their cox' full face an instant.   They were done.
The watchers' cheering almost drowned the gun.
We had hardly strength to toss our oars; our cry
Cheering the losing cutter was a sigh.
Other bright days of action have seemed great:
Wild days in a pampero off the Plate;
Good swimming days, at Hog Back or the Coves
Which the young gannet and the corbie loves;
Surf-swimming between rollers, catching breath
Between the advancing grave and breaking death,
Then shooting up into the sunbright smooth
To watch the advancing roller bare her tooth,
And days of labour also, loading, hauling;
Long days at winch or capstan, heaving, pawling;
The days with oxen, dragging stone from blasting,
And dusty days in mills, and hot days masting.
Trucking on dust-dry deckings smooth like ice,
And hunts in mighty wool-racks after mice;
Mornings with buckwheat when the fields did blanch
With White Leghorns come from the chicken ranch.
Days near the spring upon the sunburnt hill,
Plying the maul or gripping tight the drill.
Delights of work most real, delights that change
The headache life of towns to rapture strange
Not known by townsmen, nor imagined; health
That puts new glory upon mental wealth
And makes the poor man rich.
                              But that ends, too,
Health with its thoughts of life; and that bright view
That sunny landscape from life's peak, that glory,
And all a glad man's comments on life's story

BIOGRAPHY

And thoughts of marvellous towns and living men
And what pens tell and all beyond the pen
End, and are summed in words so truly dead
They raise no image of the heart and head,
The life, the man alive, the friend we knew,
The mind ours argued with or listened to,
None; but are dead, and all life's keenness, all,
Is dead as print before the funeral,
Even deader after, when the dates are sought,
And cold minds disagree with what we thought.
This many pictured world of many passions
Wears out the nations as a woman fashions,
And what life is is much to very few,
Men being so strange, so mad, and what men do
So good to watch or share; but when men count
Those hours of life that were a bursting fount,
Sparkling the dusty heart with living springs,
There seems a world, beyond our earthly things,
Gated by golden moments, each bright time
Opening to show the city white like lime,
High towered and many peopled. This made sure,
Work that obscures those moments seems impure,
Making our not-returning time of breath
Dull with the ritual and records of death,
That frost of fact by which our wisdom gives
Correctly stated death to all that lives.

Best trust the happy moments. What they gave
Makes man less fearful of the certain grave,
And gives his work compassion and new eyes.
The days that make us happy make us wise.

SHIPS

I cannot tell their wonder nor make known
Magic that once thrilled through me to the bone,
But all men praise some beauty, tell some tale,
Vent a high mood which makes the rest seem pale,
Pour their heart's blood to flourish one green leaf,
Follow some Helen for her gift of grief,
And fail in what they mean, whate'er they do:
You should have seen, man cannot tell to you
The beauty of the ships of that my city.
That beauty now is spoiled by the sea's pity;
For one may haunt the pier a score of times,
Hearing St. Nicholas bells ring out the chimes,
Yet never see those proud ones swaying home
With mainyards backed and bows a cream of foam,
Those bows so lovely-curving, cut so fine,
Those coulters of the many-bubbled brine,
As once, long since, when all the docks were filled
With that sea-beauty man has ceased to build.

Yet, though their splendour may have ceased to be,
Each played her sovereign part in making me;
Now I return my thanks with heart and lips
For the great queenliness of all those ships.

And first the first bright memory, still so clear,
An autumn evening in a golden year,
When in the last lit moments before dark
The *Chepica*, a steel-grey lovely barque,

SHIPS

Came to an anchor near us on the flood,
Her trucks aloft in sun-glow red as blood.

Then come so many ships that I could fill
Three docks with their fair hulls remembered still,
Each with her special memory's special grace,
Riding the sea, making the waves give place
To delicate high beauty; man's best strength,
Noble in every line in all their length.
Ailsa, Genista, ships, with long jibbooms,
The *Wanderer* with great beauty and strange dooms,
Liverpool (mightiest then) superb, sublime,
The *California* huge, as slow as time.
The *Copley* swift, the perfect *J. T. North*,
The loveliest barque my city has sent forth,
Dainty *John Lockett* well remembered yet,
The splendid *Argus* with her skysail set,
Stalwart *Drumcliff*, white-blocked, majestic *Sierras*,
Divine bright ships, the water's standard-bearers;
Melpomene, Euphrosyne, and their sweet
Sea-troubling sisters of the Fernie fleet;
Corunna (in whom my friend died) and the old
Long since loved *Esmeralda* long since sold.
Centurion passed in Rio, *Glaucus* spoken,
Aladdin burnt, the *Bidston* water-broken,
Yola, in whom my friend sailed, *Dawpool* trim,
Fierce-bowed *Egeria* plunging to the swim,
Stanmore wide-sterned, sweet *Cupica*, tall *Bard*,
Queen in all harbours with her moon sail yard.

Though I tell many, there must still be others,
McVickar Marshall's ships and Fernie Brothers',

[69]

Lochs, Counties, Shires, Drums, the countless lines
Whose house-flags all were once familiar signs
At high main-trucks on Mersey's windy ways
When sunlight made the wind-white water blaze.
Their names bring back old mornings, when the docks
Shone with their house-flags and their painted blocks,
Their raking masts below the Custom House
And all the marvellous beauty of their bows.

Familiar steamers, too, majestic steamers,
Shearing Atlantic roller-tops to streamers,
Umbria, Etruria, noble, still at sea,
The grandest, then, that man had brought to be.
Majestic, City of Paris, City of Rome,
Forever jealous racers, out and home.
The *Alfred Holt's* blue smoke-stacks down the stream,
The fair *Loanda* with her bows a-cream.
Booth liners, Anchor liners, Red Star liners,
The marks and styles of countless ship-designers,
The *Magdalena, Puno, Potosi*,
Lost *Cotopaxi*, all well known to me.

These splendid ships, each with her grace, her glory,
Her memory of old song or comrade's story,
Still in my mind the image of life's need,
Beauty in hardest action, beauty indeed.
"They built great ships and sailed them" sounds most brave
Whatever arts we have or fail to have;
I touch my country's mind, I come to grips
With half her purpose, thinking of these ships
That art untouched by softness, all that line
Drawn ringing hard to stand the test of brine,

[70]

TRUTH

That nobleness and grandeur, all that beauty
Born of a manly life and bitter duty,
That splendour of fine bows which yet could stand
The shock of rollers never checked by land.
That art of masts, sail crowded, fit to break,
Yet stayed to strength and backstayed into rake,
The life demanded by that art, the keen
Eye-puckered, hard-case seamen, silent, lean,—
They are grander things than all the art of towns,
Their tests are tempests and the sea that drowns,
They are my country's line, her great art done
By strong brains labouring on the thought unwon,
They mark our passage as a race of men,
Earth will not see such ships as those again.

TRUTH

Man with his burning soul
Has but an hour of breath
To build a ship of Truth
In which his soul may sail,
Sail on the sea of death.
For death takes toll
Of beauty, courage, youth,
Of all but Truth.

Life's city ways are dark,
Men mutter by; the wells
Of the great waters moan.
O death, O sea, O tide,

The waters moan like bells.
No light, no mark,
The soul goes out alone
On seas unknown.

Stripped of all purple robes,
Stripped of all golden lies,
I will not be afraid.
Truth will preserve through death;
Perhaps the stars will rise,
The stars like globes.
The ship my striving made
May see night fade.

THEY CLOSED HER EYES

FROM THE SPANISH OF DON GUSTAVO A. BÉCQUER

They closed her eyes,
They were still open;
They hid her face
With a white linen,
And, some sobbing,
Others in silence,
From the sad bedroom
All came away.

The night-light in a dish
Burned on the floor,
It flung on the wall
The bed's shadow,

[72]

And in that shadow
One saw sometimes
Drawn in sharp line
The body's shape.

The day awakened
At its first whiteness
With its thousand noises;
The town awoke
Before that contrast
Of life and strangeness,
Of light and darkness.
I thought a moment
  My God, how lonely
  The dead are!

From the house, shoulder-high
To church they bore her,
And in a chapel
They left her bier.
There they surrounded
Her pale body
With yellow candles
And black stuffs.

At the last stroke
Of the ringing for the souls
An old crone finished
Her last prayers.
She crossed the narrow nave;
The doors moaned,
And the holy place
Remained deserted.

[73]

From a clock one heard
The measured ticking,
And from some candles
The guttering.
All things there
Were so grim and sad,
So dark and rigid,
That I thought a moment,
  My God, how lonely
  The dead are!

From the high belfry
The tongue of iron
Clanged, giving out
His sad farewell.
Crape on their clothes,
Her friends and kindred
Passed in a row,
Making procession.

In the last vault,
Dark and narrow,
The pickaxe opened
A niche at one end;
There they laid her down.
Soon they bricked the place up,
And with a gesture
Bade grief farewell.

Pickaxe on shoulder
The grave-digger,
Singing between his teeth,
Passed out of sight.

THEY CLOSED HER EYES

The night came down;
It was all silent,
Lost in the shadows
I thought a moment.
  My God, how lonely
  The dead are!

In the long nights
Of bitter winter,
When the wind makes
The rafters creak,
When the violent rain
Lashes the windows,
Lonely, I remember
That poor girl.

There falls the rain
With its noise eternal.
There the north wind
Fights with the rain.
Stretched in the hollow
Of the damp bricks
Perhaps her bones
Freeze with the cold.

Does the dust return to dust?
Does the soul fly to heaven?
Is all vile matter,
Rottenness, filthiness?
I know not.   But
There is something—something
That I cannot explain,

Something that gives us
Loathing, terror,
To leave the dead
So alone, so wretched.

THE HARP

FROM THE SPANISH OF DON GUSTAVO A. BÉCQUER

In a dark corner of the room,
Perhaps forgotten by its owner,
Silent and dim with dust,
I saw the harp.

How many musics slumbered in its strings,
As the bird sleeps in the branches,
Waiting the snowy hand
That could awaken them.

Ah me, I thought, how many, many times
Genius thus slumbers in a human soul,
Waiting, as Lazarus waited, for a voice
To bid him "Rise and walk."

SONNET

FROM THE SPANISH OF DON FRANCISCO DE QUEVEDO

I saw the ramparts of my native land,
One time so strong, now dropping in decay,
Their strength destroyed by this new age's way
That has worn out and rotted what was grand.
I went into the fields: there I could see
The sun drink up the waters newly thawed,
And on the hills the moaning cattle pawed;
Their miseries robbed the day of light for me.

I went into my house: I saw how spotted,
Decaying things made that old home their prize.
My withered walking-staff had come to bend;
I felt the age had won; my sword was rotted,
And there was nothing on which I set my eyes
That was not a reminder of the end.

SONNET ON THE DEATH OF HIS WIFE

FROM THE PORTUGUESE OF ANTONIO DE FERREIRO

That blessed sunlight that once showed to me
My way to heaven more plain more certainly,
And with her bright beam banished utterly
All trace of mortal sorrow far from me,

Has gone from me, has left her prison sad,
And I am blind and alone and gone astray,
Like a lost pilgrim in a desert way
Wanting the blessed guide that once he had.

Thus with a spirit bowed and mind a blur
I trace the holy steps where she has gone,
By valleys and by meadows and by mountains,
And everywhere I catch a glimpse of her.
She takes me by the hand and leads me on,
And my eyes follow her, my eyes made fountains.

SONG

One sunny time in May
When lambs were sporting,
The sap ran in the spray
And I went courting,
And all the apple boughs
Were bright with blossom,
I picked an early rose
For my love's bosom.

And then I met her friend,
Down by the water,
Who cried "She's met her end,
That grey-eyed daughter;
That voice of hers is stilled
Her beauty broken."
O me, my love is killed,
My love unspoken.

[78]

She was too sweet, too dear,
To die so cruel,
O Death, why leave me here
And take my jewel?
Her voice went to the bone,
So true, so ringing,
And now I go alone,
Winter or springing.

THE BALLAD OF SIR BORS

Would I could win some quiet and rest, and a little ease,
In the cool grey hush of the dusk, in the dim green place of the
    trees,
Where the birds are singing, singing, singing, crying aloud
The song of the red, red rose that blossoms beyond the seas.

Would I could see it, the rose, when the light begins to fail,
And a lone white star in the West is glimmering on the mail;
The red, red passionate rose of the sacred blood of the Christ,
In the shining chalice of God, the cup of the Holy Grail.

The dusk comes gathering grey, and the darkness dims the West,
The oxen low to the byre, and all bells ring to rest;
But I ride over the moors, for the dusk still bides and waits,
That brims my soul with the glow of the rose that ends the
    Quest.

My horse is spavined and ribbed, and his bones come through
    his hide,
My sword is rotten with rust, but I shake the reins and ride,

For the bright white birds of God that nest in the rose have
    called,
And never a township now is a town where I can bide.

It will happen at last, at dusk, as my horse limps down the fell,
A star will glow like a note God strikes on a silver bell,
And the bright white birds of God will carry my soul to Christ,
And the sight of the Rose, the Rose, will pay for the years of
    hell.

SPANISH WATERS

Spanish waters, Spanish waters, you are ringing in my ears,
Like a slow sweet piece of music from the grey forgotten
    years;
Telling tales, and beating tunes, and bringing weary thoughts
    to me
Of the sandy beach at Muertos, where I would that I could be.

There's a surf breaks on Los Muertos, and it never stops to roar,
And it's there we came to anchor, and it's there we went ashore,
Where the blue lagoon is silent amid snags of rotting trees,
Dropping like the clothes of corpses cast up by the seas.

We anchored at Los Muertos when the dipping sun was red,
We left her half-a-mile to sea, to west of Nigger Head;
And before the mist was on the Cay, before the day was done,
We were all ashore on Muertos with the gold that we had won.

SPANISH WATERS

We bore it through the marshes in a half-score battered chests,
Sinking, in the sucking quagmires, to the sunburn on our
    breasts,
Heaving over tree-trunks, gasping, damning at the flies and
    heat,
Longing for a long drink, out of silver, in the ship's cool lazareet.

The moon came white and ghostly as we laid the treasure down,
There was gear there'd make a beggarman as rich as Lima Town,
Copper charms and silver trinkets from the chests of Spanish
    crews,
Gold doubloons and double moydores, louis d'ors and portagues,

Clumsy yellow-metal earrings from the Indians of Brazil,
Uncut emeralds out of Rio, bezoar stones from Guayaquil;
Silver, in the crude and fashioned, pots of old Arica bronze,
Jewels from the bones of Incas desecrated by the Dons.

We smoothed the place with mattocks, and we took and blazed
    the tree,
Which marks yon where the gear is hid that none will ever
    see,
And we laid aboard the ship again, and south away we steers,
Through the loud surf of Los Muertos which is beating in
    my ears.

I'm the last alive that knows it. All the rest have gone their
    ways
Killed, or died, or come to anchor in the old Mulatas Cays,
And I go singing, fiddling, old and starved and in despair,
And I know where all that gold is hid, if I were only there.

It's not the way to end it all. I'm old, and nearly blind,
And an old man's past's a strange thing, for it never leaves
his mind.
And I see in dreams, awhiles, the beach, the sun's disc dipping
red,
And the tall ship, under topsails, swaying in past Nigger Head.

I'd be glad to step ashore there. Glad to take a pick and go
To the lone blazed coco-palm tree in the place no others know,
And lift the gold and silver that has mouldered there for years
By the loud surf of Los Muertos which is beating in my ears.

CARGOES

Quinquireme of Nineveh from distant Ophir,
Rowing home to haven in sunny Palestine,
With a cargo of ivory,
And apes and peacocks,
Sandalwood, cedarwood, and sweet white wine.

Stately Spanish galleon coming from the Isthmus,
Dipping through the Tropics by the palm-green shores,
With a cargo of diamonds,
Emeralds, amethysts,
Topazes, and cinnamon, and gold moidores.

Dirty British coaster with a salt-caked smoke stack,
Butting through the Channel in the mad March days,
With a cargo of Tyne coal,
Road-rails, pig-lead,
Firewood, iron-ware, and cheap tin trays.

CAPTAIN STRATTON'S FANCY

Oh some are fond of red wine, and some are fond of white,
And some are all for dancing by the pale moonlight;
But rum alone's the tipple, and the heart's delight
  Of the old bold mate of Henry Morgan.

Oh some are fond of Spanish wine, and some are fond of French,
And some'll swallow tay and stuff fit only for a wench;
But I'm for right Jamaica till I roll beneath the bench,
  Says the old bold mate of Henry Morgan.

Oh some are for the lily, and some are for the rose,
But I am for the sugar-cane that in Jamaica grows;
For it's that that makes the bonny drink to warm my copper
    nose,
  Says the old bold mate of Henry Morgan.

Oh some are fond of fiddles, and a song well sung,
And some are all for music for to lilt upon the tongue;
But mouths were made for tankards, and for sucking at the
    bung,
  Says the old bold mate of Henry Morgan.

Oh some are fond of dancing, and some are fond of dice,
And some are all for red lips, and pretty lasses' eyes;
But a right Jamaica puncheon is a finer prize
  To the old bold mate of Henry Morgan.

Oh some that's good and godly ones they hold that it's a sin
To troll the jolly bowl around, and let the dollars spin;
But I'm for toleration and for drinking at an inn,
   Says the old bold mate of Henry Morgan.

Oh some are sad and wretched folk that go in silken suits,
And there's a mort of wicked rogues that live in good reputes;
So I'm for drinking honestly, and dying in my boots,
   Like an old bold mate of Henry Morgan.

AN OLD SONG RE-SUNG

I saw a ship a-sailing, a-sailing, a-sailing,
With emeralds and rubies and sapphires in her hold;
And a bosun in a blue coat bawling at the railing,
Piping through a silver call that had a chain of gold;
The summer wind was failing and the tall ship rolled.

I saw a ship a-steering, a-steering, a-steering,
With roses in red thread worked upon her sails;
With sacks of purple amethysts, the spoils of buccaneering,
Skins of musky yellow wine, and silks in bales,
Her merry men were cheering, hauling on the brails.

I saw a ship a-sinking, a-sinking, a-sinking,
With glittering sea-water splashing on her decks,
With seamen in her spirit-room singing songs and drinking,
Pulling claret bottles down, and knocking off the necks,
The broken glass was chinking as she sank among the wrecks.

ST. MARY'S BELLS

It's pleasant in Holy Mary
By San Marie lagoon,
The bells they chime and jingle
From dawn to afternoon.
They rhyme and chime and mingle,
They pulse and boom and beat,
And the laughing bells are gentle
And the mournful bells are sweet.

Oh, who are the men that ring them,
The bells of San Marie,
Oh, who but sonsie seamen
Come in from over sea,
And merrily in the belfries
They rock and sway and hale,
And send the bells a-jangle,
And down the lusty ale.

It's pleasant in Holy Mary
To hear the beaten bells
Come booming into music,
Which throbs, and clangs, and swells,
From sunset till the daybreak,
From dawn to afternoon.
In port of Holy Mary
On San Marie lagoon.

[85]

LONDON TOWN

Oh London Town's a fine town, and London sights are rare,
And London ale is right ale, and brisk's the London air,
And busily goes the world there, but crafty grows the mind,
And London Town of all towns I'm glad to leave behind.

Then hey for croft and hop-yard, and hill, and field, and pond,
With Bredon Hill before me and Malvern Hill beyond.
The hawthorn white i' the hedgerow, and all the spring's attire
In the comely land of Teme and Lugg, and Clent, and Clee,
    and Wyre.

Oh London girls are brave girls, in silk and cloth o' gold,
And London shops are rare shops, where gallant things are sold,
And bonnily clinks the gold there, but drowsily blinks the eye,
And London Town of all towns I'm glad to hurry by.

Then, hey for covert and woodland, and ash and elm and oak,
Tewkesbury inns, and Malvern roofs, and Worcester chimney
    smoke,
The apple trees in the orchard, the cattle in the byre,
And all the land from Ludlow town to Bredon church's spire.

Oh London tunes are new tunes, and London books are wise,
And London plays are rare plays, and fine to country eyes,
But craftily fares the knave there, and wickedly fares the Jew,
And London Town of all towns I'm glad to hurry through.

THE EMIGRANT

So hey for the road, the west road, by mill and forge and fold,
Scent of the fern and song of the lark by brook, and field, and
    wold,
To the comely folk at the hearth-stone and the talk beside the
    fire,
In the hearty land, where I was bred, my land of heart's desire.

THE EMIGRANT

Going by Daly's shanty I heard the boys within
Dancing the Spanish hornpipe to Driscoll's violin,
I heard the sea-boots shaking the rough planks of the floor,
But I was going westward, I hadn't heart for more.

All down the windy village the noise rang in my ears,
Old sea boots stamping, shuffling, it brought the bitter tears,
The old tune piped and quavered, the lilts came clear and strong,
But I was going westward, I couldn't join the song.

There were the grey stone houses, the night wind blowing keen,
The hill-sides pale with moonlight, the young corn springing
    green,
The hearth nooks lit and kindly, with dear friends good to see,
But I was going westward, and the ship waited me.

PORT OF HOLY PETER

The blue laguna rocks and quivers,
   Dull gurgling eddies twist and spin,
The climate does for people's livers,
    It's a nasty place to anchor in
        Is Spanish port,
        Fever port,
        Port of Holy Peter.

The town begins on the sea-beaches,
   And the town's mad with the stinging flies,
The drinking water's mostly leeches,
    It's a far remove from Paradise
        Is Spanish port,
        Fever port,
        Port of Holy Peter.

There's sand-bagging and throat-slitting,
   And quiet graves in the sea slime,
Stabbing, of course, and rum-hitting,
    Dirt, and drink, and stink, and crime,
        In Spanish port,
        Fever port,
        Port of Holy Peter.

All the day the wind's blowing
   From the sick swamp below the hills,
All the night the plague's growing,
   And the dawn brings the fever chills,

BEAUTY

In Spanish port,
Fever port,
Port of Holy Peter.

You get a thirst there's no slaking
    You get the chills and fever-shakes,
Tongue yellow and head aching,
    And then the sleep that never wakes.
And all the year the heat's baking,
    The sea rots and the earth quakes,
        In Spanish port,
        Fever port,
        Port of Holy Peter.

BEAUTY

I have seen dawn and sunset on moors and windy hills
Coming in solemn beauty like slow old tunes of Spain:
I have seen the lady April bringing the daffodils,
Bringing the springing grass and the soft warm April rain.

I have heard the song of the blossoms and the old chant of the
    sea,
And seen strange lands from under the arched white sails of
    ships;
But the loveliest things of beauty God ever has shown to me,
Are her voice, and her hair, and eyes, and the dear red curve
    of her lips.

[89]

THE SEEKERS

Friends and loves we have none, nor wealth nor blessed abode,
But the hope of the City of God at the other end of the road.

Not for us are content, and quiet, and peace of mind,
For we go seeking a city that we shall never find.

There is no solace on earth for us—for such as we—
Who search for a hidden city that we shall never see.

Only the road and the dawn, the sun, the wind, and the rain,
And the watch fire under stars, and sleep, and the road again.

We seek the City of God, and the haunt where beauty dwells,
And we find the noisy mart and the sound of burial bells.

Never the golden city, where radiant people meet,
But the dolorous town where mourners are going about the
street.

We travel the dusty road till the light of the day is dim,
And sunset shows us spires away on the world's rim.

We travel from dawn to dusk, till the day is past and by,
Seeking the Holy City beyond the rim of the sky.

Friends and loves we have none, nor wealth nor blest abode,
But the hope of the City of God at the other end of the road.

PRAYER

When the last sea is sailed, when the last shallow's charted,
When the last field is reaped, and the last harvest stored,
When the last fire is out and the last guest departed,
Grant the last prayer that I shall pray, be good to me, O Lord.

And let me pass in a night at sea, a night of storm and thunder,
In the loud crying of the wind through sail and rope and spar,
Send me a ninth great peaceful wave to drown and roll me under
To the cold tunny-fish's home where the drowned galleons are.

And in the dim green quiet place far out of sight and hearing,
Grant I may hear at whiles the wash and thresh of the sea-foam
About the fine keen bows of the stately clippers steering
Towards the lone northern star and the fair ports of home.

DAWN

The dawn comes cold: the haystack smokes,
    The green twigs crackle in the fire,
The dew is dripping from the oaks,
And sleepy men bear milking-yokes
    Slowly towards the cattle-byre.

Down in the town a clock strikes six,
    The grey east heaven burns and glows,
The dew shines on the thatch of ricks,
A slow old crone comes gathering sticks,
    The red cock in the ox-yard crows.

Beyond the stack where we have lain
    The road runs twisted like a snake
(The white road to the land of Spain),
The road that we must foot again,
    Though the feet halt and the heart ache.

LAUGH AND BE MERRY

Laugh and be merry, remember, better the world with a song,
Better the world with a blow in the teeth of a wrong.
Laugh, for the time is brief, a thread the length of a span.
Laugh and be proud to belong to the old proud pageant of man.

Laugh and be merry: remember, in olden time.
God made Heaven and Earth for joy He took in a rhyme,
Made them, and filled them full with the strong red wine of
    His mirth,
The splendid joy of the stars: the joy of the earth.

So we must laugh and drink from the deep blue cup of the sky,
Join the jubilant song of the great stars sweeping by,
Laugh, and battle, and work, and drink of the wine outpoured
In the dear green earth, the sign of the joy of the Lord.

Laugh and be merry together, like brothers akin,
Guesting awhile in the rooms of a beautiful inn,
Glad till the dancing stops, and the lilt of the music ends.
Laugh till the game is played; and be you merry, my friends.

JUNE TWILIGHT

The twilight comes; the sun
    Dips down and sets,
The boys have done
    Play at the nets.

In a warm golden glow
    The woods are steeped.
The shadows grow;
    The bat has cheeped.

Sweet smells the new-mown hay;
    The mowers pass
Home, each his way,
    Through the grass.

The night-wind stirs the fern,
    A night-jar spins;
The windows burn
    In the inns.

Dusky it grows. The moon!
    The dews descend.
Love, can this beauty in our hearts
    End?

ROADWAYS

One road leads to London,
  One road runs to Wales,
My road leads me seawards
  To the white dipping sails.

One road leads to the river,
  As it goes singing slow;
My road leads to shipping,
  Where the bronzed sailors go.

Leads me, lures me, calls me
  To salt green tossing sea;
A road without earth's road-dust
  Is the right road for me.

A wet road heaving, shining,
  And wild with seagull's cries,
A mad salt sea-wind blowing
  The salt spray in my eyes.

My road calls me, lures me
  West, east, south, and north;
Most roads lead men homewards,
  My road leads me forth

To add more miles to the tally
  Of grey miles left behind,
In quest of that one beauty
  God put me here to find.

MIDSUMMER NIGHT

The perfect disc of the sacred moon
   Through still blue heaven serenely swims,
   And the lone bird's liquid music brims
The peace of the night with a perfect tune.

This is that holiest night of the year
   When (the mowers say) may be heard and seen
   The ghostly court of the English queen,
Who rides to harry and hunt the deer.

And the woodland creatures cower awake,
   A strange unrest is on harts and does,
   For the maiden Dian a-hunting goes,
And the trembling deer are afoot in the brake.

They start at a shaken leaf: the sound
   Of a dry twig snapped by a squirrel's foot
   Is a nameless dread: and to them the hoot
Of a mousing owl is the cry of a hound.

Oh soon the forest will ring with cries,
   The dim green coverts will flash: the grass
   Will glow as the radiant hunters pass
After the quarry with burning eyes.

The hurrying feet will range unstayed
   Of questing goddess and hunted fawn,
   Till the east is grey with the sacred dawn,
And the red cock wakens the milking maid.

THE HARPER'S SONG

This sweetness trembling from the strings
   The music of my troublous lute
   Hath timed Herodias' daughter's foot;
Setting a-clink her ankle-rings
Whenas she danced to feasted kings.

Where gemmed apparel burned and caught
   The sunset 'neath the golden dome,
   To the dark beauties of old Rome
My sorrowful lute hath haply brought
Sad memories sweet with tender thought.

When night had fallen and lights and fires
   Were darkened in the homes of men,
   Some sighing echo stirred:—and then
The old cunning wakened from the wires
The old sorrows and the old desires.

Dead Kings in long forgotten lands,
   And all dead beauteous women; some
   Whose pride imperial hath become
Old armour rusting in the sands
And shards of iron in dusty hands,

Have heard my lyre's soft rise and fall
   Go trembling down the paven ways,
   Till every heart was all ablaze—
Hasty each foot—to obey the call
To triumph or to funeral.

THE GENTLE LADY

Could I begin again the slow
  Sweet mournful music filled with tears,
  Surely the old, dead, dusty ears
Would hear; the old drowsy eyes would glow,
Old memories come; old hopes and fears,
And time restore the long ago.

THE GENTLE LADY

So beautiful, so dainty-sweet,
So like a lyre's delightful touch—
A beauty perfect, ripe, complete
That art's own hand could only smutch
And nature's self not better much.

So beautiful, so purely wrought,
Like a fair missal penned with hymns,
So gentle, so surpassing thought—
A beauteous soul in lovely limbs,
A lantern that an angel trims.

So simple-sweet, without a sin,
Like gentle music gently timed,
Like rhyme-words coming aptly in,
To round a mooned poem rhymed
To tunes the laughing bells have chimed.

THE DEAD KNIGHT

The cleanly rush of the mountain air,
And the mumbling, grumbling humble-bees,
Are the only things that wander there.
The pitiful bones are laid at ease,
The grass has grown in his tangled hair,
And a rambling bramble binds his knees.

To shrieve his soul from the pangs of hell,
The only requiem bells that rang
Were the harebell and the heather bell.
Hushed he is with the holy spell
In the gentle hymn the wind sang,
And he lies quiet, and sleeps well.
He is bleached and blanched with the summer sun;
The misty rain and the cold dew
Have altered him from the kingly one
Whom his lady loved, and his men knew,
And dwindled him to a skeleton.

The vetches have twined about his bones,
The straggling ivy twists and creeps
In his eye-sockets: the nettle keeps
Vigil about him while he sleeps.
Over his body the wind moans
With a dreary tune throughout the day,
In a chorus wistful, eerie, thin
As the gulls' cry, as the cry in the bay,
The mournful word the seas say
When tides are wandering out or in.

SORROW OF MYDATH

Weary the cry of the wind is, weary the sea,
Weary the heart and the mind and the body of me,
Would I were out of it, done with it, would I could be
   A white gull crying along the desolate sands

Outcast, derelict soul in a body accurst,
Standing drenched with the spindrift, standing athirst,
For the cool green waves of death to arise and burst
   In a tide of quiet for me on the desolate sands.

Would that the waves and the long white hair of the spray
Would gather in splendid terror, and blot me away
To the sunless place of the wrecks where the waters sway
   Gently, dreamily, quietly over desolate sands.

TWILIGHT

Twilight it is, and the far woods are dim, and the rooks cry
    and call.
Down in the valley the lamps, and the mist, and a star over all,
There by the rick, where they thresh, is the drone at an end,
Twilight it is, and I travel the road with my friend.

I think of the friends who are dead, who were dear long ago
    in the past,
Beautiful friends who are dead, though I know that death
    cannot last;
Friends with the beautiful eyes that the dust has defiled,
Beautiful souls who were gentle when I was a child.

[99]

INVOCATION

O wanderer into many brains,
O spark the emperor's purple hides,
You sow the dusk with fiery grains
When the gold horseman rides.
    O beauty on the darkness hurled,
    Be it through me you shame the world.

POSTED AS MISSING

Under all her topsails she trembled like a stag,
The wind made a ripple in her bonny red flag;
They cheered her from the shore and they cheered her from
    the pier,
And under all her topsails she trembled like a deer.

So she passed swaying, where the green seas run,
Her wind-steadied topsails were stately in the sun;
There was glitter on the water from her red port light,
So she passed swaying, till she was out of sight.

Long and long ago it was, a weary time it is,
The bones of her sailor-men are coral plants by this;
Coral plants, and shark-weed, and a mermaid's comb,
And if the fishers net them they never bring them home.

It's rough on sailors' women. They have to mangle hard,
And stitch at dungarees till their finger-ends are scarred,
Thinking of the sailor-men who sang among the crowd,
Hoisting of her topsails when she sailed so proud.

A CREED

I hold that when a person dies
  His soul returns again to earth;
Arrayed in some new flesh-disguise
  Another mother gives him birth.
With sturdier limbs and brighter brain
The old soul takes the roads again.

Such is my own belief and trust;
  This hand, this hand that holds the pen,
Has many a hundred times been dust
  And turned, as dust, to dust again;
These eyes of mine have blinked and shone
In Thebes, in Troy, in Babylon.

All that I rightly think or do,
  Or make, or spoil, or bless, or blast,
Is curse or blessing justly due
  For sloth or effort in the past.
My life's a statement of the sum
Of vice indulged, or overcome.

I know that in my lives to be
  My sorry heart will ache and burn,
And worship, unavailingly,
  The woman whom I used to spurn,
And shake to see another have
The love I spurned, the love she gave.

And I shall know, in angry words,
    In gibes, and mocks, and many a tear,
A carrion flock of homing-birds,
    The gibes and scorns I uttered here.
The brave word that I failed to speak
Will brand me dastard on the cheek.

And as I wander on the roads
    I shall be helped and healed and blessed;
Dear words shall cheer and be as goads
    To urge to heights before unguessed.
My road shall be the road I made;
All that I gave shall be repaid.

So shall I fight, so shall I tread,
    In this long war beneath the stars;
So shall a glory wreathe my head,
    So shall I faint and show the scars,
Until this case, this clogging mould,
Be smithied all to kingly gold.

WHEN BONY DEATH

When bony Death has chilled her gentle blood,
    And dimmed the brightness of her wistful eyes,
And changed her glorious beauty into mud
    By his old skill in hateful wizardries;

When an old lichened marble strives to tell
    How sweet a grace, how red a lip was hers;
When rheumy grey-beards say, "I knew her well,"
    Showing the grave to curious worshippers;

HER HEART

When all the roses that she sowed in me
   Have dripped their crimson petals and decayed,
Leaving no greenery on any tree
   That her dear hands in my heart's garden laid,

Then grant, old Time, to my green mouldering skull,
These songs may keep her memory beautiful.

HER HEART

Her heart is always doing lovely things,
   Filling my wintry mind with simple flowers;
Playing sweet tunes on my untunéd strings,
   Delighting all my undelightful hours.

She plays me like a lute, what tune she will,
   No string in me but trembles at her touch,
Shakes into sacred music, or is still,
   Trembles or stops, or swells, her skill is such.
And in the dusty tavern of my soul
   Where filthy lusts drink witches' brew for wine,
Her gentle hand still keeps me from the bowl,
   Still keeps me man, saves me from being swine.

All grace in me, all sweetness in my verse,
Is hers, is my dear girl's, and only hers.

BEING HER FRIEND

Being her friend, I do not care, not I,
   How gods or men may wrong me, beat me down;
Her word's sufficient star to travel by,
   I count her quiet praise sufficient crown.

Being her friend, I do not covet gold,
   Save for a royal gift to give her pleasure;
To sit with her, and have her hand to hold,
   Is wealth, I think, surpassing minted treasure.

Being her friend, I only covet art,
   A white pure flame to search me as I trace
In crooked letters from a throbbing heart
   The hymn to beauty written on her face.

FRAGMENTS

Troy Town is covered up with weeds,
   The rabbits and the pismires brood
On broken gold, and shards, and beads
   Where Priam's ancient palace stood.

The floors of many a gallant house
   Are matted with the roots of grass;
The glow-worm and the nimble mouse
   Among her ruins flit and pass.

[104]

FRAGMENTS

And there, in orts of blackened bone,
  The widowed Trojan beauties lie,
And Simois babbles over stone
  And waps and gurgles to the sky.

Once there were merry days in Troy,
  Her chimneys smoked with cooking meals,
The passing chariots did annoy
  The sunning housewives at their wheels.

And many a lovely Trojan maid
  Set Trojan lads to lovely things;
The game of life was nobly played,
  They played the game like Queens and Kings.

So that, when Troy had greatly passed
  In one red roaring fiery coal,
The courts the Grecians overcast
  Became a city in the soul.

In some green island of the sea,
  Where now the shadowy coral grows
In pride and pomp and empery
  The courts of old Atlantis rose.

In many a glittering house of glass
  The Atlanteans wandered there;
The paleness of their faces was
  Like ivory, so pale they were.

And hushed they were, no noise of words
  In those bright cities ever rang;
Only their thoughts, like golden birds,
  About their chambers thrilled and sang.

They knew all wisdom, for they knew
   The souls of those Egyptian Kings
Who learned, in ancient Babilu,
   The beauty of immortal things.

They knew all beauty—when they thought
   The air chimed like a stricken lyre,
The elemental birds were wrought,
   The golden birds became a fire.

And straight to busy camps and marts
   The singing flames were swiftly gone;
The trembling leaves of human hearts
   Hid boughs for them to perch upon.

And men in desert places, men
   Abandoned, broken, sick with fears,
Rose singing, swung their swords agen,
   And laughed and died among the spears.

The green and greedy seas have drowned
   That city's glittering walls and towers,
Her sunken minarets are crowned
   With red and russet water-flowers.

In towers and rooms and golden courts
   The shadowy coral lifts her sprays;
The scrawl hath gorged her broken orts,
   The shark doth haunt her hidden ways.

BORN FOR NOUGHT ELSE

But, at the falling of the tide,
  The golden birds still sing and gleam,
The Atlanteans have not died,
  Immortal things still give us dream.

The dream that fires man's heart to make,
  To build, to do, to sing or say
A beauty Death can never take,
  An Adam from the crumbled clay.

BORN FOR NOUGHT ELSE

Born for nought else, for nothing but for this,
  To watch the soft blood throbbing in her throat,
To think how comely sweet her body is,
  And learn the poem of her face by rote.

Born for nought else but to attempt a rhyme
  That shall describe her womanhood aright,
And make her holy to the end of Time,
  And be my soul's acquittal in God's sight.

Born for nought else but to expressly mark
  The music of her dear delicious ways;
Born but to perish meanly in the dark,
  Yet born to be the man to sing her praise.

Born for nought else: there is a spirit tells
My lot's a King's, being born for nothing else.

TEWKESBURY ROAD

It is good to be out on the road, and going one knows not where,
  Going through meadow and village, one knows not whither
    nor why;
Through the grey light drift of the dust, in the keen cool rush
  of the air,
  Under the flying white clouds, and the broad blue lift of
    the sky.

And to halt at the chattering brook, in the tall green fern at
  the brink
  Where the harebell grows, and the gorse, and the foxgloves
    purple and white;
Where the shy-eyed delicate deer troop down to the brook to
  drink
  When the stars are mellow and large at the coming on of the
    night.

O, to feel the beat of the rain, and the homely smell of the earth,
  Is a tune for the blood to jig to, a joy past power of words;
And the blessed green comely meadows are all a-ripple with
  mirth
  At the noise of the lambs at play and the dear wild cry of the
    birds.

THE DEATH ROOMS

My soul has many an old decaying room
   Hung with the ragged arras of the past,
Where startled faces flicker in the gloom,
   And horrid whispers set the cheek aghast.

Those dropping rooms are haunted by a death,
   A something like a worm gnawing a brain,
That bids me heed what bitter lesson saith
   The blind wind beating on the window-pane.

None dwells in those old rooms: none ever can—
   I pass them through at night with hidden head;
Lock'd rotting rooms her eyes must never scan,
   Floors that her blessed feet must never tread.

Haunted old rooms: rooms she must never know,
Where death-ticks knock and mouldering panels glow.

IGNORANCE

Since I have learned Love's shining alphabet,
   And spelled in ink what's writ in me in flame,
And borne her sacred image richly set
   Here in my heart to keep me quit of shame;

Since I have learned how wise and passing wise
  Is the dear friend whose beauty I extol,
And know how sweet a soul looks through the eyes,
  That are so pure a window to her soul;

Since I have learned how rare a woman shows
  As much in all she does as in her looks,
And seen the beauty of her shame the rose,
  And dim the beauty writ about in books;

All I have learned, and can learn, shows me this—
How scant, how slight, my knowledge of her is.

THE WATCH IN THE WOOD

When Death has laid her in his quietude,
  And dimmed the glow of her benignant star,
Her tired limbs shall rest within a wood,
  In a green glade where oaks and beeches are,

Where the shy fawns, the pretty fawns, the deer,
  With mild brown eyes shall view her spirit's husk;
The sleeping woman of her will appear,
  The maiden Dian shining through the dusk.

And, when the stars are white as twilight fails,
  And the green leaves are hushed, and the winds swoon,
The calm pure thrilling throats of nightingales
  Shall hymn her sleeping beauty to the moon.

C. L. M.

All the woods hushed—save for a dripping rose,
All the woods dim—save where a glow-worm glows.

Brimming the quiet woods with holiness,
    The lone brown birds will hymn her till the dawn,
The delicate, shy, dappled deer will press
    Soft pitying muzzles on her swathéd lawn.

The little pretty rabbits running by.
    Will pause among the dewy grass to peep,
Their thudding hearts affrighted to espy
    The maiden Dian lying there asleep.

Brown, lustrous, placid eyes of sylvan things
    Will wonder at the quiet in her face,
While from the thorny branch the singer brings
    Beauty and peace to that immortal place.

Until the grey dawn sets the woods astir
The pure birds' thrilling psalm will mourn for her.

C. L. M.

In the dark womb where I began
My mother's life made me a man.
Through all the months of human birth
Her beauty fed my common earth.
I cannot see, nor breathe, nor stir,
But through the death of some of her.

Down in the darkness of the grave
She cannot see the life she gave.
For all her love, she cannot tell
Whether I use it ill or well,
Nor knock at dusty doors to find
Her beauty dusty in the mind.

If the grave's gates could be undone,
She would not know her little son,
I am so grown. If we should meet
She would pass by me in the street,
Unless my soul's face let her see
My sense of what she did for me.

What have I done to keep in mind
My debt to her and womankind?
What woman's happier life repays
Her for those months of wretched days?
For all my mouthless body leeched
Ere Birth's releasing hell was reached?

What have I done, or tried, or said
In thanks to that dear woman dead?
Men triumph over women still,
Men trample women's rights at will,
And man's lust roves the world untamed.

*   *   *   *

O grave, keep shut lest I be shamed.

WASTE

No rose but fades: no glory but must pass:
    No hue but dims: no precious silk but frets.
Her beauty must go underneath the grass,
    Under the long roots of the violets.

O, many glowing beauties Time has hid
    In that dark, blotting box the villain sends.
He covers over with a coffin-lid
    Mothers and sons, and foes and lovely friends.

Maids that were redly-lipped and comely-skinned,
    Friends that deserved a sweeter bed than clay,
All are as blossoms blowing down the wind,
    Things the old envious villain sweeps away.

And though the mutterer laughs and church bells toll,
Death brings another April to the soul.

THIRD MATE

All the sheets are clacking, all the blocks are whining,
The sails are frozen stiff and the wetted decks are shining;
The reef's in the topsails, and it's coming on to blow,
And I think of the dear girl I left long ago.

Grey were her eyes, and her hair was long and bonny,
Golden was her hair, like the wild bees' honey.
And I was but a dog, and a mad one to despise,
The gold of her hair and the grey of her eyes.

There's the sea before me, and my home's behind me,
And beyond there the strange lands where nobody will mind me,
No one but the girls with the paint upon their cheeks,
Who sell away their beauty to whomsoever seeks.

There'll be drink and women there, and songs and laughter,
Peace from what is past and from all that follows after;
And a fellow will forget how a woman lies awake,
Lonely in the night watch crying for his sake.

Black it blows and bad and it howls like slaughter,
And the ship she shudders as she takes the water.
Hissing flies the spindrift like a wind-blown smoke,
And I think of a woman and a heart I broke.

THE WILD DUCK

Twilight.   Red in the west.
Dimness.   A glow on the wood.
The teams plod home to rest.
The wild duck come to glean.
O souls not understood,
What a wild cry in the pool;
What things have the farm ducks seen
That they cry so—huddle and cry?

Only the soul that goes.
Eager. Eager. Flying.
Over the globe of the moon,
Over the wood that glows.
Wings linked. Necks a-strain,
A rush and a wild crying.

* * * * * * *

A cry of the long pain
In the reeds of a steel lagoon.
In a land that no man knows.

CHRISTMAS, 1903

O, the sea breeze will be steady, and the tall ship's going trim,
And the dark blue skies are paling, and the white stars burning
dim;
The long night watch is over, and the long sea-roving done,
And yonder light is the Start Point light, and yonder comes the
sun.

O, we have been with the Spaniards, and far and long on the sea;
But there are the twisted chimneys, and the gnarled old inns on
the quay.
The wind blows keen as the day breaks, the roofs are white with
the rime,
And the church-bells ring as the sun comes up to call men in to
Prime.

The church-bells rock and jangle, and there is peace on the
    earth.
Peace and good will and plenty and Christmas games and mirth.
O, the gold glints bright on the wind-vane as it shifts above the
    squire's house,
And the water of the bar of Salcombe is muttering about the
    bows.

O, the salt sea tide of Salcombe, it wrinkles into wisps of foam,
And the church-bells ring in Salcombe to ring poor sailors home.
The belfry rocks as the bells ring, the chimes are merry as a song,
They ring home wandering sailors who have been homeless long.

THE WORD

My friend, my bonny friend, when we are old,
    And hand in hand go tottering down the hill,
May we be rich in love's refinèd gold,
    May love's gold coin be current with us still.

May love be sweeter for the vanished days,
    And your most perfect beauty still as dear
As when your troubled singer stood at gaze
    In the dear March of a most sacred year.

May what we are be all we might have been,
    And that potential, perfect, O my friend,
And may there still be many sheafs to glean
    In our love's acre, comrade, till the end.

And may we find, when ended is the page,
Death but a tavern on our pilgrimage.

[116]

THE EVERLASTING MERCY

TO MY WIFE

Thy place is biggyd above the sterrys cleer,
Noon erthely paleys wrouhte in so statly wyse,
Com on my freend, my brothir moost enteer,
For the I offryd my blood in sacrifise.

JOHN LYDGATE.

THE EVERLASTING MERCY

From '41 to '51
I was my folk's contrary son;
I bit my father's hand right through
And broke my mother's heart in two.
I sometimes go without my dinner
Now that I know the times I've gi'n her.

From '51 to '61
I cut my teeth and took to fun.
I learned what not to be afraid of
And what stuff women's lips are made of;
I learned with what a rosy feeling
Good ale makes floors seem like the ceiling,
And how the moon gives shiny light
To lads as roll home singing by't.
My blood did leap, my flesh did revel,
Saul Kane was tokened to the devil.

From '61 to '67
I lived in disbelief of Heaven.
I drunk, I fought, I poached, I whored,
I did despite unto the Lord.
I cursed, 'would make a man look pale,
And nineteen times I went to gaol.

Now, friends, observe and look upon me,
Mark how the Lord took pity on me.
By Dead Man's Thorn, while setting wires,
Who should come up but Billy Myers,

A friend of mine, who used to be
As black a sprig of hell as me,
With whom I'd planned, to save encroachin',
Which fields and coverts each should poach in.
Now when he saw me set my snare,
He tells me "Get to hell from there.
This field is mine," he says, "by right;
If you poach here, there'll be a fight.
Out now," he says, "and leave your wire;
It's mine."
                    "It ain't."
                              "You put."
                                        "You liar."
"You closhy put."
"You bloody liar."
"This is my field."
"This is my wire."
"I'm ruler here."
"You ain't."
"I am."
"I'll fight you for it."
"Right, by damn.
Not now, though, I've a-sprained my thumb,
We'll fight after the harvest hum.
And Silas Jones, that bookie wide,
Will make a purse five pounds a side."
Those were the words, that was the place
By which God brought me into grace.

On Wood Top Field the peewits go
Mewing and wheeling ever so;
And like the shaking of a timbrel
Cackles the laughter of the whimbrel.

THE EVERLASTING MERCY

In the old quarry-pit they say
Head-keeper Pike was made away.
He walks, head-keeper Pike, for harm,
He taps the windows of the farm;
The blood drips from his broken chin,
He taps and begs to be let in.
On Wood Top, nights, I've shaked to hark
The peewits wambling in the dark
Lest in the dark the old man might
Creep up to me to beg a light.

But Wood Top grass is short and sweet
And springy to a boxer's feet;
At harvest hum the moon so bright
Did shine on Wood Top for the fight.

When Bill was stripped down to his bends
I thought how long we two'd been friends,
And in my mind, about that wire,
I thought "He's right, I am a liar.
As sure as skilly's made in prison
The right to poach that copse is his'n.
I'll have no luck to-night," thinks I.
"I'm fighting to defend a lie.
And this moonshiny evening's fun
Is worse than aught I've ever done."
And thinking that way my heart bled so
I almost stept to Bill and said so.
And now Bill's dead I would be glad
If I could only think I had.
But no. I put the thought away
For fear of what my friends would say.

They'd backed me, see? O Lord, the sin
Done for the things there's money in.

The stakes were drove, the ropes were hitched,
Into the ring my hat I pitched.
My corner faced the Squire's park
Just where the fir trees make it dark;
The place where I begun poor Nell
Upon the woman's road to hell.
I thought of't, sitting in my corner
After the time-keep struck his warner
(Two brandy flasks, for fear of noise,
Clinked out the time to us two boys).
And while my seconds chafed and gloved me
I thought of Nell's eyes when she loved me,
And wondered how my tot would end,
First Nell cast off and now my friend;
And in the moonlight dim and wan
I knew quite well my luck was gone;
And looking round I felt a spite
At all who'd come to see me fight;
The five and forty human faces
Inflamed by drink and going to races,
Faces of men who'd never been
Merry or true or live or clean;
Who'd never felt the boxer's trim
Of brain divinely knit to limb,
Nor felt the whole live body go
One tingling health from top to toe;
Nor took a punch nor given a swing,
But just soaked deady round the ring
Until their brains and bloods were foul

Enough to make their throttles howl,
While we whom Jesus died to teach
Fought round on round, three minutes each.

And thinking that, you'll understand
I thought, "I'll go and take Bill's hand.
I'll up and say the fault was mine,
He shan't make play for these here swine."
And then I thought that that was silly,
They'd think I was afraid of Billy;
They'd think (I thought it, God forgive me)
I funked the hiding Bill could give me.
And that thought made me mad and hot.
"Think that, will they? Well, they shall not.
They shan't think that. I will not. I'm
Damned if I will. I will not."
            Time!

From the beginning of the bout
My luck was gone, my hand was out.
Right from the start Bill called the play,
But I was quick and kept away
Till the fourth round, when work got mixed,
And then I knew Bill had me fixed.
My hand was out, why, Heaven knows;
Bill punched me when and where he chose.
Through two more rounds we quartered wide,
And all the time my hands seemed tied;
Bill punched me when and where he pleased.
The cheering from my backers eased,
But every punch I heard a yell
Of "That's the style, Bill, give him hell."

No one for me, but Jimmy's light
"Straight left! Straight left!" and "Watch his right."

I don't know how a boxer goes
When all his body hums from blows;
I know I seemed to rock and spin,
I don't know how I saved my chin;
I know I thought my only friend
Was that clinked flask at each round's end
When my two seconds, Ed and Jimmy,
Had sixty seconds help to gimme.
But in the ninth, with pain and knocks
I stopped: I couldn't fight nor box.
Bill missed his swing, the light was tricky,
But I went down, and stayed down, dicky.
"Get up," cried Jim. I said, "I will."
Then all the gang yelled, "Out him, Bill.
Out him." Bill rushed . . . and Clink, Clink, Clink.
Time! and Jim's knee, and rum to drink.
And round the ring there ran a titter:
"Saved by the call, the bloody quitter."

They drove (a dodge that never fails)
A pin beneath my finger nails.
They poured what seemed a running beck
Of cold spring water down my neck;
Jim with a lancet quick as flies
Lowered the swellings round my eyes.
They sluiced my legs and fanned my face
Through all that blessed minute's grace;
They gave my calves a thorough kneading,
They salved my cuts and stopped the bleeding.

A gulp of liquor dulled the pain,
And then the two flasks clinked again.

Time!
     There was Bill as grim as death,
He rushed, I clinched, to get more breath,
And breath I got, though Billy bats
Some stinging short-arms in my slats.
And when we broke, as I foresaw,
He swung his right in for the jaw.
I stopped it on my shoulder bone,
And at the shock I heard Bill groan—
A little groan or moan or grunt
As though I'd hit his wind a bunt.
At that, I clinched, and while we clinched,
His old time right arm dig was flinched,
And when we broke he hit me light
As though he didn't trust his right,
He flapped me somehow with his wrist
As though he couldn't use his fist,
And when he hit he winced with pain.
I thought, "Your sprained thumb's crocked again."
So I got strength and Bill gave ground,
And that round was an easy round.

During the wait my Jimmy said,
"What's making Billy fight so dead?
He's all to pieces. Is he blown?"
"His thumb's out."
"No? Then it's your own.
It's all your own, but don't be rash—
He's got the goods if you've got cash,

And what one hand can do he'll do.
Be careful this next round or two."

Time.   There was Bill, and I felt sick
That luck should play so mean a trick
And give me leave to knock him out
After he'd plainly won the bout.
But by the way the man came at me
He made it plain he meant to bat me;
If you'd a seen the way he come
You wouldn't think he'd crocked a thumb.
With all his skill and all his might
He clipped me dizzy left and right;
The Lord knows what the effort cost,
But he was mad to think he'd lost,
And knowing nothing else could save him
He didn't care what pain it gave him.
He called the music and the dance
For five rounds more and gave no chance.

Try to imagine if you can
The kind of manhood in the man,
And if you'd like to feel his pain
You sprain your thumb and hit the sprain.
And hit it hard, with all your power
On something hard for half-an-hour,
While someone thumps you black and blue,
And then you'll know what Billy knew.
Bill took that pain without a sound
Till halfway through the eighteenth round,
And then I sent him down and out,
And Silas said, "Kane wins the bout."

When Bill came to, you understand,
I ripped the mitten from my hand
And went across to ask Bill shake.
My limbs were all one pain and ache,
I was so weary and so sore
I don't think I'd a stood much more.
Bill in his corner bathed his thumb,
Buttoned his shirt and glowered glum.
"I'll never shake your hand," he said.
"I'd rather see my children dead.
I've been about and had some fun with you,
But you're a liar and I've done with you.
You've knocked me out, you didn't beat me;
Look out the next time that you meet me,
There'll be no friend to watch the clock for you
And no convenient thumb to crock for you,
And I'll take care, with much delight,
You'll get what you'd a got to-night;
That puts my meaning clear, I guess,
Now get to hell; I want to dress."

I dressed.   My backers one and all
Said, "Well done you," or "Good old Saul."
"Saul is a wonder and a fly 'un,
What'll you have, Saul, at the Lion?"
With merry oaths they helped me down
The stony wood path to the town.

The moonlight shone on Cabbage Walk,
It made the limestone look like chalk.
It was too late for any people,
Twelve struck as we went by the steeple.

A dog barked, and an owl was calling,
The squire's brook was still a-falling,
The carved heads on the church looked down
On "Russell, Blacksmith of this Town,"
And all the graves of all the ghosts
Who rise on Christmas Eve in hosts
To dance and carol in festivity
For joy of Jesus Christ's Nativity
(Bell-ringer Dawe and his two sons
Beheld 'em from the bell-tower once),
Two and two about about
Singing the end of Advent out,
Dwindling down to windlestraws
When the glittering peacock craws,
As craw the glittering peacock should
When Christ's own star comes over the wood.
Lamb of the sky come out of fold
Wandering windy heavens cold.
So they shone and sang till twelve
When all the bells ring out of theirselve.
Rang a peal for Christmas morn,
Glory, men, for Christ is born.

All the old monks' singing places
Glimmered quick with flitting faces,
Singing anthems, singing hymns
Under carven cherubims.
Ringer Dawe aloft could mark
Faces at the window dark
Crowding, crowding, row on row,
Till all the Church began to glow.
The chapel glowed, the nave, the choir,

THE EVERLASTING MERCY

All the faces became fire
Below the eastern window high
To see Christ's star come up the sky.
Then they lifted hands and turned,
And all their lifted fingers burned,
Burned like the golden altar tallows,
Burned like a troop of God's own Hallows,
Bringing to mind the burning time
When all the bells will rock and chime
And burning saints on burning horses
Will sweep the planets from their courses
And loose the stars to burn up night.
Lord, give us eyes to bear the light.

We all went quiet down the Scallenge
Lest Police Inspector Drew should challenge.
But 'Spector Drew was sleeping sweet,
His head upon a charges sheet,
Under the gas jet flaring full,
Snorting and snoring like a bull,
His bull cheeks puffed, his bull lips blowing,
His ugly yellow front teeth showing.
Just as we peeped we saw him fumble
And scratch his head, and shift, and mumble.

Down in the lane so thin and dark
The tan-yards stank of bitter bark,
The curate's pigeons gave a flutter,
A cat went courting down the gutter,
And none else stirred a foot or feather.
The houses put their heads together,
Talking, perhaps, so dark and sly,

[131]

Of all the folk they'd seen go by,
Children, and men and women, merry all,
Who'd some day pass that way to burial.
It was all dark, but at the turning
The Lion had a window burning.
So in we went and up the stairs,
Treading as still as cats and hares.
The way the stairs creaked made you wonder
If dead men's bones were hidden under.
At head of stairs upon the landing
A woman with a lamp was standing;
She greet each gent at head of stairs
With "Step in, gents, and take your chairs.
The punch'll come when kettle bubble,
But don't make noise or there'll be trouble."
'Twas Doxy Jane, a bouncing girl
With eyes all sparks and hair all curl,
And cheeks all red and lips all coal,
And thirst for men instead of soul.
She's trod her pathway to the fire.
Old Rivers had his nephew by her.

I step aside from Tom and Jimmy
To find if she'd a kiss to gimme.
I blew out lamp 'fore she could speak.
She said, "If you ain't got a cheek,"
And then beside me in the dim,
"Did he beat you or you beat him?"
"Why, I beat him" (though that was wrong).
She said, "You must be turble strong.
I'd be afraid you'd beat me, too."
"You'd not," I said, "I wouldn't do."

[132]

"Never?"
"No, never."
"Never?"
"No."
"O Saul. Here's missus. Let me go."
It wasn't missus, so I didn't,
Whether I mid do or I midn't,
Until she'd promised we should meet
Next evening, six, at top of street,
When we could have a quiet talk
On that low wall up Worcester Walk.
And while we whispered there together
I give her silver for a feather
And felt a drunkenness like wine
And shut out Christ in husks and swine.
I felt the dart strike through my liver.
God punish me for't and forgive her.

Each one could be a Jesus mild,
Each one has been a little child,
A little child with laughing look,
A lovely white unwritten book;
A book that God will take, my friend,
As each goes out at journey's end.
The Lord Who gave us Earth and Heaven
Takes that as thanks for all He's given.
The book he lent is given back
All blotted red and smutted black.

"Open the door," said Jim, "and call."
Jane gasped "They'll see me. Loose me, Saul."

She pushed me by, and ducked downstair
With half the pins out of her hair.
I went inside the lit room rollen
Her scented handkerchief I'd stolen.
"What would you fancy, Saul?" they said.
"A gin punch hot and then to bed."
"Jane, fetch the punch bowl to the gemmen;
And mind you don't put too much lemon.
Our good friend Saul has had a fight of it,
Now smoke up, boys, and make a night of it."

The room was full of men and stink
Of bad cigars and heavy drink.
Riley was nodding to the floor
And gurgling as he wanted more.
His mouth was wide, his face was pale,
His swollen face was sweating ale;
And one of those assembled Greeks
Had corked black crosses on his cheeks.
Thomas was having words with Goss,
He "wouldn't pay, the fight was cross."
And Goss told Tom that "cross or no,
The bets go as the verdicts go,
By all I've ever heard or read of.
So pay, or else I'll knock your head off."
Jim Gurvil said his smutty say
About a girl down Bye Street way,
And how the girl from Froggatt's circus
Died giving birth in Newent work'us.
And Dick told how the Dymock wench
Bore twins, poor things, on Dog Hill bench;
And how he'd owned to one in Court

And how Judge made him sorry for't.
Jack set a jew's harp twanging drily;
"Gimme another cup," said Riley.
A dozen more were in their glories
With laughs and smokes and smutty stories;
And Jimmy joked and took his sup
And sang his song of "Up, come up."
Jane brought the bowl of stewing gin
And poured the egg and lemon in,
And whisked it up and served it out
While bawdy questions went about.
Jack chucked her chin, and Jim accost her
With bits out of the "Maid of Gloster."
And fifteen arms went round her waist.
(And then men ask, Are Barmaids chaste?)

O young men, pray to be kept whole
From bringing down a weaker soul.
Your minute's joy so meet in doin'
May be the woman's door to ruin;
The door to wandering up and down,
A painted whore at half a crown.
The bright mind fouled, the beauty gay
All eaten out and fallen away,
By drunken days and weary tramps
From pub to pub by city lamps
Till men despise the game they started
Till health and beauty are departed,
And in a slum the reeking hag
Mumbles a crust with toothy jag,
Or gets the river's help to end
The life too wrecked for man to mend.

We spat and smoked and took our swipe
Till Silas up and tap his pipe,
And begged us all to pay attention
Because he'd several things to mention.
We'd seen the fight (Hear, hear. That's you);
But still one task remained to do,
That task was his, he didn't shun it,
To give the purse to him as won it.
With this remark, from start to out
He'd never seen a brisker bout.
There was the purse. At that he'd leave it.
Let Kane come forward to receive it.

I took the purse and hemmed and bowed,
And called for gin punch for the crowd;
And when the second bowl was done,
I called, "Let's have another one."
Si's wife come in and sipped and sipped
(As women will) till she was pipped.
And Si hit Dicky Twot a clouter
Because he put his arm about her;
But after Si got overtasked
She sat and kissed whoever asked.
My Doxy Jane was splashed by this,
I took her on my knee to kiss.
And Tom cried out, "O damn the gin;
Why can't we all have women in?
Bess Evans, now, or Sister Polly,
Or those two housemaids at the Folly?
Let someone nip to Biddy Price's,
They'd all come in a brace of trices.
Rose Davies, Sue, and Betsy Perks;

[136]

One man, one girl, and damn all Turks."
But, no. "More gin," they cried; "Come on.
We'll have the girls in when it's gone."
So round the gin went, hot and heady,
Hot Hollands punch on top of deady.

Hot Hollands punch on top of stout
Puts madness in and wisdom out.
From drunken man to drunken man
The drunken madness raged and ran.
"I'm climber Joe who climbed the spire."
"You're climber Joe the bloody liar."
"Who says I lie?" "I do."
                              "You lie,
I climbed the spire and had a fly."
"I'm French Suzanne, the Circus Dancer,
I'm going to dance a bloody Lancer."
"If I'd my rights I'm Squire's heir."
"By rights I'd be a millionaire."
"By rights I'd be the lord of you,
But Farmer Scriggins had his do,
He done me, so I've had to hoove it,
I've got it all wrote down to prove it.
And one of these dark winter nights
He'll learn I mean to have my rights;
I'll bloody him a bloody fix,
I'll bloody burn his bloody ricks."

From three long hours of gin and smokes,
And two girls' breath and fifteen blokes,
A warmish night, and windows shut,

The room stank like a fox's gut.
The heat and smell and drinking deep
Began to stun the gang to sleep.
Some fell downstairs to sleep on the mat,
Some snored it sodden where they sat.
Dick Twot had lost a tooth and wept,
But all the drunken others slept.
Jane slept beside me in the chair,
And I got up; I wanted air.

I opened window wide and leaned
Out of that pigstye of the fiend
And felt a cool wind go like grace
About the sleeping market-place.
The clock struck three, and sweetly, slowly,
The bells chimed Holy, Holy, Holy;
And in a second's pause there fell
The cold note of the chapel bell,
And then a cock crew, flapping wings,
And summat made me think of things.
How long those ticking clocks had gone
From church and chapel, on and on,
Ticking the time out, ticking slow
To men and girls who'd come and go,
And how they ticked in belfry dark
When half the town was bishop's park,
And how they'd rung a chime full tilt
The night after the church was built,
And how that night was Lambert's Feast,
The night I'd fought and been a beast.
And how a change had come. And then
I thought, "You tick to different men."

What with the fight and what with drinking
And being awake alone there thinking,
My mind began to carp and tetter,
"If this life's all, the beasts are better."
And then I thought, "I wish I'd seen
The many towns this town has been;
I wish I knew if they'd a got
A kind of summat we've a-not,
If them as built the church so fair
Were half the chaps folk say they were;
For they'd the skill to draw their plan,
And skill's a joy to any man;
And they'd the strength, not skill alone,
To build it beautiful in stone;
And strength and skill together thus
O, they were happier men than us.

But if they were, they had to die
The same as every one and I.
And no one lives again, but dies,
And all the bright goes out of eyes,
And all the skill goes out of hands,
And all the wise brain understands,
And all the beauty, all the power
Is cut down like a withered flower.
In all the show from birth to rest
I give the poor dumb cattle best."

I wondered, then, why life should be,
And what would be the end of me
When youth and health and strength were gone
And cold old age came creeping on?

A keeper's gun? The Union ward?
Or that new quod at Hereford?
And looking round I felt disgust
At all the nights of drink and lust,
And all the looks of all the swine
Who'd said that they were friends of mine;
And yet I knew, when morning came,
The morning would be just the same,
For I'd have drinks and Jane would meet me
And drunken Silas Jones would greet me,
And I'd risk quod and keeper's gun
Till all the silly game was done.
"For parson chaps are mad, supposin'
A chap can change the road he's chosen."
And then the Devil whispered, "Saul,
Why should you want to live at all?
Why fret and sweat and try to mend?
It's all the same thing in the end.
But when it's done," he said, "it's ended.
Why stand it, since it can't be mended?"
And in my heart I heard him plain,
"Throw yourself down and end it, Kane."

"Why not?" said I. "Why not? But no.
I won't. I've never had my go.
I've not had all the world can give.
Death by and by, but first I'll live.
The world owes me my time of times,
And that time's coming now, by crimes."

A madness took me then. I felt
I'd like to hit the world a belt.

I felt that I could fly through air,
A screaming star with blazing hair,
A rushing comet, crackling, numbing
The folk with fear of judgment coming,
A 'Lijah in a fiery car,
Coming to tell folk what they are.
"That's what I'll do," I shouted loud,
"I'll tell this sanctimonious crowd
This town of window peeping, prying,
Maligning, peering, hinting, lying,
Male and female human blots
Who would, but daren't be, whores and sots,
That they're so steeped in petty vice
That they're less excellent than lice,
That they're so soaked in petty virtue
That touching one of them will dirt you,
Dirt you with the stain of mean
Cheating trade and going between,
Pinching, starving, scraping, hoarding,
Spying through the chinks of boarding
To see if Sue, the prentice lean,
Dares to touch the margarine.
Fawning, cringing, oiling boots,
Raging in the crowd's pursuits,
Flinging stones at all the Stephens,
Standing firm with all the evens
Making hell for all the odd,
All the lonely ones of God,
Those poor lonely ones who find
Dogs more mild than human kind.
For dogs," I said, "are nobles born
To most of you, you cockled corn.

I've known dogs to leave their dinner,
Nosing a kind heart in a sinner.
Poor old Crafty wagged his tail
The day I first came home from jail.
When all my folk, so primly clad,
Glowered black and thought me mad,
And muttered how they'd been respected,
While I was what they'd all expected.
(I've thought of that old dog for years,
And of how near I come to tears.)

But you, you minds of bread and cheese,
Are less divine that that dog's fleas.
You suck blood from kindly friends,
And kill them when it serves your ends.
Double traitors, double black,
Stabbing only in the back,
Stabbing with the knives you borrow
From the friends you bring to sorrow.
You stab all that's true and strong,
Truth and strength you say are wrong,
Meek and mild, and sweet and creeping,
Repeating, canting, cadging, peeping,
That's the art and that's the life
To win a man his neighbour's wife.
All that's good and all that's true,
You kill that, so I'll kill you."

At that I tore my clothes in shreds
And hurled them on the window leads;
I flung my boots through both the winders

And knocked the glass to little flinders;
The punch bowl and the tumblers followed,
And then I seized the lamps and holloed,
And down the stairs, and tore back bolts,
As mad as twenty blooded colts;
And out into the street I pass,
As mad as two-year-olds at grass,
A naked madman waving grand
A blazing lamp in either hand.
I yelled like twenty drunken sailors,
"The devil's come among the tailors."
A blaze of flame behind me streamed,
And then I clashed the lamps and screamed
"I'm Satan, newly come from hell."
And then I spied the fire bell.

I've been a ringer, so I know
How best to make a big bell go.
So on to bell-rope swift I swoop,
And stick my one foot in the loop
And heave a down-swig till I groan,
"Awake, you swine, you devil's own."
I made the fire-bell awake,
I felt the bell-rope throb and shake;
I felt the air mingle and clang
And beat the walls a muffled bang,
And stifle back and boom and bay
Like muffled peals on Boxing Day,
And then surge up and gather shape,
And spread great pinions and escape;
And each great bird of clanging shrieks
O Fire! Fire, from iron beaks.

My shoulders cracked to send around
Those shrieking birds made out of sound
With news of fire in their bills.
(They heard 'em plain beyond Wall Hills.)

Up go the winders, out come heads,
I heard the springs go creak in beds;
But still I heave and sweat and tire,
And still the clang goes "Fire, Fire!"
"Where is it, then? Who is it, there?
You ringer, stop, and tell us where."
"Run round and let the Captain know."
"It must be bad, he's ringing so,"
"It's in the town, I see the flame;
Look there! Look there, how red it came."
"Where is it, then? O stop the bell."
I stopped and called: "It's fire of hell;
And this is Sodom and Gomorrah,
And now I'll burn you up, begorra."

By this the firemen were mustering,
The half-dressed stable men were flustering,
Backing the horses out of stalls
While this man swears and that man bawls,
"Don't take th' old mare. Back, Toby, back.
Back, Lincoln. Where's the fire, Jack?"
"Damned if I know. Out Preston way."
"No. It's at Chancey's Pitch, they say."
"It's sixteen ricks at Pauntley burnt."
"You back old Darby out, I durn't."
They ran the big red engine out,

And put 'em to with damn and shout.
And then they start to raise the shire,
"Who brought the news, and where's the fire?"
They'd moonlight, lamps, and gas to light 'em.
I give a screech-owl's screech to fright 'em,
And snatch from underneath their noses
The nozzles of the fire hoses.
"I am the fire. Back, stand back,
Or else I'll fetch your skulls a crack;
D'you see these copper nozzles here?
They weigh ten pounds apiece, my dear;
I'm fire of hell come up this minute
To burn this town, and all that's in it.
To burn you dead and burn you clean,
You cogwheels in a stopped machine,
You hearts of snakes, and brains of pigeons,
You dead devout of dead religions,
You offspring of the hen and ass,
By Pilate ruled, and Caiaphas.
Now your account is totted. Learn
Hell's flames are loose and you shall burn."

At that I leaped and screamed and ran,
I heard their cries go, "Catch him, man."
"Who was it?" "Down him." "Out him, Ern."
"Duck him at pump, we'll see who'll burn."
A policeman clutched, a fireman clutched,
A dozen others snatched and touched.
"By God, he's stripped down to his buff."
"By God, we'll make him warm enough."
"After him," "Catch him," Out him," "Scrob him."
"We'll give him hell." "By God, we'll mob him."

"We'll duck him, scrout him, flog him, fratch him."
"All right," I said. "But first you'll catch him."

The men who don't know to the root
The joy of being swift of foot,
Have never known divine and fresh
The glory of the gift of flesh,
Nor felt the feet exult, nor gone
Along a dim road, on and on,
Knowing again the bursting glows,
The mating hare in April knows,
Who tingles to the pads with mirth
At being the swiftest thing on earth.
O, if you want to know delight,
Run naked in an autumn night,
And laugh, as I laughed then, to find
A running rabble drop behind,
And whang, on every door you pass,
Two copper nozzles, tipped with brass,
And doubly whang at every turning,
And yell, "All hell's let loose, and burning."

I beat my brass and shouted fire
At doors of parson, lawyer, squire,
At all three doors I threshed and slammed
And yelled aloud that they were damned.
I clodded squire's glass with turves
Because he spring-gunned his preserves.
Through parson's glass my nozzle swishes
Because he stood for loaves and fishes,
But parson's glass I spared a tittle.

He give me a orange once when little,
And he who gives a child a treat
Makes joy-bells ring in Heaven's street,
And he who gives a child a home
Builds palaces in Kingdom come,
And she who gives a baby birth
Brings Saviour Christ again to Earth,
For life is joy, and mind is fruit,
And body's precious earth and root.
But lawyer's glass—well, never mind,
Th'old Adam's strong in me, I find.
God pardon man, and may God's son
Forgive the evil things I've done.

What more? By Dirty Lane I crept
Back to the Lion, where I slept.
The raging madness hot and floodin'
Boiled itself out and left me sudden,
Left me worn out and sick and cold,
Aching as though I'd all grown old;
So there I lay, and there they found me
On door-mat, with a curtain round me.
Si took my heels and Jane my head
And laughed, and carried me to bed.
And from the neighbouring street they reskied
My boots and trousers, coat and weskit;
They bath-bricked both the nozzles bright
To be mementoes of the night,
And knowing what I should awake with
They flannelled me a quart to slake with,
And sat and shook till half past two
Expecting Police Inspector Drew.

I woke and drank, and went to meat
In clothes still dirty from the street.
Down in the bar I heard 'em tell
How someone rang the fire bell,
And how th' inspector's search had thriven,
And how five pounds reward was given.
And Shepherd Boyce, of Marley, glad us
By saying it was blokes from mad'us,
Or two young rips lodged at the Prince
Whom none had seen nor heard of since,
Or that young blade from Worcester Walk
(You know how country people talk).
Young Joe the ostler come in sad,
He said th'old mare had bit his dad.
He said there'd come a blazing screeching
Daft Bible-prophet chap a-preaching,
Had put th'old mare in such a taking
She'd thought the bloody earth was quaking.
And others come and spread a tale
Of cut-throats out of Gloucester jail,
And how we needed extra cops
With all them Welsh come picking hops:
With drunken Welsh in all our sheds
We might be murdered in our beds.

By all accounts, both men and wives
Had had the scare up of their lives.

I ate and drank and gathered strength,
And stretched along the bench full length,
Or crossed to window seat to pat

Black Silas Jones's little cat.
At four I called, "You devil's own,
The second trumpet shall be blown.
The second trump, the second blast;
Hell's flames are loosed, and judgment's passed.
Too late for mercy now. Take warning.
I'm death and hell and Judgment morning."
I hurled the bench into the settle,
I banged the table on the kettle,
I sent Joe's quart of cider spinning.
"Lo, here begins my second inning."
Each bottle, mug, and jug and pot
I smashed to crocks in half a tot;
And Joe, and Si, and Nick, and Percy
I rolled together topsy versy.
And as I ran I heard 'em call,
"Now damn to hell, what's gone with Saul?"

Out into street I ran uproarious
The devil dancing in me glorious.
And as I ran I yell and shriek
"Come on, now, turn the other cheek."
Across the way by almshouse pump
I see old puffing parson stump.
Old parson, red-eyed as a ferret
From nightly wrestlings with the spirit;
I ran across, and barred his path.
His turkey gills went red as wrath
And then he froze, as parsons can.
"The police will deal with you, my man."
"Not yet," said I, "not yet they won't;
And now you'll hear me, like or don't.

The English Church both is and was
A subsidy of Caiaphas.
I don't believe in Prayer nor Bible,
They're lies all through, and you're a libel,
A libel on the Devil's plan
When first he miscreated man.
You mumble through a formal code
To get which martyrs burned and glowed.

I look on martyrs as mistakes,
But still they burned for it at stakes;
Your only fire's the jolly fire
Where you can guzzle port with Squire,
And back and praise his damned opinions
About his temporal dominions.
You let him give the man who digs,
A filthy hut unfit for pigs,
Without a well, without a drain,
With mossy thatch that lets in rain,
Without a 'lotment, 'less he rent it,
And never meat, unless he scent it,
But weekly doles of 'leven shilling
To make a grown man strong and willing,
To do the hardest work on earth
And feed his wife when she gives birth,
And feed his little children's bones.
I tell you, man, the Devil groans.
With all your main and all your might
You back what is against what's right;
You let the Squire do things like these,
You back him in't and give him ease,
You take his hand, and drink his wine,

And he's a hog, but you're a swine.
For you take gold to teach God's ways
And teach man how to sing God's praise.
And now I'll tell you what you teach
In downright honest English speech.

"You teach the ground-down starving man
That Squire's greed's Jehovah's plan.
You get his learning circumvented
Lest it should make him discontented
(Better a brutal, starving nation
Than men with thoughts above their station),
You let him neither read nor think,
You goad his wretched soul to drink
And then to jail, the drunken boor;
O sad intemperance of the poor.
You starve his soul till it's rapscallion,
Then blame his flesh for being stallion.
You send your wife around to paint
The golden glories of "restraint."
How moral exercise bewild'rin'
Would soon result in fewer children.
You work a day in Squire's fields
And see what sweet restraint it yields,
A woman's day at turnip picking,
Your heart's too fat for plough or ricking.

"And you whom luck taught French and Greek
Have purple flaps on either cheek,
A stately house, and time for knowledge,
And gold to send your sons to college,
That pleasant place, where getting learning
Is also key to money earning.

But quite your damndest want of grace
Is what you do to save your face;
The way you sit astride the gates
By padding wages out of rates;
Your Christmas gifts of shoddy blankets
That every working soul may thank its
Loving parson, loving squire
Through whom he can't afford a fire.
Your well-packed bench, your prison pen,
To keep them something less than men;
Your friendly clubs to help 'em bury,
Your charities of midwifery.
Your bidding children duck and cap
To them who give them workhouse pap.
O, what you are, and what you preach,
And what you do, and what you teach
Is not God's Word, nor honest schism,
But Devil's cant and pauperism."

By this time many folk had gathered
To listen to me while I blathered;
I said my piece, and when I'd said it,
I'll do old purple parson credit,
He sunk (as sometimes parsons can)
His coat's excuses in the man.
"You think that Squire and I are kings
Who made the existing state of things,
And made it ill.   I answer, No,
States are not made, nor patched; they grow,
Grow slow through centuries of pain
And grow correctly in the main,
But only grow by certain laws

Of certain bits in certain jaws.
You want to doctor that. Let be.
You cannot patch a growing tree.
Put these two words beneath your hat,
These two: securus judicat.
The social states of human kinds
Are made by multitudes of minds,
And after multitudes of years
A little human growth appears
Worth having, even to the soul
Who sees most plain it's not the whole.

This state is dull and evil, both,
I keep it in the path of growth;
You think the Church an outworn fetter;
Kane, keep it, till you've built a better.
And keep the existing social state;
I quite agree it's out of date,
One does too much, another shirks,
Unjust, I grant; but still . . . it works.
To get the whole world out of bed
And washed, and dressed, and warmed, and fed,
To work, and back to bed again,
Believe me, Saul, costs worlds of pain.
Then, as to whether true or sham
That book of Christ, Whose priest I am;
The Bible is a lie, say you,
Where do you stand, suppose it true?
Good-bye. But if you've more to say,
My doors are open night and day.
Meanwhile, my friend, 'twould be no sin
To mix more water in your gin.

We're neither saints nor Philip Sidneys,
But mortal men with mortal kidneys."

He took his snuff, amd wheezed a greeting,
And waddled off to mothers' meeting;
I hung my head upon my chest,
I give old purple parson best.
For while the Plough tips round the Pole
The trained mind outs the upright soul,
As Jesus said the trained mind might,
Being wiser than the sons of light,
But trained men's minds are spread so thin
They let all sorts of darkness in;
Whatever light man finds they doubt it
They love, not light, but talk about it.

But parson'd proved to people's eyes
That I was drunk, and he was wise;
And people grinned and women tittered,
And little children mocked and twittered.
So, blazing mad, I stalked to bar
To show how noble drunkards are,
And guzzled spirits like a beast,
To show contempt for Church and priest,
Until, by six, my wits went round
Like hungry pigs in parish pound.
At half past six, rememb'ring Jane,
I staggered into street again
With mind made up (or primed with gin)
To bash the cop who'd run me in;
For well I knew I'd have to cock up
My legs that night inside the lock-up,

And it was my most fixed intent
To have a fight before I went.
Our Fates are strange, and no one knows his;
Our lovely Saviour Christ disposes.

Jane wasn't where we'd planned, the jade.
She'd thought me drunk and hadn't stayed.
So I went up the Walk to look for her
And lingered by the little brook for her,
And dowsed my face, and drank at spring,
And watched two wild duck on the wing.
The moon come pale, the wind come cool,
A big pike leapt in Lower Pool,
The peacock screamed, the clouds were straking,
My cut cheek felt the weather breaking;
An orange sunset waned and thinned
Foretelling rain and western wind,
And while I watched I heard distinct
The metals on the railway clinked.
The blood-edged clouds were all in tatters,
The sky and earth seemed mad as hatters;
They had a death look, wild and odd,
Of something dark foretold by God.
And seeing it so, I felt so shaken
I wouldn't keep the road I'd taken,
But wandered back towards the inn
Resolved to brace myself with gin.
And as I walked, I said, "It's strange,
There's Death let loose to-night, and Change."

In Cabbage Walk I made a haul
Of two big pears from lawyer's wall,

And, munching one, I took the lane
Back into Market-place again.
Lamp-lighter Dick had passed the turning.
And all the Homend lamps were burning.
The windows shone, the shops were busy,
But that strange Heaven made me dizzy.
The sky had all God's warning writ
In bloody marks all over it,
And over all I thought there was
A ghastly light besides the gas.
The Devil's tasks and Devil's rages
Were giving me the Devil's wages.

In Market-place it's always light,
The big shop windows make it bright;
And in the press of people buying
I spied a little fellow crying
Because his mother'd gone inside
And left him there, and so he cried.
And mother'd beat him when she found him,
And mother's whip would curl right round him,
And mother'd say he'd done't to crost her,
Though there being crowds about he'd lost her.

Lord, give to men who are old and rougher
The things that little children suffer,
And let keep bright and undefiled
The young years of the little child.
I pat his head at edge of street
And gi'm my second pear to eat.
Right under lamp, I pat his head,
"I'll stay till mother come," I said,

And stay I did, and joked and talked,
And shoppers wondered as they walked.
"There's that Saul Kane, the drunken blaggard,
Talking to little Jimmy Jaggard.
The drunken blaggard reeks of drink."
"Whatever will his mother think?"
"Wherever has his mother gone?
Nip round to Mrs. Jaggard's, John,
And say her Jimmy's out again,
In Market-place, with boozer Kane."
"When he come out to-day he staggered.
O, Jimmy Jaggard, Jimmy Jaggard."
"His mother's gone inside to bargain,
Run in and tell her, Polly Margin,
And tell her poacher Kane is tipsy
And selling Jimmy to a gipsy."
"Run in to Mrs. Jaggard, Ellen,
Or else, dear knows, there'll be no tellin',
And don't dare leave yer till you've fount her,
You'll find her at the linen counter."
I told a tale, to Jim's delight,
Of where the tom-cats go by night,
And how when moonlight come they went
Among the chimneys black and bent,
From roof to roof, from house to house,
With little baskets full of mouse
All red and white, both joint and chop
Like meat out of a butcher's shop;
Then all along the wall they creep
And everyone is fast asleep,
And honey-hunting moths go by,
And by the bread-batch crickets cry;

[157]

Then on they hurry, never waiting
To lawyer's backyard cellar grating
Where Jaggard's cat, with clever paw,
Unhooks a broke-brick's secret door;
Then down into the cellar black,
Across the wood slug's slimy track,
Into an old cask's quiet hollow,
Where they've got seats for what's to follow;
Then each tom-cat lights little candles,
And O, the stories and the scandals,
And O, the songs and Christmas carols,
And O, the milk from little barrels.
They light a fire fit for roasting
(And how good mouse-meat smells when toasting),
Then down they sit to merry feast
While moon goes west and sun comes east.

Sometimes they make so merry there
Old lawyer come to head of stair
To 'fend with fist and poker took firm
His parchments channelled by the bookworm,
And all his deeds, and all his packs
Of withered ink and sealing wax;
And there he stands, with candle raised,
And listens like a man amazed,
Or like a ghost a man stands dumb at,
He says, "Hush! Hush! I'm sure there's summat."
He hears outside the brown owl call,
He hears the death-tick tap the wall,
The gnawing of the wainscot mouse,
The creaking up and down the house,
The unhooked window's hinges ranging,

The sounds that say the wind is changing.
At last he turns, and shakes his head,
"It's nothing, I'll go back to bed."

And just then Mrs. Jaggard came
To view and end her Jimmy's shame.

She made one rush and gi'm a bat
And shook him like a dog a rat.
"I can't turn round but what you're straying.
I'll give you tales and gipsy playing.
I'll give you wand'ring off like this
And listening to whatever 'tis,
You'll laugh the little side of the can,
You'll have the whip for this, my man;
And not a bite of meat nor bread
You'll touch before you go to bed.
Some day you'll break your mother's heart,
After God knows she's done her part,
Working her arms off day and night
Trying to keep your collars white.
Look at your face, too, in the street.
What dirty filth've you found to eat?
Now don't you blubber here, boy, or
I'll give you sum't to blubber for."
She snatched him off from where we stand
And knocked the pear-core from his hand,
And looked at me, "You Devil's limb,
How dare you talk to Jaggard's Jim;
You drunken, poaching, boozing brute, you,
If Jaggard was a man he'd shoot you."
She glared all this, but didn't speak,
She gasped, white hollows in her cheek;

Jimmy was writhing, screaming wild,
The shoppers thought I'd killed the child.

I had to speak, so I begun.
"You'd oughtn't beat your little son;
He did no harm, but seeing him there
I talked to him and gi'm a pear;
I'm sure the poor child meant no wrong,
It's all my fault he stayed so long,
He'd not have stayed, mum, I'll be bound
If I'd not chanced to come around.
It's all my fault he stayed, not his.
I kept him here, that's how it is."
"Oh! And how dare you, then?" says she,
"How dare you tempt my boy from me?
How dare you do't, you drunken swine,
Is he your child or is he mine?
A drunken sot they've had the beak to,
Has got his dirty whores to speak to,
His dirty mates with whom he drink,
Not little children, one would think.
Look on him, there," she says, "look on him
And smell the stinking gin upon him,
The lowest sot, the drunknest liar,
The dirtiest dog in all the shire:
Nice friends for any woman's son
After ten years, and all she's done.

"For I've had eight, and buried five,
And only three are left alive.
I've given them all we could afford.
I've taught them all to fear the Lord.

They've had the best we had to give,
The only three the Lord let live.

"For Minnie whom I loved the worst
Died mad in childbed with her first.
And John and Mary died of measles,
And Rob was drowned at the Teasels.
And little Nan, dear little sweet,
A cart run over in the street;
Her little shift was all one stain,
I prayed God put her out of pain.
And all the rest are gone or going
The road to hell, and there's no knowing
For all I've done and all I've made them
I'd better not have overlaid them.
For Susan went the ways of shame
The time the 'till'ry regiment came,
And t'have her child without a father
I think I'd have her buried rather.
And Dicky boozes, God forgimme,
And now't's to be the same with Jimmy.
And all I've done and all I've bore
Has made a drunkard and a whore,
A bastard boy who wasn't meant,
And Jimmy gwine where Dicky went;
For Dick began the self-same way
And my old hairs are going gray,
And my poor man's a withered knee,
And all the burden falls on me.
"I've washed eight little children's limbs,
I've taught eight little souls their hymns,
I've risen sick and lain down pinched

And borne it all and never flinched;
But to see him, the town's disgrace,
With God's commandments broke in's face,
Who never worked, not he, nor earned,
Nor will do till the seas are burned,
Who never did since he was whole
A hand's turn for a human soul,
But poached and stole and gone with women,
And swilled down gin enough to swim in,
To see him only lift one finger
To make my little Jimmy linger.
In spite of all his mother's prayers,
And all her ten long years of cares,
And all her broken spirit's cry
That drunkard's finger puts them by,
And Jimmy turns. And now I see
That just as Dick was, Jim will be,
And all my life will have been vain.
I might have spared myself the pain,
And done the world a blessed riddance
If I'd a drowned 'em all like kittens.
And he the sot, so strong and proud,
Who'd make white shirts of's mother's shroud,
He laughs now, it's a joke to him,
Though it's the gates of hell to Jim.

"I've had my heart burnt out like coal,
And drops of blood wrung from my soul
Day in, day out, in pain and tears,
For five and twenty wretched years;
And he, he's ate the fat and sweet,
And loafed and spat at top of street,

And drunk and leched from day till morrow,
And never known a moment's sorrow.
He come out drunk from th' inn to look
The day my little Nan was took;
He sat there drinking, glad and gay,
The night my girl was led astray;
He praised my Dick for singing well,
The night Dick took the road to hell;
And when my corpse goes stiff and blind,
Leaving four helpless souls behind,
He will be there still, drunk and strong.
It do seem hard. It do seem wrong.
But 'Woe to him by whom the offence,'
Says our Lord Jesus' Testaments.
Whatever seems, God doth not slumber
Though he lets pass times without number.
He'll come with trump to call his own,
And this world's way'll be overthrown.
He'll come with glory and with fire
To cast great darkness on the liar,
To burn the drunkard and the treacher,
And do his judgment on the lecher,
To glorify the spirits' faces
Of those whose ways were stony places
Who chose with Ruth the better part;
O Lord, I see Thee as Thou art,
O God, the fiery four-edged sword,
The thunder of the wrath outpoured,
The fiery four-faced creatures burning,
And all the four-faced wheels all turning,
Coming with trump and fiery saint.
Jim, take me home, I'm turning faint."

They went, and some cried, "Good old sod."
"She put it to him straight, by God."

Summat she was, or looked, or said,
Went home and made me hang my head.
I slunk away into the night
Knowing deep down that she was right.
I'd often heard religious ranters,
And put them down as windy canters,
But this old mother made me see
The harm I done by being me.
Being both strong and given to sin
I 'tracted weaker vessels in.
So back to bar to get more drink,
I didn't dare begin to think,
And there were drinks and drunken singing,
As though this life were dice for flinging;
Dice to be flung, and nothing furder,
And Christ's blood just another murder.
"Come on, drinks round, salue, drink hearty,
Now, Jane, the punch-bowl for the party.
If any here won't drink with me
I'll knock his bloody eyes out. See?
Come on, cigars round, rum for mine,
Sing us a smutty song, some swine."
But though the drinks and songs went round
That thought remained, it was not drowned.
And when I'd rise to get a light
I'd think, "What's come to me to-night?"

There's always crowds when drinks are standing.
The house doors slammed along the landing,

The rising wind was gusty yet,
And those who came in late were wet;
And all my body's nerves were snappin'
With sense of summat 'bout to happen,
And music seemed to come and go
And seven lights danced in a row.
There used to be a custom then,
Miss Bourne, the Friend, went round at ten
To all the pubs in all the place,
To bring the drunkards' souls to grace;
Some sulked, of course, and some were stirred,
But none give her a dirty word.
A tall pale woman, grey and bent,
Folk said of her that she was sent.
She wore Friends' clothes, and women smiled,
But she'd a heart just like a child.
She come to us near closing time
When we were at some smutty rhyme,
And I was mad, and ripe for fun;
I wouldn't a minded what I done.
So when she come so prim and grey
I pound the bar and sing, "Hooray,
Here's Quaker come to bless and kiss us,
Come, have a gin and bitters, missus,
Or may be Quaker girls so prim
Would rather start a bloody hymn.
Now Dick, oblige. A hymn, you swine,
Pipe up the 'Officer of the Line,'
A song to make one's belly ache,
Or 'Nell and Roger at the Wake,'
Or that sweet song, the talk in town,
'The lady fair and Abel Brown.'

'O, who's that knocking at the door,'
Miss Bourne'll play the music score."
The men stood dumb as cattle are,
They grinned, but thought I'd gone too far,
There come a hush and no one break it,
They wondered how Miss Bourne would take it.
She up to me with black eyes wide,
She looked as though her spirit cried;
She took my tumbler from the bar
Beside where all the matches are
And poured it out upon the floor dust,
Among the fag-ends, spit and saw-dust.

"Saul Kane," she said, "when next you drink,
Do me the gentleness to think
That every drop of drink accursed
Makes Christ within you die of thirst,
That every dirty word you say
Is one more flint upon His way,
Another thorn about His head,
Another mock by where He tread,
Another nail, another cross.
All that you are is that Christ's loss."
The clock run down and struck a chime
And Mrs. Si said, "Closing time."

The wet was pelting on the pane
And something broke inside my brain,
I heard the rain drip from the gutters
And Silas putting up the shutters,
While one by one the drinkers went;
I got a glimpse of what it meant,
How she and I had stood before

In some old town by some old door
Waiting intent while someone knocked
Before the door for ever locked;
She was so white that I was scared,
A gas jet, turned the wrong way, flared,
And Silas snapped the bars in place.
Miss Bourne stood white and searched my face.
When Silas done, with ends of tunes
He 'gan a gathering the spittoons,
His wife primmed lips and took the till.
Miss Bourne stood still and I stood still,
And "Tick. Slow. Tick. Slow " went the clock.
She said, "He waits until you knock."
She turned at that and went out swift,
Si grinned and winked, his missus sniffed.

I heard her clang the Lion door,
I marked a drink-drop roll to floor;
It took up scraps of sawdust, furry,
And crinkled on, a half inch, blurry;
A drop from my last glass of gin;
And someone waiting to come in,
A hand upon the door latch gropen
Knocking the man inside to open.
I know the very words I said,
They bayed like bloodhounds in my head.
"The water's going out to sea
And there's a great moon calling me;
But there's a great sun calls the moon,
And all God's bells will carol soon
For joy and glory and delight
Of someone coming home to-night."

Out into darkness, out to night,
My flaring heart gave plenty light,
So wild it was there was no knowing
Whether the clouds or stars were blowing;
Blown chimney pots and folk blown blind,
And puddles glimmering like my mind,
And chinking glass from windows banging,
And inn signs swung like people hanging,
And in my heart the drink unpriced,
The burning cataracts of Christ.

I did not think, I did not strive,
The deep peace burnt my me alive;
The bolted door had broken in,
I knew that I had done with sin.
I knew that Christ had given me birth
To brother all the souls on earth,
And every bird and every beast
Should share the crumbs broke at the feast.

O glory of the lighted mind.
How dead I'd been, how dumb, how blind.
The station brook, to my new eyes,
Was babbling out of Paradise,
The waters rushing from the rain
Were singing Christ has risen again.
I thought all earthly creatures knelt
From rapture of the joy I felt.
The narrow station-wall's brick ledge,
The wild hop withering in the hedge,
The lights in huntsmans' upper storey
Were parts of an eternal glory,

Were God's eternal garden flowers.
I stood in bliss at this for hours.

O glory of the lighted soul.
The dawn came up on Bradlow Knoll,
The dawn with glittering on the grasses,
The dawn which pass and never passes.

"It's dawn," I said, "And chimney's smoking,
And all the blessed fields are soaking.
It's dawn, and there's an engine shunting;
And hounds, for huntsman's going hunting.
It's dawn, and I must wander north
Along the road Christ led me forth."

So up the road I wander slow
Past where the snowdrops used to grow
With celandines in early springs,
When rainbows were triumphant things
And dew so bright and flowers so glad,
Eternal joy to lass and lad.
And past the lovely brook I paced,
The brook whose source I never traced,
The brook, the one of two which rise
In my green dream in Paradise,
In wells where heavenly buckets clink
To give God's wandering thirsty drink
By those clean cots of carven stone
Where the clear water sings alone.
Then down, past that white-blossomed pond,
And past the chestnut trees beyond,
And past the bridge the fishers knew,
Where yellow flag flowers once grew,

Where we'd go gathering cops of clover,
In sunny June times long since over.
O clover-cops half white, half red,
O beauty from beyond the dead.
O blossom, key to earth and heaven,
O souls that Christ has new forgiven.

Then down the hill to gipsies' pitch
By where the brook clucks in the ditch.
A gipsy's camp was in the copse,
Three felted tents, with beehive tops,
And round black marks where fires had been,
And one old waggon painted green,
And three ribbed horses wrenching grass,
And three wild boys to watch me pass,
And one old woman by the fire
Hulking a rabbit warm from wire.
I loved to see the horses bait.
I felt I walked at Heaven's gate,
That Heaven's gate was opened wide
Yet still the gipsies camped outside.
The waste souls will prefer the wild,
Long after life is meek and mild.
Perhaps when man has entered in
His perfect city free from sin,
The campers will come past the walls
With old lame horses full of galls,
And waggons hung about with withies,
And burning coke in tinker's stithies,
And see the golden town, and choose,
And think the wild too good to lose.
And camp outside, as these camped then

With wonder at the entering men.
So past, and past the stone heap white
That dewberry trailers hid from sight,
And down the field so full of springs,
Where mewing peewits clap their wings,
And past the trap made for the mill
Into the field below the hill.
There was a mist along the stream,
A wet mist, dim, like in a dream;
I heard the heavy breath of cows,
And waterdrops from th'alder boughs;
And eels, or snakes, in dripping grass,
Whipping aside to let me pass.
The gate was backed against the ryme
To pass the cows at milking time.
And by the gate as I went out
A moldwarp rooted earth wi's snout.
A few steps up the Callows' Lane
Brought me above the mist again,
The two great fields arose like death
Above the mists of human breath.

All earthly things that blessèd morning
Were everlasting joy and warning.
The gate was Jesus' way made plain,
The mole was Satan foiled again,
Black blinded Satan snouting way
Along the red of Adam's clay;
The mist was error and damnation,
The lane the road unto salvation.
Out of the mist into the light,
O blessèd gift of inner sight.

The past was faded like a dream;
There come the jingling of a team,
A ploughman's voice, a clink of chain,
Slow hoofs, and harness under strain.
Up the slow slope a team came bowing,
Old Callow at his autumn ploughing,
Old Callow, stooped above the hales,
Ploughing the stubble into wales.
His grave eyes looking straight ahead,
Shearing a long straight furrow red;
His plough-foot high to give it earth
To bring new food for men to birth.
O wet red swathe of earth laid bare,
O truth, O strength, O gleaming share,
O patient eyes that watch the goal,
O ploughman of the sinner's soul.
O Jesus, drive the coulter deep
To plough my living man from sleep.

Slow up the hill the plough team plod,
Old Callow at the task of God,
Helped by man's wit, helped by the brute,
Turning a stubborn clay to fruit,
His eyes forever on some sign
To help him plough a perfect line.
At top of rise the plough team stopped,
The fore-horse bent his head and cropped.
Then the chains chack, the brasses jingle,
The lean reins gather through the cringle,
The figures move against the sky,
The clay wave breaks as they go by.
I kneeled there in the muddy fallow,

I knew that Christ was there with Callow,
That Christ was standing there with me,
That Christ had taught me what to be,
That I should plough, and as I ploughed
My Saviour Christ would sing aloud,
And as I drove the clods apart
Christ would be ploughing in my heart,
Through rest-harrow and bitter roots,
Through all my bad life's rotten fruits.

O Christ who holds the open gate,
O Christ who drives the furrow straight,
O Christ, the plough, O Christ, the laughter
Of holy white birds flying after,
Lo, all my heart's field red and torn,
And Thou wilt bring the young green corn,
The young green corn divinely springing,
The young green corn forever singing;
And when the field is fresh and fair
Thy blessèd feet shall glitter there,
And we will walk the weeded field,
And tell the golden harvest's yield,
The corn that makes the holy bread
By which the soul of man is fed,
The holy bread, the food unpriced,
Thy everlasting mercy, Christ.

The share will jar on many a stone,
Thou wilt not let me stand alone;
And I shall feel (thou wilt not fail),
Thy hand on mine upon the hale.

[173]

Near Bullen Bank, on Gloucester Road,
Thy everlasting mercy showed
The ploughman patient on the hill
Forever there, forever still,
Ploughing the hill with steady yoke
Of pine-trees lightning-struck and broke.
I've marked the May Hill ploughman stay
There on his hill, day after day
Driving his team against the sky,
While men and women live and die.
And now and then he seems to stoop
To clear the coulter with the scoop,
Or touch an ox to haw or gee
While Severn stream goes out to sea.
The sea with all her ships and sails,
And that great smoky port in Wales,
And Gloucester tower bright i' the sun,
All know that patient wandering one.
And sometimes when they burn the leaves
The bonfires' smoking trails and heaves,
And girt red flamës twink and twire
As though he ploughed the hill afire.
And in men's hearts in many lands
A spiritual ploughman stands
Forever waiting, waiting now,
The heart's "Put in, man, zook the plough."

By this the sun was all one glitter,
The little birds were all in twitter;
Out of a tuft a little lark
Went higher up than I could mark,
His little throat was all one thirst

To sing until his heart should burst
To sing aloft in golden light
His song from blue air out of sight.
The mist drove by, and now the cows
Came plodding up to milking house.
Followed by Frank, the Callows' cowman,
Who whistled "Adam was a ploughman."
There come such cawing from the rooks,
Such running chuck from little brooks,
One thought it March, just budding green,
With hedgerows full of celandine.
An otter 'out of stream and played,
Two hares come loping up and stayed;
Wide-eyed and tender-eared but bold.
Sheep bleated up by Penny's fold.
I heard a partridge covey call,
The morning sun was bright on all.
Down the long slope the plough team drove
The tossing rooks arose and hove.
A stone struck on the share.   A word
Came to the team.   The red earth stirred.

I crossed the hedge by shooter's gap,
I hitched my boxer's belt a strap,
I jumped the ditch and crossed the fallow:
I took the hales from farmer Callow.

How swift the summer goes,
Forget-me-not, pink, rose.
The young grass when I started
And now the hay is carted,
And now my song is ended,
And all the summer spended;
The blackbird's second brood
Routs beech leaves in the wood;
The pink and rose have speeded,
Forget-me-not has seeded.
Only the winds that blew,
The rain that makes things new,
The earth that hides things old,
And blessings manifold.

O lovely lily clean,
O lily springing green,
O lily bursting white,
Dear lily of delight,
Spring in my heart agen
That I may flower to men.

GREAT HAMPDEN.   June, 1911.

NOTE

"The Everlasting Mercy" first appeared in *The English Review* for October, 1911. I thank the Editor and Proprietors of that paper for permitting me to reprint it here. The persons and events described in the poem are entirely imaginary, and no reference is made or intended to any living person.

JOHN MASEFIELD.

THE WIDOW IN THE BYE STREET

THE WIDOW IN THE BYE STREET [1]

PART I

Down Bye Street, in a little Shropshire town,
There lived a widow with her only son:
She had no wealth nor title to renown,
Nor any joyous hours, never one.
She rose from ragged mattress before sun
And stitched all day until her eyes were red,
And had to stitch, because her man was dead.

Sometimes she fell asleep, she stitched so hard,
Letting the linen fall upon the floor;
And hungry cats would steal in from the yard,
And mangy chickens pecked about the door,
Craning their necks so ragged and so sore
To search the room for bread-crumbs, or for mouse,
But they got nothing in the widow's house.

Mostly she made her bread by hemming shrouds
For one rich undertaker in the High Street,
Who used to pray that folks might die in crowds
And that their friends might pay to let them lie sweet;
And when one died the widow in the Bye Street
Stitched night and day to give the worm his dole.
The dead were better dressed than that poor soul.

[1] Copyright in the United Kingdom and U. S. A., 1912.

THE WIDOW IN THE BYE STREET

Her little son was all her life's delight,
For in his little features she could find
A glimpse of that dead husband out of sight,
Where out of sight is never out of mind.
And so she stitched till she was nearly blind,
Or till the tallow candle end was done,
To get a living for her little son.

Her love for him being such she would not rest,
It was a want which ate her out and in,
Another hunger in her withered breast
Pressing her woman's bones against the skin.
To make him plump she starved her body thin.
And he, he ate the food, and never knew,
He laughed and played as little children do.

When there was little sickness in the place
She took what God would send, and what God sent
Never brought any colour to her face
Nor life into her footsteps when she went.
Going, she trembled always withered and bent,
For all went to her son, always the same,
He was first served whatever blessing came.

Sometimes she wandered out to gather sticks,
For it was bitter cold there when it snowed.
And she stole hay out of the farmer's ricks
For bands to wrap her feet in while she sewed,
And when her feet were warm and the grate glowed
She hugged her little son, her heart's desire,
With "Jimmy, ain't it snug beside the fire?"

THE WIDOW IN THE BYE STREET

So years went on till Jimmy was a lad
And went to work as poor lads have to do,
And then the widow's loving heart was glad
To know that all the pains she had gone through,
And all the years of putting on the screw,
Down to the sharpest turn a mortal can,
Had borne their fruit, and made her child a man.

He got a job at working on the line,
Tipping the earth down, trolly after truck,
From daylight till the evening, wet or fine,
With arms all red from wallowing in the muck,
And spitting, as the trolly tipped, for luck,
And singing "Binger" as he swung the pick,
Because the red blood ran in him so quick.

So there was bacon then, at night, for supper
In Bye Street there, where he and mother stay;
And boots they had, not leaky in the upper,
And room rent ready on the settling day;
And beer for poor old mother, worn and grey,
And fire in frost; and in the widow's eyes
It seemed the Lord had made earth paradise.

And there they sat of evenings after dark
Singing their song of "Binger," he and she,
Her poor old cackle made the mongrels bark
And "You sing Binger, mother," carols he;
"By crimes, but that's a good song, that her be:"
And then they slept there in the room they shared,
And all the time fate had his end prepared.

One thing alone made life not perfect sweet:
The mother's daily fear of what would come
When woman and her lovely boy should meet,
When the new wife would break up the old home.
Fear of that unborn evil struck her dumb,
And when her darling and a woman met,
She shook and prayed, "Not her, O God; not yet."

"Not yet, dear God, my Jimmy took from me."
Then she would subtly question with her son.
"Not very handsome. I don't think her be?"
"God help the man who marries such an one."
Her red eyes peered to spy the mischief done.
She took great care to keep the girls away,
And all her trouble made him easier prey.

There was a woman out at Plaister's End,
Light of her body, fifty to the pound,
A copper coin for any man to spend,
Lovely to look on when the wits were drowned.
Her husband's skeleton was never found,
It lay among the rocks at Glydyr Mor
Where he drank poison finding her a whore.

She was not native there, for she belonged
Out Milford way, or Swansea; no one knew.
She had the piteous look of someone wronged,
"Anna," her name, a widow, last of Triw.
She had lived at Plaister's End a year or two;
At Callow's cottage, renting half an acre;
She was a hen-wife and a perfume-maker.

THE WIDOW IN THE BYE STREET

Secret she was; she lived in reputation;
But secret unseen threads went floating out:
Her smile, her voice, her face, were all temptation,
All subtle flies to trouble man the trout;
Man to entice, entrap, entangle, flout. . .
To take and spoil, and then to cast aside:
Gain without giving was the craft she plied.

And she complained, poor lonely widowed soul,
How no one cared, and men were rutters all;
While true love is an ever burning goal
Burning the brighter as the shadows fall.
And all love's dogs went hunting at the call,
Married or not she took them by the brain,
Sucked at their hearts and tossed them back again.

Like the straw fires lit on Saint John's Eve,
She burned and dwindled in her fickle heart;
For if she wept when Harry took his leave,
Her tears were lures to beckon Bob to start.
And if, while loving Bob, a tinker's cart
Came by, she opened window with a smile
And gave the tinker hints to wait a while.

She passed for pure; but, years before, in Wales,
Living at Mountain Ash with different men,
Her less discretion had inspired tales
Of certain things she did, and how, and when.
Those seven years of youth; we are frantic then.
She had been frantic in her years of youth,
The tales were not more evil than the truth.

THE WIDOW IN THE BYE STREET

She had two children as the fruits of trade,
Though she drank bitter herbs to kill the curse,
Both of them sons, and one she overlaid,
The other one the parish had to nurse.
Now she grew plump with money in her purse,
Passing for pure a hundred miles, I guess,
From where her little son wore workhouse dress.

There with the Union boys he came and went,
A parish bastard fed on bread and tea,
Wearing a bright tin badge in furthest Gwent,
And no one knowing who his folk could be.
His mother never knew his new name: she,—
She touched the lust of those who served her turn,
And chief among her men was Shepherd Ern.

A moody, treacherous man of bawdy mind,
Married to that mild girl from Ercall Hill,
Whose gentle goodness made him more inclined
To hotter sauces sharper on the bill.
The new lust gives the lecher the new thrill,
The new wine scratches as it slips the throat,
The new flag is so bright by the old boat.

Ern was her man to buy her bread and meat,
Half of his weekly wage was hers to spend,
She used to mock, "How is your wife, my sweet?"
Or wail, "O, Ernie, how is this to end?"
Or coo, "My Ernie is without a friend,
She cannot understand my precious life,"
And Ernie would go home and beat his wife.

So the four souls are ranged, the chess-board set,
The dark, invisible hand of secret Fate
Brought it to come to being that they met
After so many years of lying in wait.
While we least think it he prepares his Mate.
Mate, and the King's pawn played, it never ceases
Though all the earth is dust of taken pieces.

PART II

October Fair-time is the time for fun,
For all the street is hurdled into rows
Of pens of heifers blinking at the sun,
And Lemster sheep which pant and seem to doze,
And stalls of hardbake and galanty shows,
And cheapjacks smashing crocks, and trumpets blowing,
And the loud organ of the horses going.

There you can buy blue ribbons for your girl
Or take her in a swing-boat tossing high,
Or hold her fast when all the horses whirl
Round to the steam pipe whanging at the sky,
Or stand her cockshies at the cocoa-shy,
Or buy her brooches with her name in red,
Or Queen Victoria done in gingerbread.

Then there are rifle shots at tossing balls,
"And if you hit you get a good cigar,"
And strength-whackers for lads to lamm with mauls,
And Cheshire cheeses on a greasy spar.
The country folk flock in from near and far,
Women and men, like blowflies to the roast,
All love the fair; but Anna loved it most.

THE WIDOW IN THE BYE STREET

Anna was all agog to see the fair;
She made Ern promise to be there to meet her,
To arm her round to all the pleasures there,
And buy her ribbons for her neck, and treat her,
So that no woman at the fair should beat her
In having pleasure at a man's expense.
She planned to meet him at the chapel fence.

So Ernie went; and Jimmy took his mother,
Dressed in her finest with a Monmouth shawl,
And there was such a crowd she thought she'd smother,
And O, she loved a pep'mint above all.
Clash go the crockeries where the cheapjacks bawl,
Baa go the sheep, thud goes the waxwork's drum,
And Ernie cursed for Anna hadn't come.

He hunted for her up and down the place,
Raging and snapping like a working brew.
"If you're with someone else I'll smash his face,
And when I've done for him I'll go for you."
He bought no fairings as he'd vowed to do
For his poor little children back at home
Stuck at the glass "to see till father come."

Not finding her, he went into an inn,
Busy with ringing till and scratching matches.
Where thirsty drovers mingled stout with gin
And three or four Welsh herds were singing catches.
The swing-doors clattered, letting in in snatches
The noises of the fair, now low, now loud.
Ern called for beer and glowered at the crowd.

THE WIDOW IN THE BYE STREET

While he was glowering at his drinking there,
In came the gipsy Bessie, hawking toys;
A bold-eyed strapping harlot with black hair,
One of the tribe which camped at Shepherd's Bois.
She lured him out of inn into the noise
Of the steam-organ where the horses spun,
And so the end of all things was begun.

Newness in lust, always the old in love.
"Put up your toys," he said, "and come along,
We'll have a turn of swing boats up above,
And see the murder when they strike the gong."
"Don't 'ee," she giggled. "My, but ain't you strong.
And where's your proper girl? You don't know me."
"I do." "You don't." "Why, then, I will," said he.

Anna was late because the cart which drove her
Called for her late (the horse had broke a trace),
She was all dressed and scented for her lover,
Her bright blue blouse had imitation lace,
The paint was red as roses on her face,
She hummed a song, because she thought to see
How envious all the other girls would be.

When she arrived and found her Ernie gone,
Her bitter heart thought, "This is how it is.
Keeping me waiting while the sports are on:
Promising faithful, too, and then to miss.
O, Ernie, won't I give it you for this."
And looking up she saw a couple cling,
Ern with his arm round Bessie in the swing.

THE WIDOW IN THE BYE STREET

Ern caught her eye and spat, and cut her dead,
Bessie laughed hardly, in the gipsy way.
Anna, though blind with fury, tossed her head,
Biting her lips until the red was grey,
For bitter moments given, bitter pay,
The time for payment comes, early or late,
No earthly debtor but accounts to Fate.

She turned aside, telling with bitter oaths
What Ern should suffer if he turned agen,
And there was Jimmy stripping off his clothes
Within a little ring of farming men.
"Now, Jimmy, put the old tup into pen."
His mother, watching, thought her heart would curdle,
To see Jim drag the old ram to the hurdle.

Then the ram butted and the game began,
Till Jimmy's muscles cracked and the ram grunted.
The good old wrestling game of Ram and Man,
At which none knows the hunter from the hunted.
"Come and see Jimmy have his belly bunted."
"Good tup. Good Jim. Good Jimmy. Sick him, Rover,
By dang, but Jimmy's got him fairly over."

Then there was clap of hands and Jimmy grinned
And took five silver shillings from his backers,
And said th' old tup had put him out of wind
Or else he'd take all comers at the Whackers.
And some made rude remarks of rams and knackers,
And mother shook to get her son alone,
So's to be sure he hadn't broke a bone.

THE WIDOW IN THE BYE STREET

None but the lucky man deserves the fair,
For lucky men have money and success,
Things that a whore is very glad to share,
Or dip, at least, a finger in the mess.
Anne, with her raddled cheeks and Sunday dress,
Smiled upon Jimmy, seeing him succeed,
As though to say, "You are a man, indeed."

All the great things of life are swiftly done,
Creation, death, and love the double gate.
However much we dawdle in the sun
We have to hurry at the touch of Fate;
When Life knocks at the door no one can wait,
When Death makes his arrest we have to go.
And so with Love, and Jimmy found it so.

Love, the sharp spear, went pricking to the bone,
In that one look, desire and bitter aching,
Longing to have that woman all alone
For her dear beauty's sake all else forsaking;
And sudden agony that set him shaking
Lest she, whose beauty made his heart's blood cruddle,
Should be another man's to kiss and cuddle.

She was beside him when he left the ring,
Her soft dress brushed against him as he passed her;
He thought her penny scent a sweeter thing
Than precious ointment out of alabaster;
Love, the mild servant, makes a drunken master.
She smiled, half sadly, out of thoughtful eyes,
And all the strong young man was easy prize.

[189]

She spoke, to take him, seeing him a sheep,
"How beautiful you wrastled with the ram,
It made me all go tremble just to peep,
I am that fond of wrastling, that I am.
Why, here's your mother, too. Good evening, ma'am.
I was just telling Jim how well he done,
How proud you must be of so fine a son."

Old mother blinked, while Jimmy hardly knew
Whether he knew the woman there or not;
But well he knew, if not, he wanted to,
Joy of her beauty ran in him so hot,
Old trembling mother by him was forgot,
While Anna searched the mother's face, to know
Whether she took her for a whore or no.

The woman's maxim, "Win the woman first,"
Made her be gracious to the withered thing.
"This being in crowds do give one such a thirst,
I wonder if they've tea going at 'The King'?
My throat's that dry my very tongue do cling,
Perhaps you'd take my arm, we'd wander up
(If you'd agree) and try and get a cup.

Come, ma'am, a cup of tea would do you good
There's nothing like a nice hot cup of tea
After the crowd and all the time you've stood;
And 'The King's' strict, it isn't like 'The Key.'
Now, take my arm, my dear, and lean on me."
And Jimmy's mother, being nearly blind,
Took Anna's arm, and only thought her kind.

[190]

THE WIDOW IN THE BYE STREET

So off they set, with Anna talking to her,
How nice the tea would be after the crowd,
And mother thinking half the time she knew her,
And Jimmy's heart's blood ticking quick and loud,
And Death beside him knitting at his shroud,
And all the High Street babbling with the fair,
And white October clouds in the blue air.

So tea was made, and down they sat to drink;
O the pale beauty sitting at the board
There is more death in women than we think,
There is much danger in the soul adored,
The white hands bring the poison and the cord;
Death has a lodge in lips as red as cherries,
Death has a mansion in the yew tree berries.

They sat there talking after tea was done,
And Jimmy blushed at Anna's sparkling looks,
And Anna flattered mother on her son,
Catching both fishes on her subtle hooks.
With twilight, tea and talk in ingle-nooks,
And music coming up from the dim street,
Mother had never known a fair so sweet.

Now cow-bells clink, for milking-time is come,
The drovers stack the hurdles into carts,
New masters drive the straying cattle home,
Many a young calf from his mother parts,
Hogs straggle back to sty by fits and starts;
The farmers take a last glass at the inns,
And now the frolic of the fair begins.

THE WIDOW IN THE BYE STREET

All of the side shows of the fair are lighted,
Flares and bright lights, and brassy cymbals clanging,
"Beginning now" and "Everyone's invited,"
Shatter the pauses of the organ's whanging,
The Oldest Show on Earth and the Last Hanging,
"The Murder in the Red Barn," with real blood,
The rifles crack, the Sally shy-sticks thud.

Anna walked slowly homewards with her prey,
Holding old tottering mother's weight upon her,
And pouring in sweet poison on the way
Of "Such a pleasure, ma'am, and such an honour,"
And "One's so safe with such a son to con her
Through all the noises and through all the press,
Boys daredn't squirt tormenters on her dress."

At mother's door they stop to say "Goodnight."
And mother must go in to set the table.
Anna pretended that she felt a fright
To go alone through all the merry babel:
"My friends are waiting at 'The Cain and Abel,'
Just down the other side of Market Square,
It'd be a mercy if you'd set me there."

So Jimmy came, while mother went inside;
Anna has got her victim in her clutch.
Jimmy, all blushing, glad to be her guide,
Thrilled by her scent, and trembling at her touch.
She was all white and dark, and said not much;
She sighed, to hint that pleasure's grave was dug,
And smiled within to see him such a mug.

They passed the doctor's house among the trees,
She sighed so deep that Jimmy asked her why.
"I'm too unhappy upon nights like these,
When everyone has happiness but I!"
"Then, aren't you happy?" She appeared to cry,
Blinked with her eyes, and turned away her head:
"Not much; but some men understand," she said.

Her voice caught lightly on a broken note,
Jimmy half-dared but dared not touch her hand,
Yet all his blood went pumping in his throat
Beside the beauty he could understand,
And Death stopped knitting at the muffling band.
"The shroud is done," he muttered, "toe to chin."
He snapped the ends, and tucked his needles in.

Jimmy, half stammering, choked, "Has any man—"
He stopped, she shook her head to answer "No."
"Then tell me." "No. Perhaps some day, if I can.
It hurts to talk of some things ever so.
But you're so different. There, come, we must go.
None but unhappy women know how good
It is to meet a soul who's understood."
"No. Wait a moment. May I call you Anna?"

"Perhaps. There must be nearness 'twixt us two."
Love in her face hung out his bloody banner,
And all love's clanging trumpets shocked and blew
"When we got up to-day we never knew."
"I'm sure I didn't think, nor you did." "Never."
"And now this friendship's come to us forever."

"Now, Anna, take my arm, dear." "Not to-night,
That must come later when we know our minds,
We must agree to keep this evening white,
We'll eat the fruit to-night and save the rinds."
And all the folk whose shadows darked the blinds,
And all the dancers whirling in the fair,
Were wretched worms to Jim and Anna there.

"How wonderful life is," said Anna, lowly.
"But it begins again with you for friend."
In the dim lamplight Jimmy thought her holy,
A lovely fragile thing for him to tend,
Grace beyond measure, beauty without end.
"Anna," he said; "Good-night. This is the door.
I never knew what people meant before,"

"Good-night, my friend. Good-bye." "But oh, my sweet,
The night's quite early yet, don't say good-bye,
Come just another short turn down the street,
The whole life's bubbling up for you and I.
Somehow I feel to-morrow we may die.
Come just as far as to the blacksmith's light."
But "No," said Anna; "not to-night. Good-night."

All the tides triumph when the white moon fills
Down in the race the toppling waters shout,
The breakers shake the bases of the hills,
There is a thundering where the streams go out,
And the wise shipman puts his ship about
Seeing the gathering of those waters wan,
But what when love makes high tide in a man?

THE WIDOW IN THE BYE STREET

Jimmy walked home with all his mind on fire,
One lovely face forever set in flame.
He shivered as he went, like tautened wire,
Surge after surge of shuddering in him came
And then swept out repeating one sweet name
"Anna, oh Anna," to the evening star.
Anna was sipping whiskey in the bar.

So back to home and mother Jimmy wandered,
Thinking of Plaister's End and Anna's lips.
He ate no supper worth the name, but pondered
On Plaister's End hedge, scarlet with ripe hips,
And of the lovely moon there in eclipse,
And how she must be shining in the house
Behind the hedge of those old dog-rose boughs.

Old mother cleared away. The clock struck eight.
"Why, boy, you've left your bacon, lawks a me,
So that's what comes of having tea so late,
Another time you'll go without your tea.
Your father liked his cup, too, didn't he,
Always 'another cup' he used to say,
He never went without on any day.

How nice the lady was and how she talked,
I've never had a nicer fair, not ever."
"She said she'd like to see us if we walked
To Plaister's End, beyond by Watersever.
Nice-looking woman, too, and that, and clever;
We might go round one evening, p'raps, we two;
Or I might go, if it's too far for you."

"No," said the mother, "we're not folk for that;
Meet at the fair and that, and there an end.
Rake out the fire and put out the cat,
These fairs are sinful, tempting folk to spend.
Of course she spoke polite and like a friend;
Of course she had to do, and so I let her,
But now it's done and past, so I forget her."

"I don't see why forget her. Why forget her?
She treat us kind. She weren't like everyone.
I never saw a woman I liked better,
And he's not easy pleased, my father's son.
So I'll go round some night when work is done."
"Now, Jim, my dear, trust mother, there's a dear."
"Well, so I do, but sometimes you're so queer."

She blinked at him out of her withered eyes
Below her lashless eyelids red and bleared.
Her months of sacrifice had won the prize,
Her Jim had come to what she always feared.
And yet she doubted, so she shook and peered
And begged her God not let a woman take
The lovely son whom she had starved to make.

Doubting, she stood the dishes in the rack,
"We'll ask her in some evening, then," she said,
"How nice her hair looked in the bit of black."
And still she peered from eyes all dim and red
To note at once if Jimmy drooped his head,
Or if his ears blushed when he heard her praised,
And Jimmy blushed and hung his head and gazed.

[196]

"This is the end," she thought. "This is the end.
I'll have to sew again for Mr. Jones,
Do hems when I can hardly see to mend,
And have the old ache in my marrow bones.
And when his wife's in child-bed, when she groans,
She'll send for me until the pains have ceased,
And give me leavings at the christening feast.

And sit aslant to eye me as I eat,
'You're only wanted here, ma'am, for to-day,
Just for the christ'ning party, for the treat,
Don't ever think I mean to let you stay;
Two's company, three's none, that's what I say.'
Life can be bitter to the very bone
When one is poor, and woman, and alone,"

"Jimmy," she said, still doubting. "Come, my dear,
Let's have our 'Binger,' 'fore we go to bed."
And then "The parson's dog," she cackled clear,
"Lep over stile," she sang, nodding her head.
"His name was little Binger." "Jim," she said,
"Binger, now, chorus" . . . Jimmy kicked the hob,
The sacrament of song died in a sob.

Jimmy went out into the night to think
Under the moon so steady in the blue.
The woman's beauty ran in him like drink,
The fear that men had loved her burnt him through;
The fear that even then another knew
All the deep mystery which women make
To hide the inner nothing made him shake.

"Anna, I love you, and I always shall."
He looked towards Plaister's End beyond Cot Hills.
A white star glimmered in the long canal,
A droning from the music came in thrills.
Love is a flame to burn out human wills,
Love is a flame to set the will on fire,
Love is a flame to cheat men into mire.

One of the three, we make Love what we choose.
But Jimmy did not know, he only thought
That Anna was too beautiful to lose,
That she was all the world and he was naught,
That it was sweet, though bitter, to be caught.
"Anna, I love you." Underneath the moon,
"I shall go mad unless I see you soon."

The fair's lights threw aloft a misty glow.
The organ whangs, the giddy horses reel,
The rifles cease, the folk begin to go,
The hands unclamp the swing boats from the wheel,
There is a smell of trodden orange peel;
The organ drones and dies, the horses stop,
And then the tent collapses from the top.

The fair is over, let the people troop,
The drunkards stagger homewards down the gutters,
The showmen heave in an excited group,
The poles tilt slowly down, the canvas flutters,
The mauls knock out the pins, the last flare sputters.
"Lower away." "Go easy." "Lower, lower."
"You've dang near knock my skull in. Loose it slower."

THE WIDOW IN THE BYE STREET

"Back in the horses." "Are the swing boats loaded?"
"All right to start." "Bill, where's the cushion gone?
The red one for the Queen?" "I think I stowed it."
"You think, you think. Lord, where's that cushion, John?"
"It's in that ditty box you're sitting on,
What more d'you want?" A concertina plays
Far off as wandering lovers go their ways.

Up the dim Bye Street to the market-place
The dead bones of the fair are borne in carts,
Horses and swing boats at a funeral pace
After triumphant hours quickening hearts;
A policeman eyes each waggon as it starts,
The drowsy showmen stumble half asleep,
One of them cat calls, having drunken deep.

So out, over the pass, into the plain,
And the dawn finds them filling empty cans
In some sweet-smelling dusty country lane,
Where a brook chatters over rusty pans.
The iron chimneys of the caravans
Smoke as they go. And now the fair has gone
To find a new pitch somewhere further on.

But as the fair moved out two lovers came,
Ernie and Bessie loitering out together;
Bessie with wild eyes, hungry as a flame,
Ern like a stallion tugging at a tether.
It was calm moonlight, and October weather,
So still, so lovely, as they topped the ridge.
They brushed by Jimmy standing on the bridge.

And, as they passed, they gravely eyed each other,
And the blood burned in each heart beating there;
And out into the Bye Street tottered mother,
Without her shawl, in the October air.
"Jimmy," she cried, "Jimmy." And Bessie's hair
Drooped on the instant over Ernie's face,
And the two lovers clung in an embrace.

"O, Ern." "My own, my Bessie." As they kissed
Jimmy was envious of the thing unknown.
So this was Love, the something he had missed,
Woman and man athirst, aflame, alone.
Envy went knocking at his marrow-bone,
And Anna's face swam up so dim, so fair,
Shining and sweet, with poppies in her hair.

PART III

After the fair, the gang began again.
Tipping the trolleys down the banks of earth.
The truck of stone clanks on the endless chain,
A clever pony guides it to its berth.
"Let go." It tips, the navvies shout for mirth
To see the pony step aside, so wise,
But Jimmy sighed, thinking of Anna's eyes.

And when he stopped his shovelling he looked
Over the junipers towards Plaister way,
The beauty of his darling had him hooked,
He had no heart for wrastling with the clay.
"O Lord Almighty, I must get away;
 O Lord, I must. I must just see my flower.
Why, I could run there in the dinner hour."

THE WIDOW IN THE BYE STREET

The whistle on the pilot engine blew,
The men knocked off, and Jimmy slipped aside
Over the fence, over the bridge, and through,
And then ahead along the water-side,
Under the red-brick rail-bridge, arching wide,
Over the hedge, across the fields, and on;
The foreman asked: "Where's Jimmy Gurney gone?"

It is a mile and more to Plaister's End,
But Jimmy ran the short way by the stream,
And there was Anna's cottage at the bend,
With blue smoke on the chimney, faint as steam.
"God, she's at home," and up his heart a gleam
Leapt like a rocket on November nights,
And shattered slowly in a burst of lights.

Anna was singing at her kitchen fire,
She was surprised, and not well pleased to see
A sweating navvy, red with heat and mire,
Come to her door, whoever he might be.
But when she saw that it was Jimmy, she
Smiled at his eyes upon her, full of pain,
And thought, "But, still, he mustn't come again.

People will talk; boys are such crazy things;
But he's a dear boy though he is so green."
So, hurriedly, she slipped her apron strings,
And dabbed her hair, and wiped her fingers clean,
And came to greet him languid as a queen,
Looking as sweet, as fair, as pure, as sad,
As when she drove her loving husband mad.

"Poor boy," she said, "Poor boy, how hot you are."
She laid a cool hand to his sweating face.
"How kind to come. Have you been running far?
I'm just going out; come up the road a pace.
O dear, these hens; they're all about the place."
So Jimmy shooed the hens at her command,
And got outside the gate as she had planned.

"Anna, my dear, I love you; love you, true;
I had to come—I don't know—I can't rest—
I lay awake all night, thinking of you.
Many must love you, but I love you best."
"Many have loved me, yes, dear," she confessed,
She smiled upon him with a tender pride,
"But my love ended when my husband died.

"Still, we'll be friends, dear friends, dear, tender friends;
Love with its fever's at an end for me.
Be by me gently now the fever ends,
Life is a lovelier thing than lovers see,
I'd like to trust a man, Jimmy," said she,
"May I trust you?" "Oh, Anna dear, my dear——"
"Don't come so close," she said, "with people near.

Dear, don't be vexed; it's very sweet to find
One who will understand; but life is life,
And those who do not know are so unkind.
But you'll be by me, Jimmy, in the strife,
I love you though I cannot be your wife;
And now be off, before the whistle goes,
Or else you'll lose your quarter, goodness knows."

"When can I see you, Anna? Tell me, dear.
To-night? To-morrow? Shall I come to-night?"
"Jimmy, my friend, I cannot have you here;
But when I come to town perhaps we might.
Dear, you must go; no kissing; you can write,
And I'll arrange a meeting when I learn
What friends are doing" (meaning Shepherd Ern).

"Good-bye, my own." "Dear Jim, you understand.
If we were only free, dear, free to meet,
Dear, I would take you by your big, strong hand
And kiss your dear boy eyes so blue and sweet;
But my dead husband lies under the sheet,
Dead in my heart, dear, lovely, lonely one,
So, Jim, my dear, my loving days are done.

But though my heart is buried in his grave
Something might be—friendship and utter trust—
And you, my dear starved little Jim shall have
Flowers of friendship from my dead heart's dust;
Life would be sweet if men would never lust.
Why do you, Jimmy? Tell me sometime, dear,
Why men are always what we women fear.

Not now. Good-bye; we understand, we two,
And life, oh, Jim, how glorious life is;
This sunshine in my heart is due to you;
I was so sad, and life has given this.
I think 'I wish I had something of his,'
Do give me something, will you be so kind?
Something to keep you always in my mind."

"I will," he said. "Now go, or you'll be late."
He broke from her and ran, and never dreamt
That as she stood to watch him from the gate
Her heart was half amusement, half contempt,
Comparing Jim the squab, red and unkempt,
In sweaty corduroys, with Shepherd Ern.
She blew him kisses till he passed the turn.

The whistle blew before he reached the line;
The foreman asked him what the hell he meant,
Whether a duke had asked him out to dine,
Or if he thought the bag would pay his rent?
And Jim was fined before the foreman went.
But still his spirit glowed from Anna's words,
Cooed in the voice so like a singing bird's.

"O Anna, darling, you shall have a present;
I'd give you golden gems if I were rich,
And everything that's sweet and all that's pleasant."
He dropped his pick as though he had a stitch,
And stared tow'rds Plaister's End, past Bushe's Pitch.
O beauty, what I have to give I'll give,
All mine is yours, beloved, while I live."

All through the afternoon his pick was slacking,
His eyes were always turning west and south,
The foreman was inclined to send him packing,
But put it down to after fair-day drouth;
He looked at Jimmy with an ugly mouth,
And Jimmy slacked, and muttered in a moan,
"My love, my beautiful, my very own."

[204]

So she had loved. Another man had had her;
She had been his with passion in the night;
An agony of envy made him sadder,
Yet stabbed a pang of bitter-sweet delight—
O he would keep his image of her white.
The foreman cursed, stepped up, and asked him flat
What kind of gum tree he was gaping at.

It was Jim's custom, when the pay day came,
To take his weekly five and twenty shilling
Back in the little packet to his dame:
Not taking out a farthing for a filling,
Nor twopence for a pot, for he was willing
That she should have it all to save or spend.
But love makes many lovely customs end.

Next pay day came, and Jimmy took the money,
But not to mother, for he meant to buy
A thirteen shilling locket for his honey,
Whatever bellies hungered and went dry,
A silver heart-shape with a ruby eye
He bought the thing and paid the shopman's price,
And hurried off to make the sacrifice.

"Is it for me? You dear, dear generous boy.
How sweet of you. I'll wear it in my dress.
When you're beside me life is such a joy,
You bring the sun to solitariness."
She brushed his jacket with a light caress,
His arms went round her fast, she yielded meek;
He had the happiness to kiss her cheek.

"My dear, my dear." "My very dear, my Jim,
How very kind my Jimmy is to me;
I ache to think that some are harsh to him;
Not like my Jimmy, beautiful and free.
My darling boy, how lovely it would be
If all would trust as we two trust each other."
And Jimmy's heart grew hard against his mother.

She, poor old soul, was waiting in the gloom
For Jimmy's pay, that she could do the shopping.
The clock ticked out a solemn tale of doom;
Clogs on the bricks outside went clippa-clopping,
The owls were coming out and dew was dropping.
The bacon burnt, and Jimmy not yet home.
The clock was ticking dooms out like a gnome.

"What can have kept him that he doesn't come?
O God, they'd tell me if he'd come to hurt."
The unknown, unseen evil struck her numb,
She saw his body bloody in the dirt,
She saw the life blood pumping through the shirt,
She saw him tipsy in the navvies' booth,
She saw all forms of evil but the truth.

At last she hurried up the line to ask
If Jim were hurt or why he wasn't back.
She found the watchman wearing through his task;
Over the fire basket in his shack;
Behind, the new embankment rose up black.
"Gurney?" he said. He'd got to see a friend."
"Where?" "I dunno. I think out Plaister's End."

Thanking the man, she tottered down the hill,
The long-feared fang had bitten to the bone.
The brook beside her talked as water will
That it was lonely singing all alone,
The night was lonely with the water's tone,
And she was lonely to the very marrow.
Love puts such bitter poison on Fate's arrow.

She went the long way to them by the mills,
She told herself that she must find her son.
The night was ominous of many ills;
The soughing larch-clump almost made her run,
Her boots hurt (she had got a stone in one)
And bitter beaks were tearing at her liver
That her boy's heart was turned from her forever.

She kept the lane, past Spindle's past the Callows',
Her lips still muttering prayers against the worst,
And there were people coming from the sallows,
Along the wild duck patch by Beggar's Hurst.
Being in moonlight mother saw them first,
She saw them moving in the moonlight dim,
A woman with a sweet voice saying "Jim."

Trembling she grovelled down into the ditch,
They wandered past her pressing side to side.
"O Anna, my belov'd, if I were rich."
It was her son, and Anna's voice replied,
"Dear boy, dear beauty boy, my love and pride."
And he: "It's but a silver thing, but I
Will earn you better lockets by and bye."

"Dear boy, you mustn't." "But I mean to do."
"What was that funny sort of noise I heard?"
"Where?"
"In the hedge; a sort of sob or coo.
Listen. It's gone." "It may have been a bird."
Jim tossed a stone but mother never stirred.
She hugged the hedgerow, choking down her pain,
While the hot tears were blinding in her brain.

The two passed on, the withered woman rose,
For many minutes she could only shake,
Staring ahead with trembling little "Oh's,"
The noise a very frightened child might make.
"O God, dear God, don't let the woman take
My little son, God, not my little Jim.
O God, I'll have to starve if I lose him."

So back she trembled, nodding with her head,
Laughing and trembling in the bursts of tears,
Her ditch-filled boots both squelching in the tread,
Her shopping-bonnet sagging to her ears,
Her heart too dumb with brokenness for fears.
The nightmare whickering with the laugh of death
Could not have added terror to her breath.

She reached the house, and: "I'm all right," said she,
"I'll just take off my things; but I'm all right,
I'd be all right with just a cup of tea,
If I could only get this grate to light,
The paper's damp and Jimmy's late to-night;
'Belov'd, if I was rich,' was what he said,
Oh, Jim, I wish that God would kill me dead."

[208]

While she was blinking at the unlit grate,
Scratching the moistened match-heads off the wood,
She heard Jim coming, so she reached his plate,
And forked the over-frizzled scraps of food.
"You're late," she said, "and this yer isn't good,
Whatever makes you come in late like this?"
"I've been to Plaister's End, that's how it is."

    M. You've been to Plaister's End?"
    J. "Yes."
    M. I've been staying
For money for the shopping ever so.
Down here we can't get victuals without paying,
There's no trust down the Bye Street, as you know,
And now it's dark and it's too late to go.
You've been to Plaister's End. What took you there?"
    J. "The lady who was with us at the fair."

    M. "The lady, eh? The lady?"
    J. "Yes, the lady."
    M. "You've been to see her?"
    J. "Yes."

    M. "What happened then?"
    J. "I saw her."
    M. "Yes. And what filth did she trade ye?
Or d'you expect your locket back agen?
I know the rotten ways of whores with men.
What did it cost ye?"
    J. "What did what cost?"
    M. "It."
Your devil's penny for the devil's bit."

J. "I don't know what you mean."
    M. "Jimmy, my own.
Don't lie to mother, boy, for mother knows.
I know you and that lady to the bone,
And she's a whore, that thing you call a rose,
A whore who takes whatever male thing goes;
A harlot with the devil's skill to tell
The special key of each man's door to hell."

    J. "She's not.   She's nothing of the kind, I tell 'ee."
    M. "You can't tell women like a woman can;
A beggar tells a lie to fill his belly,
A strumpet tells a lie to win a man,
Women were liars since the world began;
And she's a liar, branded in the eyes,
A rotten liar, who inspires lies."

    J. "I say she's not."
    M. "No, don't 'ee, Jim, my dearie,
You've seen her often in the last few days,
She's given a love as makes you come in weary
To lie to me before going out to laze.
She's tempted you into the devil's ways,
She's robbing you, full fist, of what you earn,
In God's Name, what's she giving in return?"

    J. "Her faith, my dear, and that's enough for me."
    M. "Her faith.   Her faith.   Oh, Jimmy, listen, dear;
Love doesn't ask for faith, my son, not he;
He asks for life throughout the live-long year,
And life's a test for any plough to ere.
Life tests a plough in meadows made of stones,
   Love takes a toll of spirit, mind and bones.

I know a woman's portion when she loves,
It's hers to give, my darling, not to take;
It isn't lockets, dear, nor pairs of gloves,
It isn't marriage bells nor wedding cake,
It's up and cook, although the belly ache;
And bear the child, and up and work again,
And count a sick man's grumble worth the pain.

Will she do this, and fifty times as much?"
    J. "No. I don't ask her."
    M. "No. I warrant, no.
She's one to get a young fool in her clutch,
And you're a fool to let her trap you so.
She love you? She? O Jimmy, let her go;
I was so happy, dear, before she came,
And now I'm going to the grave in shame.

I bore you, Jimmy, in this very room.
For fifteen years I got you all you had,
You were my little son, made in my womb,
Left all to me, for God had took your dad,
You were a good son, doing all I bade,
Until this strumpet came from God knows where,
And now you lie, and I am in despair.

Jimmy, I won't say more. I know you think
That I don't know, being just a withered old,
With chaps all fallen in and eyes that blink,
And hands that tremble so they cannot hold.
A bag of bones to put in churchyard mould,
A red-eyed hag beside your evening star."
And Jimmy gulped, and thought, "By God, you are."

[211]

"Well, if I am, my dear, I don't pretend.
I got my eyes red, Jimmy, making you.
My dear, before our love time's at an end
Think just a minute what it is you do.
If this were right, my dear, you'd tell me true;
You don't, and so it's wrong; you lie; and she
Lies too, or else you wouldn't lie to me.

Women and men have only got one way
And that way's marriage; other ways are lust.
If you must marry this one, then you may
If you'll not drop her."
    J. "No."
    M. "I say you must.
Or bring my hairs with sorrow to the dust.
Marry your whore, you'll pay, and there an end.
My God, you shall not have a whore for friend.

By God, you shall not, not while I'm alive.
Never, so help me God, shall that thing be.
If she's a woman fit to touch she'll wive,
If not she's whore, and she shall deal with me.
And may God's blessed mercy help us see
And may He make my Jimmy count the cost,
My little boy who's lost, as I am lost."

People in love cannot be won by kindness,
And opposition makes them feel like martyrs.
When folk are crazy with drunken blindness
  It's best to flog them with each other's garters,
And have the flogging done by Shropshire carters,

Born under Ercall where the white stones lie;
Ercall that smells of honey in July.

Jimmy said nothing in reply, but thought
That mother was an old, hard, jealous thing.
"I'll love my girl through good and ill report,
I shall be true whatever grief it bring."
And in his heart he heard the death-bell ring
For mother's death, and thought what it would be
To bury her in churchyard and be free.

He saw the narrow grave under the wall,
Home without mother nagging at his dear,
And Anna there with him at evenfall,
Bidding him dry his eyes and be of cheer.
"The death that took poor mother brings me near,
Nearer than we have ever been before,
Near as the dead one came, but dearer, more."

"Good-night, my son," said mother. "Night," he said.
He dabbed her brow wi's lips and blew the light,
She lay quite silent crying on the bed,
Stirring no limb, but crying through the night,
He slept, convinced that he was Anna's knight.
And when he went to work he left behind
Money for mother crying herself blind.

After that night he came to Anna's call,
He was a fly in Anna's subtle weavings,
Mother had no more share in him at all;
All that the mother had was Anna's leavings.
There were more lies, more lockets, more deceivings,

Taunts from the proud old woman, lies from him,
And Anna's coo of "Cruel. Leave her, Jim."

Also the foreman spoke: "You make me sick,
You come-day-go-day-God-send-plenty-beer.
You put less mizzle on your bit of Dick,
Or get your time, I'll have no slackers here,
I've had my eye on you too long, my dear."
And Jimmy pondered while the man attacked,
"I'd see her all day long if I were sacked."

And trembling mother thought, "I'll go to see'r.
She'd give me back my boy if she were told
Just what he is to me, my pretty dear:
She wouldn't leave me starving in the cold,
Like what I am." But she was weak and old.
She thought, "But if I ast her, I'm afraid
He'd hate me ever after," so she stayed.

PART IV

Bessie, the gipsy, got with child by Ern,
She joined her tribe again at Shepherd's Meen,
In that old quarry overgrown with fern,
Where goats are tethered on the patch of green.
There she reflected on the fool she'd been,
And plaited kipes and waited for the bastard,
And thought that love was glorious while it lasted.

And Ern the moody man went moody home,
To that most gentle girl from Ercall Hill,
And bade her take a heed now he had come,
Or else, by cripes, he'd put her through the mill.

He didn't want her love, he'd had his fill,
Thank you, of her, the bread and butter sack.
And Anna heard that Shepherd Ern was back.

"Back. And I'll have him back to me," she muttered,
"This lovesick boy of twenty, green as grass,
Has made me wonder if my brains are buttered,
He, and his lockets, and his love, the ass.
I don't know why he comes. Alas! alas!
God knows I want no love; but every sun
I bolt my doors on some poor loving one.

It breaks my heart to turn them out of doors,
I hear them crying to me in the rain;
One, with a white face, curses, one implores,
"Anna, for God's sake, let me in again,
Anna, belov'd, I cannot bear the pain."
Like hoovey sheep bleating outside a fold,
"Anna, belov'd, I'm in the wind and cold."

I want no men. I'm weary to the soul
Of men like moths about a candle flame,
Of men like flies about a sugar bowl,
Acting alike, and all wanting the same,
My dreamed-of swirl of passion never came,
No man has given me the love I dreamed,
But in the best of each one something gleamed.

If my dear darling were alive, but he. . .
He was the same; he didn't understand.
The eyes of that dead child are haunting me,
I only turned the blanket with my hand.
It didn't hurt, he died as I had planned.

A little skinny creature, weak and red;
It looked so peaceful after it was dead.

I have been all alone, in spite of all.
Never a light to help me place my feet:
I have had many a pain and many a fall.
Life's a long headache in a noisy street,
Love at the budding looks so very sweet,
Men put such bright disguises on their lust,
And then it all goes crumble into dust.

Jimmy the same, dear, lovely Jimmy, too,
He goes the self-same way the others went:
I shall bring sorrow to those eyes of blue.
He asks the love I'm sure I never meant.
Am I to blame? And all his money spent!
Men make this shutting doors such cruel pain.
O, Ern, I want you in my life again."

On Sunday afternoons the lovers walk
Arm within arm, dressed in their Sunday best,
The man with the blue necktie sucks a stalk,
The woman answers when she is addressed.
On quiet country stiles they sit to rest,
And after fifty years of wear and tear
  They think how beautiful their courtships were.

Jimmy and Anna met to walk together
The Sunday after Shepherd Ern returned;
And Anna's hat was lovely with a feather
Bought and dyed blue with money Jimmy earned.
They walked towards Callows Farm, and Anna yearned:

[216]

THE WIDOW IN THE BYE STREET

"Dear boy," she said, "This road is dull to-day,
Suppose we turn and walk the other way."

They turned, she sighed. "What makes you sigh?" he asked.
"Thinking," she said, "thinking and grieving, too.
Perhaps some wicked woman will come masked
Into your life, my dear, to ruin you.
And trusting every woman as you do
It might mean death to love and be deceived;
You'd take it hard, I thought, and so I grieved."

"Dear one, dear Anna." "O my lovely boy,
Life is all golden to the fingers tips.
What will be must be: but to-day's a joy.
Reach me that lovely branch of scarlet hips."
He reached and gave; she put it to her lips.
"And here," she said, "we come to Plaister Turns,"
And then she chose the road to Shepherd Ern's.

As the deft angler, when the fishes rise,
Flicks on the broadening circle over each
The delicatest touch of dropping flies,
Then pulls more line and whips a longer reach,
Longing to feel the rod bend, the reel screech,
And the quick comrade net the monster out,
So Anna played the fly over her trout.

Twice she passed, thrice, she with the boy beside her,
A lovely fly, hooked for a human heart,
She passed his little gate, while Jimmy eyed her,
Feeling her beauty tear his soul apart:
Then did the great trout rise, the great pike dart,

THE WIDOW IN THE BYE STREET

The gate went clack, a man came up the hill,
The lucky strike had hooked him through the gill.

Her breath comes quick, her tired beauty glows,
She would not look behind, she looked ahead,
It seemed to Jimmy she was like a rose,
A golden white rose faintly flushed with red.
Her eyes danced quicker at the approaching tread,
Her finger nails dug sharp into her palm.
She yearned to Jimmy's shoulder, and kept calm.

"Evening," said Shepherd Ern.   She turned and eyed him,
Cold and surprised, but interested too,
To see how much he felt the hook inside him,
And how much he surmised, and Jimmy knew,
And if her beauty still could make him do
The love tricks he had gambolled in the past.
A glow shot through her that her fish was grassed.

"Evening," she said.   "Good evening."   Jimmy felt
Jealous and angry at the shepherd's tone;
He longed to hit the fellow's nose a belt,
He wanted his beloved his alone.
A fellow's girl should be a fellow's own.
Ern gave the lad a glance and turned to Anna,
Jim might have been in China by his manner.

"Still walking out?"   "As you are."   "I'll be bound."
"Can you talk gipsy yet, or plait a kipe?"
"I'll teach you if I can when I come round."
"And when will that be?"   "When the time is ripe."
And Jimmy longed to hit the man a swipe

Under the chin to knock him out of time,
But Anna stayed: she still had twigs to lime.

"Come, Anna, come, my dear," he muttered low.
She frowned, and blinked and spoke again to Ern.
I hear the gipsy has a row to hoe."
"The more you hear," he said, "the less you'll learn."
"We've come out," she said, "to take a turn;
Suppose you come along: the more the merrier."
"All right," he said, "but how about the terrier?"

He cocked an eye at Jimmy. "Does he bite?"
Jimmy blushed scarlet. "He's a dear," said she.
Ern walked a step, "Will you be in tonight?"
She shook her head, "I doubt if that may be.
Jim, here's a friend who wants to talk to me,
So will you go and come another day?"
"By crimes, I won't!" said Jimmy, "I shall stay."

" I thought he bit," said Ern, and Anna smiled,
And Jimmy saw the smile and watched her face
While all the jealous devils made him wild;
A third in love is always out of place;
And then her gentle body full of grace
Leaned to him sweetly as she tossed her head,
"Perhaps we two'll be getting on," she said.

They walked, but Jimmy turned to watch the third.
"I'm here, not you," he said; the shepherd grinned:
Anna was smiling sweet without a word;
She got the scarlet berry branch unpinned.
"It's cold," she said, "this evening, in the wind."

A quick glance showed that Jimmy didn't mind her,
She beckoned with the berry branch behind her.

Then dropped it gently on the broken stones,
Preoccupied, unheeding, walking straight,
Saying "You jealous boy," in even tones,
Looking so beautiful, so delicate,
Being so very sweet: but at her gate
She felt her shoe unlaced and looked to know
If Ern had taken up the sprig or no.

He had, she smiled. "Anna," said Jimmy sadly,
"That man's not fit to be a friend of yourn,
He's nobbut just an oaf; I love you madly,
  And hearing you speak kind to'm made me burn.
Who is he, then?" She answered "Shepherd Ern,
A pleasant man, an old, old friend of mine."
"By cripes, then, Anna, drop him, he's a swine."

"Jimmy," she said, "you must have faith in me,
Faith's all the battle in a love like ours.
You must believe, my darling, don't you see,
That life to have its sweets must have its sours.
Love isn't always two souls picking flowers.
You must have faith. I give you all I can.
What, can't I say 'Good evening' to a man?"

"Yes," he replied, "but not a man like him."
"Why not a man like him?" she said, "What next?"
By this they'd reached her cottage in the dim,
Among the daisies that the cold had kexed.
"Because I say. Now, Anna, don't be vexed."

"I'm more than vexed," she said, "with words like these.
'You say,' indeed. How dare you. Leave me, please."

"Anna, my Anna." "Leave me." She was cold,
Proud and imperious with a lifting lip,
Blazing within, but outwardly controlled;
He had a colt's first instant of the whip.
The long lash curled to cut a second strip.
"You to presume to teach. Of course, I know
You're mother's Sunday scholar, aren't you? Go."

She slammed the door behind her, clutching skirts.
"Anna." He heard her bedroom latches thud.
He learned at last how bitterly love hurts;
He longed to cut her throat and see her blood,
To stamp her blinking eyeballs into mud.
"Anna, by God!" Love's many torments make
That tune soon change to "Dear, for Jesus' sake."

He beat the door for her. She never stirred,
But primming bitter lips before her glass;
Admired her hat as though she hadn't heard,
And tried her front hair parted, and in mass.
She heard her lover's hasty footsteps pass.
"He's gone," she thought. She crouched below the pane,
And heard him cursing as he tramped the lane.

Rage ran in Jimmy as he tramped the night;
Rage, strongly mingled with a youth's disgust
At finding a beloved woman light,
And all her precious beauty dirty dust;
A tinsel-varnish gilded over lust.

[221]

THE WIDOW IN THE BYE STREET

Nothing but that.   He sat him down to rage,
Beside the stream whose waters never age.

Plashing, it slithered down the tiny fall
To eddy wrinkles in the trembling pool
With that light voice whose music cannot pall,
Always the note of solace, flute-like, cool.
And when hot-headed man has been a fool,
He could not do a wiser thing than go
To that dim pool where purple teazels grow.

He glowered there until suspicion came,
Suspicion, anger's bastard, with mean tongue,
To mutter to him till his heart was flame,
And every fibre of his soul was wrung,
That even then Ern and his Anna clung
Mouth against mouth in passionate embrace.
There was no peace for Jimmy in the place.

Raging he hurried back to learn the truth.
The little swinging wicket glimmered white,
The chimney jagged the skyline like a tooth,
Bells came in swoons, for it was Sunday night.
The garden was all dark, but there was light
Up in the little room where Anna slept:
The hot blood beat his brain; he crept, he crept.

Clutching himself to hear, clutching to know,
Along the path, rustling with withered leaves,
Up to the apple, too decayed to blow,
Which crooked a palsied finger at the eaves.
And up the lichened trunk his body heaves.

Dust blinded him, twigs snapped, the branches shook,
He leaned along a mossy bough to look.

Nothing at first, except a guttering candle
Shaking amazing shadows on the ceiling.
Then Anna's voice upon a bar of "Randal,
Where have you been?" and voice and music reeling,
Trembling, as though she sang with flooding feeling.
The singing stopped midway upon the stair,
Then Anna showed in white with loosened hair.

Her back was towards him, and she stood awhile,
Like a wild creature tossing back her mane,
And then her head went back, he saw a smile
On the half face half turned towards the pane;
Her eyes closed, and her arms went out again.
Jim gritted teeth, and called upon his Maker,
She dropped into a man's arms there to take her.

Agony first, sharp, sudden, like a knife,
Then down the tree to batter at the door;
"Open there. Let me in. I'll have your life.
You Jezebel of hell, you painted whore.
Talk about faith, I'll give you faith galore."
The window creaked, a jug of water came
Over his head and neck with certain aim.

"Clear out," said Ern; "I'm here, not you, to-night,
Clear out. We whip young puppies when they yap."
"If you're a man," said Jim, "come down and fight,
I'll put a stopper on your ugly chap."
"Go home," said Ern; "go home and get your pap.

To kennel, pup, and bid your mother bake
Some soothing syrup in your puppy-cake."

There was a dibble sticking in the bed,
Jim wrenched it out and swung it swiftly round,
And sent it flying at the shepherd's head:
"I'll give you puppy-cake. Take that, you hound."
The broken glass went clinking to the ground,
The dibble balanced, checked, and followed flat.
"My God," said Ern, "I'll give you hell for that."

He flung the door ajar with "Now, my pup—
Hold up the candle, Anna—now, we'll see."
"By crimes, come on," said Jimmy; "put them up.
Come, put them up, you coward, here I be."
And Jim, eleven stone, what chance had he
Against fourteen? but what he could he did;
Ern swung his right: "That settles you, my kid."

Jimmy went down and out: "The kid," said Ern.
"A kid, a sucking puppy; hold the light."
And Anna smiled: "It gave me such a turn.
You look so splendid, Ernie, when you fight."
She looked at Jim with: "Ern, is he all right?"
"He's coming to." She shuddered, "Pah, the brute,
What things he said; " she stirred him with her foot.

"You go inside," said Ern, "and bolt the door,
I'll deal with him." She went and Jimmy stood.
"Now, pup," said Ern, "don't come round here no more.
I'm here, not you, let that be understood.
I tell you frankly, pup, for your own good."

"Give me my hat," said Jim. He passed the gate,
And as he tottered off he called, "You wait."

"Thanks, I don't have to," Shepherd Ern replied;
"You'll do whatever waiting's being done."
The door closed gently as he went inside,
The bolts jarred in the channels one by one.
"I'll give you throwing bats about, my son.
Anna." "My dear?" "Where are you?" "Come and find."
The light went out, the windows stared out blind,

Blind as blind eyes forever seeing dark.
And in the dim the lovers went upstairs,
Her eyes fast closed, the shepherd's burning stark,
His lips entangled in her straying hairs,
Breath coming short as in a convert's prayers,
Her stealthy face all drowsy in the dim
And full of shudders as she yearned to him.

Jim crossed the water, cursing in his tears,
"By cripes, you wait. My God, he's with her now,
And all her hair pulled down over her ears;
Loving the blaggard like a filthy sow.
I saw her kiss him from the apple bough.
They say a whore is always full of wiles.
O God, how sweet her eyes are when she smiles.

Curse her and curse her. No, my God, she's sweet,
It's all a helly nightmare. I shall wake.
If it were all a dream I'd kiss her feet,
I wish it were a dream for Jesus' sake.
One thing: I bet I made his guzzle ache,

[225]

I cop it fair before he sent me down,
I'll cop him yet some evening on the crown.

O God, O God, what pretty ways she had.
He's kissing all her skin, so white and soft.
She's kissing back. I think I'm going mad.
Like rutting rattens in the apple loft.
She held that light she carried high aloft
Full in my eyes for him to hit me by,
I had the light all dazzling in my eye.

She had her dress all clutched up to her shoulder,
And all her naked arm was all one gleam.
It's going to freeze to-night, it's turning colder.
I wish there was more water in the stream,
I'd drownd myself. Perhaps it's all a dream,
And by and bye I'll wake and find it stuff.
By crimes, the pain I suffer's real enough."

About two hundred yards from Gunder Loss
He stopped to shudder, leaning on the gate,
He bit the touchwood underneath the moss;
"Rotten, like her," he muttered in his hate;
He spat it out again with "But, you wait,
We'll see again, before to-morrow's past,
In this life he laughs longest who laughs last."

All through the night the stream ran to the sea,
The different water always saying the same,
Cat-like, and then a tinkle, never glee,
A lonely little child alone in shame.
An otter snapped a thorn twig when he came,
It drifted down, it passed the Hazel Mill,
It passed the Springs; but Jimmy stayed there still.

THE WIDOW IN THE BYE STREET

Over the pointed hill-top came the light,
Out of the mists on Ercall came the sun,
Red like a huntsman hallowing after night,
Blowing a horn to rouse up everyone;
Through many glittering cities he had run,
Splashing the wind vanes on the dewy roofs
With golden sparks struck by his horses' hoofs.

The watchman rose, rubbing his rusty eyes,
He stirred the pot of cocoa for his mate;
The fireman watched his head of power rise.
"What time?" he asked.
    "You haven't long to wait."
"Now, is it time?"
    "Yes. Let her ripple." Straight
The whistle shrieked its message, "Up to work!
Up, or be fined a quarter if you shirk."

Hearing the whistle, Jimmy raised his head,
"The warning call, and me in Sunday clo'es;
I'd better go; I've time. The sun looks red,
I feel so stiff I'm very nearly froze."
So over brook and through the fields he goes,
And up the line among the navvies' smiles,
"Young Jimmy Gurney's been upon the tiles."

The second whistle blew and work began,
Jimmy worked too, not knowing what he did,
He tripped and stumbled like a drunken man;
He muddled all, whatever he was bid,
The foreman cursed, "Good God, what ails the kid?
Hi! Gurney. You. We'll have you crocking soon,
You take a lie down till the afternoon."

"I won't," he answered. "Why the devil should I?
I'm here, I mean to work. I do my piece,
Or would do if a man could, but how could I
When you come nagging round and never cease?
Well, take the job and give me my release,
I want the sack, now give it, there's my pick;
Give me the sack." The sack was given quick.

PART V

Dully he got his time-check from the keeper.
"Curse her," he said; "and that's the end of whores "—
He stumbled drunkenly across a sleeper—
"Give all you have and get kicked out—a-door."
He cashed his time-check at the station stores.
"Bett'ring yourself, I hope, Jim," said the master;
"That's it," said Jim; "and so I will do, blast her."

Beyond the bridge, a sharp turn to the right
Leads to "The Bull and Boar," the carters' rest;
An inn so hidden it is out of sight
To anyone not coming from the west,
The high embankment hides it with its crest.
Far up above, the Chester trains go by,
The drinkers see them sweep against the sky.

Canal men used it when the bargers came,
The navvies used it when the line was making;
The pigeons strut and sidle, ruffling, tame,
The chuckling brook in front sets shadows shaking.
Cider and beer for thirsty workers' slaking,
A quiet house; like all that God controls,
It is Fate's instrument on human souls.

[228]

Thither Jim turned. "And now I'll drink," he said.
"I'll drink and drink—I never did before—
I'll drink and drink until I'm mad or dead,
For that's what comes of meddling with a whore."
He called for liquor at "The Bull and Boar";
Moody he drank; the woman asked him why:
"Have you had trouble?" "No," he said, "I'm dry.

Dry and burnt up, so give's another drink;
That's better, that's much better, that's the sort,"
And then he sang, so that he should not think,
His Binger-Bopper song, but cut it short.
His wits were working like a brewer's wort,
Until among them came the vision gleaming
Of Ern with bloody nose and Anna screaming.

"That's what I'll do," he muttered; "knock him out,
And kick his face in with a running jump.
I'll not have dazzled eyes this second bout,
And she can wash the fragments under pump."
It was his ace; but Death had played a trump.
Death the blind beggar chuckled, nodding dumb,
"My game; the shroud is ready, Jimmy—come."

Meanwhile, the mother, waiting for her child,
Had tottered out a dozen times to search.
"Jimmy," she said, "you'll drive your mother wild;
Your father's name's too good a name to smirch,
Come home, my dear, she'll leave you in the lurch;
He was so good, my little Jim, so clever;
He never stop a night, away, not ever.

[229]

He never slept a night away till now,
Never, not once, in all the time he's been.
It's the Lord's will, they say, and we must bow,
But O, it's like a knife, it cuts so keen!
He'll work in's Sunday clothes, it'll be seen,
And then they'll laugh, and say 'It isn't strange;
He slept with her, and so he couldn't change.'

Perhaps," she thought, "I'm wrong; perhaps he's dead;
Kllled himself like; folk do in love, they say.
He never tells what passes in his head,
And he's been looking late so old and grey.
A railway train has cut his head away,
Like the poor hare we found at Maylow's shack.
O God, have pity, bring my darling back!"

All the high stars went sweeping through the sky,
The sun made all the orient clean, clear gold.
"O blessed God," she prayed, "do let me die,
Or bring my wand'ring lamb back into fold.
The whistle's gone, and all the bacon's cold;
I must know somehow if he's on the line,
He could have bacon sandwich when he dine."

She cut the bread, and started, short of breath,
Up the canal now draining for the rail;
A poor old woman pitted against death,
Bringing her pennyworth of love for bail.
Wisdom, beauty, and love may not avail.
She was too late. "Yes, he was here; oh, yes.
He chucked his job and went." "Where?" "Home, I guess."

"Home, but he hasn't been home." "Well, he went.
Perhaps you missed him, mother." "Or perhaps
He took the field path yonder through the bent.
He very likely done that, don't he, chaps?"
The speaker tested both his trouser straps
And took his pick. "He's in the town," he said.
"He'll be all right, after a bit in bed."

She trembled down the high embankment's ridge,
Glad, though too late; not yet too late, indeed.
For forty yards away, beyond the bridge,
Jimmy still drank, the devil still sowed seed.
"A bit in bed," she thought, "is what I need.
I'll go to 'Bull and Boar' and rest a bit,
They've got a bench outside; they'd let me sit."

Even as two soldiers on a fortress wall
See the bright fire streak of a coming shell,
Catch breath, and wonder "Which way will it fall?
To you? to me? or will it all be well?"
Ev'n so stood life and death, and could not tell
Whether she'd go to th' inn and find her son,
Or take the field and let the doom be done.

"No, not the inn," she thought. "People would talk.
I couldn't in the open daytime; no.
I'll just sit here upon the timber balk,
I'll rest for just a minute and then go."
Resting, her old tired heart began to glow,
Glowed and gave thanks, and thought itself in clover,
"He's lost his job, so now she'll throw him over."

Sitting, she saw the rustling thistle-kex,
The picks flash bright above, the trolleys tip.
The bridge-stone shining, full of silver specks,
And three swift children running down the dip.
A Stoke Saint Michael carter cracked his whip,
The water in the runway made its din.
She half heard singing coming from the inn.

She turned, and left the inn, and took the path
And "Brother Life, you lose," said Brother Death,
"Even as the Lord of all appointed hath
In this great miracle of blood and breath."
He doeth all things well, as the book saith,
He bids the changing stars fulfil their turn,
His hand is on us when we least discern.

Slowly she tottered, stopping with the stitch,
Catching her breath, "O lawks, a dear, a dear.
How the poor tubings in my heart do twitch,
It hurts like the rheumatics very near."
And every painful footstep drew her clear
From that young life she bore with so much pain.
She never had him to herself again.

Out of the inn came Jimmy, red with drink,
Crying: "I'll show her. Wait a bit. I'll show her .
You wait a bit. I'm not the kid you think.
I'm Jimmy Gurney, champion tupper-thrower,
When I get done with her you'll never know her,
Nor him you won't. Out of my way, you fowls,
Or else I'll rip the red things off your jowls."

THE WIDOW IN THE BYE STREET

He went across the fields to Plaister's End.
There was a lot of water in the brook,
Sun and white cloud and weather on the mend
For any man with any eyes to look.
He found old Callow's plough-bat, which he took.
"My innings now, my pretty dear," said he.
"You wait a bit. I'll show you. Now you'll see."

Her chimney smoke was blowing blue and faint,
The wise duck shook a tail across the pool,
The blacksmith's shanty smelt of burning paint,
Four newly tired cartwheels hung to cool.
He had loved the place when under Anna's rule.
Now he clenched teeth and flung aside the gate,
There at the door they stood. He grinned "Now wait."

Ern had just brought her in a wired hare,
She stood beside him stroking down the fur.
"O, Ern, poor thing, look how its eyes do stare."
"It isn't *it*," he answered. "It's a her."
She stroked the breast and plucked away a bur,
She kissed the pads, and leapt back with a shout,
"My God, he's got the spudder. Ern. Look out."

Ern clenched his fists. Too late. He felt no pain,
Only incredible haste in something swift,
A shock that made the sky black on his brain,
Then stillness, while a little cloud went drift.
The weight upon his thigh bones wouldn't lift;
Then poultry in a long procession came,
Grey-legged, doing the goose-step, eyes like flame.

Grey-legged old cocks and hens sedate in age,
Marching with jerks as though they moved on springs,
With sidelong hate in round eyes red with rage,
And shouldered muskets clipped by jealous wings,
Then an array of horns and stupid things:
Sheep on a hill with harebells, hare for dinner.
"Hare." A slow darkness covered up the sinner.

"But little time is right hand fain of blow."
Only a second changes life to death;
Hate ends before the pulses cease to go,
There is great power in the stop of breath.
There's too great truth in what the dumb thing saith,
Hate never goes so far as that, nor can.
"I am what life becomes. D'you hate me, man?"

Hate with his babbling instant, red and damning,
Passed with his instant, having drunken red.
"You've killed him."
"No, I've not, he's only shamming.
Get up."
"He can't."
"O God, he isn't dead."
"O God."
"Here. Get a basin. Bathe his head.
Ernie, for God's sake, what are you playing at?
I only give him one, like, with the bat."

Man cannot call the brimming instant back;
Time's an affair of instants spun to days;
If man must make an instant gold, or black,
Let him, he may, but Time must go his ways.
Life may be duller for an instant's blaze.

Life's an affair of instants spun to years,
Instants are only cause of all these tears.

Then Anna screamed aloud. "Help. Murder. Murder."
"By God, it is," he said. "Through you, you slut."
Backing, she screamed, until the blacksmith heard her.
"Hurry," they cried, "the woman's throat's being cut."
Jim had his coat off by the water butt.
"He might come to," he said, "with wine or soup.
I only hit him once, like, with the scoop."

"Splash water on him, chaps. I only meant
To hit him just a clip, like, nothing more.
There. Look. He isn't dead, his eyelids went.
And he went down. O God, his head's all tore.
I've washed and washed: it's all one gob of gore.
He don't look dead to you? What? Nor to you?
Not kill, the clip I give him, couldn't do."

"God send; he looks damn bad," the blacksmith said.
"Py Cot," his mate said, "she wass altogether;
She hass an illness look of peing ted."
"Here. Get a glass," the smith said, "and a feather."
"Wass you at fightings or at playings whether?
"Here, get a glass and feather. Quick's the word."
The glass was clear. The feather never stirred.

"By God, I'm sorry, Jim. That settles it."
"By God. I've killed him, then."
                              "The doctor might."
"Try, if you like; but that's a nasty hit."
"Doctor's gone by. He won't be back till night."
"Py Cot, the feather was not looking right."

"By Jesus, chaps, I never meant to kill 'un.
Only to bat. I'll go to p'leece and tell 'un.

O Ern, for God's sake speak, for God's sake speak."
No answer followed: Ern had done with dust,
"The p'leece is best," the smith said, "or a beak.
I'll come along; and so the lady must.
Evans, you bring the lady, will you just?
Tell 'em just how it come, lad. Come your ways;
And Joe, you watch the body where it lays."

They walked to town, Jim on the blacksmith's arm.
Jimmy was crying like a child, and saying,
"I never meant to do him any harm."
His teeth went clack, like bones at mummers playing,
And then he trembled hard and broke out praying,
"God help my poor old mother. If he's dead,
I've brought her my last wages home," he said.

He trod his last free journey down the street;
Treading the middle road, and seeing both sides,
The school, the inns, the butchers selling meat,
The busy market where the town divides.
Then past the tanpits full of stinking hides,
And up the lane to death, as weak as pith.
"By God, I hate this, Jimmy," said the smith.

PART VI

Anna in black, the judge in scarlet robes,
A fuss of lawyers' people coming, going,
The windows shut, the gas alight in globes,

[236]

Evening outside, and pleasant weather blowing.
"They'll hang him?" "I suppose so; there's no knowing."
"A pretty piece, the woman, ain't she, John?
He killed the fellow just for carrying on."

"She give her piece to counsel pretty clear."
"Ah, that she did, and when she stop she smiled."
"She's had a-many men, that pretty dear;
She's drove a-many fellow pretty wild."
"More silly idiots they to be beguiled."
"Well, I don't know." "Well, I do. See her eyes?
Mystery, eh? A woman's mystery's lies."

"Perhaps." "No p'raps about it, that's the truth.
I know these women; they're a rotten lot."
"You didn't use to think so in your youth."
"No; but I'm wiser now, and not so hot.
Married or buried, *I* say, wives or shot,
These unmanned, unattached Maries and Susans
Make life no better than a proper nuisance."

"Well, I don't know." "Well, if you don't you will."
"I look on women as as good as men."
"Now, that's the kind of talk that makes me ill.
When have they been as good? I ask you when?"
"Always they have." "They haven't. Now and then
P'raps one or two was neither hen nor fury."
"One for your mother, that. Here comes the jury."

Guilty. Thumbs down. No hope. The judge passed sentence:
"A frantic passionate youth, unfit for life,
A fitting time afforded for repentance,

Then certain justice with a pitiless knife.
For her, his wretched victim's widowed wife,
Pity. For her who bore him, pity. (Cheers.)
The jury were exempt for seven years."

All bowed; the Judge passed to the robing-room,
Dismissed his clerks, disrobed, and knelt and prayed
As was his custom after passing doom,
Doom upon life, upon the thing not made.
"O God, who made us out of dust, and laid
Thee in us bright, to lead us to the truth,
O God, have pity upon this poor youth.

Show him Thy grace, O God, before he die;
Shine in his heart; have mercy upon me
Who deal the laws men make to travel by
Under the sun upon the path to Thee;
O God, Thou knowest I'm as blind as he,
As blind, as frantic, not so single, worse,
Only Thy pity spared me from the curse.

Thy pity, and Thy mercy, God, did save,
Thy bounteous gifts, not any grace of mine,
From all the pitfalls leading to the grave,
From all the death-feasts with the husks and swine.
God, who hast given me all things, now make shine
Bright in this sinner's heart that he may see.
God, take this poor boy's spirit back to Thee."

Then trembling with his hands, for he was old,
He went to meet his college friend, the Dean,
The loiterers watched him as his carriage rolled.

"There goes the Judge," said one, and one was keen:
"Hanging that wretched boy, that's where he's been."
A policeman spat, two lawyers talked statistics,
"'Crime passionel' in Agricultural Districts."

"They'd oughtn't hang a boy:" but one said "Stuff.
This sentimental talk is rotten, rotten.
The law's the law and not half strict enough,
Forgers and murderers are misbegotten,
Let them be hanged and let them be forgotten.
A rotten fool should have a rotten end;
Mend them, you say? The rotten never mend."

And one "Not mend? The rotten not, perhaps.
The rotting would; so would the just infected.
A week in quod has ruined lots of chaps
Who'd all got good in them till prison wrecked it."
And one, "Society must be protected."
"He's just a kid. She trapped him." "No, she didden."
"He'll be reprieved." "He mid be and he midden."

So the talk went; and Anna took the train,
Too sad for tears, and pale; a lady spoke
Asking if she were ill or suffering pain?
"Neither," she said; but sorrow made her choke,
"I'm only sick because my heart is broke.
My friend, a man, my oldest friend here, died.
I had to see the man who killed him, tried.

He's to be hanged. Only a boy. My friend.
I thought him just a boy; I didn't know.
And Ern was killed, and now the boy's to end,

[239]

And all because he thought he loved me so."
"My dear," the lady said; and Anna, "Oh,
It's very hard to bear the ills men make,
He thought he loved, and it was all mistake."

"My dear," the lady said; "you poor, poor woman,
Have you no friends to go to?" "I'm alone.
I've parents living, but they're both inhuman,
And none can cure what pierces to the bone.
I'll have to leave and go where I'm not known.
Begin my life again." Her friend said "Yes.
Certainly that. But leave me your address:

For I might hear of something; I'll enquire,
Perhaps the boy might be reprieved or pardoned.
Couldn't we ask the rector or the squire
To write and ask the Judge? He can't be hardened.
What do you do? Is it housework? Have you gardened?
Your hands are very white and soft to touch."
"Lately I've not had heart for doing much."

So the talk passes as the train descends
Into the vale, and halts, and starts to climb
To where the apple-bearing country ends
And pleasant-pastured hills rise sweet with thyme,
Where clinking sheepbells make a broken chime
And sunwarm gorses rich the air with scent
And kestrels poise for mice, there Anna went.

There, in the April, in the garden-close,
One heard her in the morning singing sweet,
Calling the birds from the unbudded rose,

Offering her lips with grains for them to eat.
The redbreasts come with little wiry feet,
Sparrows and tits and all wild feathery things,
Brushing her lifted face with quivering wings.

Jimmy was taken down into a cell,
He did not need a hand, he made no fuss.
The men were kind: "For what the kid done . . . well—
The same might come to any one of us."
They brought him bits of cake at tea time: thus
The love that fashioned all in human ken,
Works in the marvellous hearts of simple men.

And in the nights (they watched him night and day)
They told him bits of stories through the grating,
Of how the game went at the football play,
And how the rooks outside had started mating.
And all the time they knew the rope was waiting,
And every evening friend would say to friend,
"I hope we've not to drag him at the end."

And poor old mother came to see her son,
"The Lord has gave," she said, "The Lord has took;
I loved you very dear, my darling one,
And now there's none but God where we can look.
We've got God's promise written in His Book,
He will not fail; but oh, it do seem hard."
She hired a room outside the prison yard.

"Where did you get the money for the room?
And how are you living, mother; how'll you live?"
"It's what I'd saved to put me in the tomb,

[241]

I'll want no tomb but what the parish give."
"Mother, I lied to you that time, O forgive,
I brought home half my wages, half I spent,
And you went short that week to pay the rent.

I went to see'r, I spent my money on her,
And you who bore me paid the cost in pain.
You went without to buy the clothes upon her:
A hat, a locket, and a silver chain.
O mother dear, if all might be again,
Only from last October, you and me;
O mother dear, how different it would be.

We were so happy in the room together,
Singing at 'Binger-Bopper,' weren't us, just?
And going a-hopping in the summer weather,
And all the hedges covered white with dust,
And blackberries, and that, and traveller's trust.
I thought her wronged, and true, and sweet, and wise,
The devil takes sweet shapes when he tells lies.

Mother, my dear, will you forgive your son?"
"God knows I do, Jim, I forgive you, dear;
You didn't know, and couldn't, what you done.
God pity all poor people suffering here,
And may His mercy shine upon us clear,
And may we have His Holy Word for mark,
To lead us to His Kingdom through the dark."

"Amen. Amen," said Jimmy; then they kissed.
The warders watched, the little larks were singing,
A plough team jangled, turning at the rist;

THE WIDOW IN THE BYE STREET

Beyond, the mild cathedral bells were ringing,
The elm-tree rooks were cawing at the springing:
O beauty of the time when winter's done,
And all the fields are laughing at the sun!

"I s'pose they've brought the line beyond the Knapp?"
"Ah, and beyond the Barcle, so they say."
"Hearing the rooks begin reminds a chap.
Look queer, the street will, with the lock away;
O God, I'll never see it." "Let us pray.
Don't think of that, but think," the mother said,
"Of men going on long after we are dead.

Red helpless little things will come to birth,
And hear the whistles going down the line,
And grow up strong and go about the earth,
And have much happier times than yours and mine;
And some day one of them will get a sign,
And talk to folk, and put an end to sin,
And then God's blessed kingdom will begin.

God dropped a spark down into everyone,
And if we find and fan it to a blaze
It'll spring up and glow, like—like the sun,
And light the wandering out of stony ways.
God warms his hands at man's heart when he prays,
And light of prayer is spreading heart to heart;
It'll light all where now it lights a part.

And God who gave His mercies takes His mercies,
And God who gives beginning gives the end.
I dread my death; but it's the end of curses,

A rest for broken things too broke to mend.
O Captain Christ, our blessed Lord and Friend,
We are two wandered sinners in the mire,
Burn our dead hearts with love out of Thy fire.

And when thy death comes, Master, let us bear it
As of Thy will, however hard to go;
Thy Cross is infinite for us to share it,
Thy help is infinite for us to know.
And when the long trumpets of the Judgment blow
May our poor souls be glad and meet agen,
And rest in Thee." "Say, 'Amen,' Jim." "Amen."

* * * * * *

There was a group outside the prison gate,
Waiting to hear them ring the passing bell,
Waiting as empty people always wait
For the strong toxic of another's hell.
And mother stood there, too, not seeing well,
Praying through tears to let His will be done,
And not to hide His mercy from her son.

Talk in the little group was passing quick.
"It's nothing now to what it was, to watch."
"Poor wretched kid, I bet he's feeling sick."
"Eh? What d'you say, chaps? Someone got a match?"
"They draw a bolt and drop you down a hatch
And break your neck, whereas they used to strangle
In the old times, when you could see them dangle."

Someone said, "Off hats," when the bell began.
Mother was whimpering now upon her knees.
A broken ringing like a beaten pan,

THE WIDOW IN THE BYE STREET

It sent the sparrows wavering to the trees.
The wall-top grasses whickered in the breeze,
The broken ringing clanged, clattered and clanged,
As though men's bees were swarming, not men hanged.

Now certain Justice with the pitiless knife.
The white, sick chaplain snuffling at the nose,
"I am the resurrection and the life."
The bell still clangs, the small procession goes,
The prison warders ready ranged in rows.
"Now, Gurney, come, my dear; it's time," they said.
And ninety seconds later he was dead.

Some of life's sad ones are too strong to die,
Grief doesn't kill them as it kills the weak,
Sorrow is not for those who sit and cry
Lapped in the love of turning t'other cheek,
But for the noble souls austere and bleak
Who have had the bitter dose and drained the cup
And wait for Death face fronted, standing up.

As the last man upon the sinking ship,
Seeing the brine creep brightly on the deck,
Hearing aloft the slatting topsails rip,
Ripping to rags among the topmast's wreck,
Yet hoists the new red ensign without speck,
That she, so fair, may sink with colours flying,
So the old widowed mother kept from dying.

She tottered home, back to the little room,
It was all over for her, but for life;
She drew the blinds, and trembled in the gloom;

THE WIDOW IN THE BYE STREET

"I sat here thus when I was wedded wife;
Sorrow sometimes, and joy; but always strife.
Struggle to live except just at the last,
O God, I thank Thee for the mercies past.

Harry, my man, when we were courting; eh . . .
The April morning up the Cony-gree.
How grand he looked upon our wedding day.
'I wish we'd had the bells,' he said to me;
And we'd the moon that evening, I and he,
And dew come wet, oh, I remember how,
And we come home to where I'm sitting now.

And he lay dead here, and his son was born here;
He never saw his son, his little Jim.
And now I'm all alone here, left to mourn here,
And there are all his clothes, but never him.
He's down under the prison in the dim,
With quicklime working on him to the bone,
The flesh I made with many and many a groan.

Oh, how his little face come, with bright hair.
Dear little face. We made this room so snug;
He sit beside me in his little chair,
I give him real tea sometimes in his mug.
He liked the velvet in the patchwork rug.
He used to stroke it, did my pretty son,
He called it Bunny, little Jimmy done.

And then he ran so, he was strong at running,
Always a strong one, like his dad at that.
In summertimes I done my sewing sunning,

And he'd be sprawling, playing with the cat.
And neighbours brought their knitting out to chat
Till five o'clock; he had his tea at five;
How sweet life was when Jimmy was alive."

* * * * *

Darkness and midnight, and the midnight chimes.
Another four-and-twenty hours begin.
Darkness again, and many, many times,
The alternating light and darkness spin
Until the face so thin is still more thin,
Gazing each earthly evening, wet or fine,
For Jimmy coming from work along the line.

Over her head the Chester wires hum,
Under the bridge the rocking engines flash.
"He's very late this evening, but he'll come
And bring his little packet full of cash
(Always he does), and supper's cracker hash,
That is his favourite food excepting bacon.
They say my boy was hanged; but they're mistaken."

And sometimes she will walk the cindery mile,
Singing, as she and Jimmy used to do,
Singing "The parson's dog lep over a stile,"
Along the path where water lilies grew.
The stars are placid on the evening's blue,
Burning like eyes so calm, so unafraid,
On all that God has given and man has made.

Burning they watch, and mothlike owls come out,
The redbreast warbles shrilly once and stops;
The homing cowman gives his dog a shout,

THE WIDOW IN THE BYE STREET

The lamps are lighted in the village shops.
Silence; the last bird passes; in the copse
The hazels cross the moon, a nightjar spins,
Dew wets the grass, the nightingale begins.

Singing her crazy song the mother goes,
Singing as though her heart were full of peace,
Moths knock the petals from the dropping rose,
Stars make the glimmering pool a golden fleece,
The moon droops west, but still she does not cease,
The little mice peep out to hear her sing,
Until the inn-man's cockerel shakes his wing.

And in the sunny dawns of hot Julys,
The labourers going to meadow see her there.
Rubbing the sleep out of their heavy eyes,
They lean upon the parapet to stare;
They see her plaiting basil in her hair,
Basil, the dark red wound-wort, cops of clover,
The blue self-heal and golden Jacks of Dover.

Dully they watch her, then they turn to go
To that high Shropshire upland of late hay;
Her singing lingers with them as they mow,
And many times they try it, now grave, now gay,
Till, with full throat, over the hills away,
They lift it clear; oh, very clear it towers
Mixed with the swish of many falling flowers.

DAUBER

DAUBER

I

Four bells were struck, the watch was called on deck,
All work aboard was over for the hour,
And some men sang and others played at check,
Or mended clothes or watched the sunset glower.
The bursting west was like an opening flower,
And one man watched it till the light was dim,
But no one went across to talk to him.

He was the painter in that swift ship's crew,
Lampman and painter—tall, a slight-built man,
Young for his years, and not yet twenty-two;
Sickly, and not yet brown with the sea's tan.
Bullied and damned at since the voyage began,
"Being neither man nor seaman by his tally,"
He bunked with the idlers just abaft the galley.

His work began at five; he worked all day,
Keeping no watch and having all night in.
His work was what the mate might care to say;
He mixed red lead in many a bouilli tin;
His dungarees were smeared with paraffin.
"Go drown himself" his round-house mates advised him,
And all hands called him "Dauber" and despised him.

Si, the apprentice, stood beside the spar,
Stripped to the waist, a basin at his side,
Slushing his hands to get away the tar,

And then he washed himself and rinsed and dried;
Towelling his face, hair-towzelled, eager eyed,
He crossed the spar to Dauber, and there stood
Watching the gold of heaven turn to blood.

They stood there by the rail while the swift ship
Tore on out of the tropics, straining her sheets,
Whitening her trackway to a milky strip,
Dim with green bubbles and twisted water meets,
Her clacking tackle tugged at pins and cleats,
Her great sails bellied stiff, her great masts leaned:
They watched how the seas struck and burst and greened.

Si talked with Dauber, standing by the side.
"Why did you come to sea, painter?" he said.
"I want to be a painter," he replied,
"And know the sea and ships from A to Z,
And paint great ships at sea before I'm dead;
Ships under skysails running down the Trade—
Ships and the sea; there's nothing finer made.

"But there's so much to learn, with sails and ropes,
And how the sails look, full or being furled,
And how the lights change in the troughs and slopes,
And the sea's colours up and down the world,
And how a storm looks when the sprays are hurled
High as the yard (they say) I want to see;
There's none ashore can teach such things to me.

"And then the men and rigging, and the way
Ships move, running or beating, and the poise
At the roll's end, the checking in the sway—

I want to paint them perfect, short of the noise;
And then the life, the half-decks full of boys,
The fo'c's'les with the men there, dripping wet:
I know the subjects that I want to get.

"It's not been done, the sea, not yet been done,
From the inside, by one who really knows;
I'd give up all if I could be the one,
But art comes dear the way the money goes.
So I have come to sea, and I suppose
Three years will teach me all I want to learn
And make enough to keep me till I earn."

Even as he spoke his busy pencil moved,
Drawing the leap of water off the side
Where the great clipper trampled iron-hooved,
Making the blue hills of the sea divide,
Shearing a glittering scatter in her stride,
And leaping on full tilt with all sails drawing,
Proud as a war-horse, snuffing battle, pawing.

"I cannot get it yet—not yet," he said;
"That leap and light, and sudden change to green,
And all the glittering from the sunset's red,
And the milky colours where the bursts have been,
And then the clipper striding like a queen
Over it all, all beauty to the crown.
I see it all, I cannot put it down.

"It's hard not to be able. There, look there!
I cannot get the movement nor the light;
Sometimes it almost makes a man despair

[253]

To try and try and never get it right.
Oh, if I could—oh, if I only might,
I wouldn't mind what hells I'd have to pass,
Not if the whole world called me fool and ass."

Down sank the crimson sun into the sea,
The wind cut chill at once, the west grew dun.
"Out sidelights!" called the mate. "Hi, where is he?"
The Boatswain called, "Out sidelights, damn you! Run!"
"He's always late or lazing," murmured one—
"The Dauber, with his sketching." Soon the tints
Of red and green passed on dark waterglints.

Darker it grew, still darker, and the stars
Burned golden, and the fiery fishes came.
The wire-note loudened from the straining spars;
The sheet-blocks clacked together always the same;
The rushing fishes streaked the seas with flame,
Racing the one speed noble as their own:
What unknown joy was in those fish unknown!

Just by the round-house door, as it grew dark,
The Boatswain caught the Dauber with, "Now, you;
Till now I've spared you, damn you! now you hark:
I've just had hell for what you didn't do;
I'll have you broke and sent among the crew
If you get me more trouble by a particle.
Don't you forget, you daubing, useless article!

"You thing, you twice-laid thing from Port Mahon!"
Then came the Cook's "Is that the Dauber there?
Why don't you leave them stinking paints alone?

They stink the house out, poisoning all the air.
Just take them out." "Where to?" "I don't care where.
I won't have stinking paint here." From their plates:
"That's right; wet paint breeds fever," growled his mates.

He took his still wet drawings from the berth
And climbed the ladder to the deck-house top;
Beneath, the noisy half-deck rang with mirth,
For two ship's boys were putting on the strop:
One, clambering up to let the skylight drop,
Saw him bend down beneath a boat and lay
His drawings there, till all were hid away.

And stand there silent, leaning on the boat,
Watching the constellations rise and burn,
Until the beauty took him by the throat,
So stately is their glittering overturn;
Armies of marching eyes, armies that yearn
With banners rising and falling, and passing by
Over the empty silence of the sky.

The Dauber sighed there looking at the sails,
Wind-steadied arches leaning on the night,
The high trucks traced on heaven and left no trails;
The moonlight made the topsails almost white,
The passing sidelight seemed to drip green light.
And on the clipper rushed with fire-bright bows;
He sighed, "I'll never do't," and left the house.

"Now," said the reefer, "up! Come Sam; come, Si,
Dauber's been hiding something." Up they slid,
Treading on naked tiptoe stealthily

To grope for treasure at the long-boat skid.
"Drawings!" said Sam.   "Is this what Dauber hid?
Lord!   I expected pudding, not this rot.
Still, come, we'll have some fun with what we've got."

They smeared the paint with turpentine until
They could remove with mess-clouts every trace
Of quick perception caught by patient skill,
And lines that had brought blood into his face.
They wiped the pigments off and did erase,
With knives, all sticking clots.   When they had done.
Under the boat they laid them every one.

All he had drawn since first he came to sea,
His six weeks' leisure fruits, they laid them there.
They chuckled then to think how mad he'd be
Finding his paintings vanished into air.
Eight bells were struck, and feet from everywhere
Went shuffling aft to muster in the dark;
The mate's pipe glowed above, a dim red spark.

Names in the darkness passed and voices cried;
The red spark glowed and died, the faces seemed
As things remembered when a brain has died,
To all but high intenseness deeply dreamed.
Like hissing spears the fishes' fire streamed,
And on the clipper rushed with tossing mast,
A bath of flame broke round her as she passed.

The watch was set, the night came, and the men
Hid from the moon in shadowed nooks to sleep,
Bunched like the dead; still, like the dead, as when

DAUBER

Plague in a city leaves none even to weep.
The ship's track brightened to a mile-broad sweep;
The mate there felt her pulse, and eyed the spars:
South-west by south she staggered under the stars.

Down in his bunk the Dauber lay awake
Thinking of his unfitness for the sea.
Each failure, each derision, each mistake,
There in the life not made for such as he;
A morning grim with trouble sure to be,
A noon of pain from failure, and a night
Bitter with men's contemning and despite.

This in the first beginning, the green leaf,
Still in the Trades before bad weather fell;
What harvest would he reap of hate and grief
When the loud Horn made every life a hell?
When the sick ship lay over, clanging her bell,
And no time came for painting or for drawing,
But all hands fought, and icy death came clawing?

Hell, he expected,—hell. His eyes grew blind;
The snoring from his messmates droned and snuffled,
And then a gush of pity calmed his mind.
The cruel torment of his thought was muffled,
Without, on deck, an old, old, seaman shuffled,
Humming his song, and through the open door
A moonbeam moved and thrust along the floor.

The green bunk curtains moved, the brass rings clicked,
The Cook cursed in his sleep, turning and turning,
The moonbeams' moving finger touched and picked,

And all the stars in all the sky were burning.
"This is the art I've come for, and am learning,
The sea and ships and men and travelling things.
It is most proud, whatever pain it brings."

He leaned upon his arm and watched the light
Sliding and fading to the steady roll;
This he would some day paint, the ship at night,
And sleeping seamen tired to the soul;
The space below the bunks as black as coal,
Gleams upon chests, upon the unlit lamp,
The ranging door hook, and the locker clamp.

This he would paint, and that, and all these scenes,
And proud ships carrying on, and men their minds,
And blues of rollers toppling into greens,
And shattering into white that bursts and blinds,
And scattering ships running erect like hinds,
And men in oilskins beating down a sail
High on the yellow yard, in snow, in hail.

With faces ducked down from the slanting drive
Of half-thawed hail mixed with half-frozen spray,
The roaring canvas like a thing alive,
Shaking the mast, knocking their hands away,
The foot-ropes jerking to the tug and sway,
The savage eyes salt-reddened at the rims,
And icicles on the south-wester brims.

And sunnier scenes would grow under his brush,
The tropic dawn with all things dropping dew,
The darkness and the wonder and the hush,

[258]

The insensate grey before the marvel grew;
Then the veil lifted from the trembling blue,
The walls of sky burst in, the flower, the rose,
All the expanse of heaven a mind that glows.

He turned out of his bunk; the Cook still tossed,
One of the other two spoke in his sleep.
A cockroach scuttled where the moonbeam crossed;
Outside there was the ship, the night, the deep.
"It is worth while," the youth said; "I will keep
To my resolve, I'll learn to paint all this.
My Lord, my God, how beautiful it is!"

Outside was the ship's rush to the wind's hurry,
A resonant wire-hum from every rope,
The broadening bow-wash in a fiery flurry,
The leaning masts in their majestic slope,
And all things strange with moonlight: filled with hope
By all that beauty going as man bade,
He turned and slept in peace.   Eight bells were made.

II

Next day was Sunday, his free painting day,
While the fine weather held, from eight till eight.
He rose when called at five, and did array
The round-house gear, and set the kit-bags straight;
Then kneeling down, like housemaid at a grate,
He scrubbed the deck with sand until his knees
Were blue with dye from his wet dungarees.

Soon all was clean, his Sunday tasks were done;
His day was clear for painting as he chose.
The wetted decks were drying in the sun,
The men coiled up, or swabbed, or sought repose.
The drifts of silver arrows fell and rose
As flying fish took wing; the breakfast passed,
Wasting good time, but he was free at last.

Free for two hours and more to tingle deep,
Catching a likeness in a line or tint,
The canvas running up in a proud sweep,
Wind-wrinkled at the clews, and white like lint,
The glittering of the blue waves into glint;
Free to attempt it all, the proud ship's pawings,
The sea, the sky—he went to fetch his drawings.

Up to the deck-house top he quickly climbed,
He stooped to find them underneath the boat.
He found them all obliterated, slimed,
Blotted, erased, gone from him line and note.
They were all spoiled: a lump came in his throat,
Being vain of his attempts, and tender skinned—
Beneath the skylight watching reefers grinned.

He clambered down, holding the ruined things.
"Bosun," he called, "look here, did you do these:
Wipe off my paints and cut them into strings,
And smear them till you can't tell chalk from cheese?
Don't stare, but did you do it? Answer, please."
The Bosun turned: "I'll give you a thick ear!
Do it! I didn't. Get to hell from here!

"I touch your stinking daubs? The Dauber's daft."
A crowd was gathering now to hear the fun;
The reefers tumbled out, the men laid aft,
The Cook blinked, cleaning a mess kid in the sun.
"What's up with Dauber now?" said everyone.
"Someone has spoiled my drawings—look at this!"
"Well, that's a dirty trick, by God, it is!"

"It is," said Sam, "a low-down dirty trick,
To spoil a fellow's work in such a way,
And if you catch him, Dauber, punch him sick,
For he deserves it, be he who he may."
A seaman shook his old head wise and grey.
"It seems to me," he said, "who ain't no judge,
Them drawings look much better now they're smudge."

"Where were they, Dauber? On the deck-house? Where?"
"Under the long-boat, in a secret place."
"The blackguard must have seen you put them there.
He is a swine! I tell him to his face:
I didn't think we'd anyone so base."
"Nor I," said Dauber. "There was six weeks' time
Just wasted in these drawings: it's a crime!"

"Well, don't you say we did it," growled his mates,
"And as for crime, be damned! the things were smears—
Best overboard, like you, with shot for weights;
Thank God they're gone, and now go shake your ears."
The Dauber listened, very near to tears.
"Dauber, if I were you," said Sam again,
"I'd aft, and see the Captain and complain."

[261]

A sigh came from the assembled seamen there.
Would he be such a fool for their delight
As go to tell the Captain? Would he dare?
And would the thunder roar, the lightning smite?
There was the Captain come to take a sight,
Handling his sextant by the chart-house aft.
The Dauber turned, the seamen thought him daft.

The Captain took his sights—a mate below
Noted the times; they shouted to each other,
The Captain quick with "Stop," the answer slow,
Repeating slowly one height then another.
The swooping clipper stumbled through the smother,
The ladder brasses in the sunlight burned,
The Dauber waited till the Captain turned.

There stood the Dauber, humbled to the bone,
Waiting to speak. The Captain let him wait,
Glanced at the course, and called in even tone,
"What is the man there wanting, Mr. Mate?"
The logship clattered on the grating straight,
The reel rolled to the scuppers with a clatter,
The Mate came grim: "Well, Dauber, what's the matter?"

"Please, sir, they spoiled my drawings." "Who did?" "They."
"Who's they?" "I don't quite know, sir." "Don't quite
    know, sir?
Then why are you aft to talk about it, hey?
Whom d'you complain of?" "No one." "No one?" "No,
    sir."
"Well, then, go forward till you've found them. Go, sir.

If you complain of someone, then I'll see.
Now get to hell! and don't come bothering me."

"But, sir, they washed them off, and some they cut.
Look here, sir, how they spoiled them." "Never mind.
Go shove your head inside the scuttle butt,
And that will make you cooler. You will find
Nothing like water when you're mad and blind.
Where were the drawings? in your chest, or where?"
"Under the long-boat, sir; I put them there."

"Under the long-boat, hey? Now mind your tip.
I'll have the skids kept clear with nothing round them;
The long-boat ain't a store in this here ship.
Lucky for you it wasn't I who found them.
If I had seen them, Dauber, I'd have drowned them.
Now you be warned by this. I tell you plain—
Don't stow your brass-rags under boats again.

"Go forward to your berth." The Dauber turned.
The listeners down below them winked and smiled,
Knowing how red the Dauber's temples burned,
Having lost the case about his only child.
His work was done to nothing and defiled,
And there was no redress: the Captain's voice
Spoke, and called "Painter," making him rejoice.

The Captain and the Mate conversed together.
"Drawings, you tell me, Mister?" "Yes, sir; views:
Wiped off with turps, I gather that's his blether.
He says they're things he can't afford to lose.
He's Dick, who came to sea in dancing shoes,

[263]

And found the dance a bear dance. They were hidden
Under the long-boat's chocks, which I've forbidden."

"Wiped off with turps?" The Captain sucked his lip.
"Who did it, Mister?" "Reefers, I suppose;
Them devils do the most pranks in a ship;
The round-house might have done it, Cook or Bose."
"I can't take notice of it till he knows.
How does he do his work?" "Well, no offence;
He tries; he does his best. He's got no sense."

"Painter," the Captain called; the Dauber came.
"What's all this talk of drawings? What's the matter?"
"They spoiled my drawings, sir." "Well, who's to blame?
The long-boat's there for no one to get at her;
You broke the rules, and if you choose to scatter
Gear up and down where it's no right to be,
And suffer as result, don't come to me.

"Your place is in the round-house, and your gear
Belongs where you belong. Who spoiled your things?
Find out who spoiled your things and fetch him here."
"But, sir, they cut the canvas into strings."
"I want no argument nor questionings.
Go back where you belong and say no more,
And please remember that you're not on shore."

The Dauber touched his brow and slunk away—
They eyed his going with a bitter eye.
"Dauber," said Sam, "what did the Captain say?"
The Dauber drooped his head without reply.
"Go forward, Dauber, and enjoy your cry."

DAUBER

The Mate limped to the rail; like little feet
Over his head the drumming reef-points beat.

The Dauber reached the berth and entered in.
Much mockery followed after as he went,
And each face seemed to greet him with the grin
Of hounds hot following on a creature spent.
"Aren't you a fool?" each mocking visage meant.
"Who did it, Dauber? What did Captain say?
It is a crime, and there'll be hell to pay."

He bowed his head, the house was full of smoke;
The Sails was pointing shackles on his chest.
"Lord, Dauber, be a man and take a joke"—
He puffed his pipe—"and let the matter rest.
Spit brown, my son, and get a hairy breast;
Get shoulders on you at the crojick braces,
And let this painting business go to blazes.

"What good can painting do to anyone?
I don't say never do it; far from that—
No harm in sometimes painting just for fun.
Keep it for fun, and stick to what you're at.
Your job's to fill your bones up and get fat;
Rib up like Barney's bull, and thick your neck.
Throw paints to hell, boy; you belong on deck."

"That's right," said Chips; "it's down-right good advice.
Painting's no good; what good can painting do
Up on a lower topsail stiff with ice,
With all your little fish-hooks frozen blue?
Painting won't help you at the weather clew,

Nor pass your gaskets for you, nor make sail.
Painting's a balmy job not worth a nail."

The Dauber did not answer; time was passing.
He pulled his easel out, his paints, his stool.
The wind was dropping, and the sea was glassing—
New realms of beauty waited for his rule;
The draught out of the crojick kept him cool.
He sat to paint, alone and melancholy.
"No turning fools," the Chips said, "from their folly."

He dipped his brush and tried to fix a line,
And then came peace, and gentle beauty came,
Turning his spirit's water into wine,
Lightening his darkness with a touch of flame:
O, joy of trying for beauty, ever the same,
You never fail, your comforts never end;
O, balm of this world's way; O, perfect friend!

III

They lost the Trades soon after; then came calm,
Light little gusts and rain, which soon increased
To glorious northers shouting out a psalm
At seeing the bright blue water silver fleeced;
Hornwards she rushed, trampling the seas to yeast.
There fell a rain-squall in a blind day's end
When for an hour the Dauber found a friend.

Out of the rain the voices called and passed,
The stay-sails flogged, the tackle yanked and shook.
Inside the harness-room a lantern cast

DAUBER

Light and wild shadows as it ranged its hook.
The watch on deck was gathered in the nook,
They had taken shelter in that secret place,
Wild light gave wild emotions to each face.

One beat the beef-cask, and the others sang
A song that had brought anchors out of seas
In ports where bells of Christians never rang,
Nor any sea mark blazed among the trees.
By forlorn swamps, in ice, by windy keys,
That song had sounded; now it shook the air
From these eight wanderers brought together there.

Under the poop-break, sheltering from the rain,
The Dauber sketched some likeness of the room,
A note to be a prompting to his brain,
A spark to make old memory reillume.
"Dauber," said someone near him in the gloom,
"How goes it, Dauber?" It was reefer Si.
"There's not much use in trying to keep dry."

They sat upon the sail-room doorway coaming,
The lad held forth like youth, the Dauber listened
To how the boy had had a taste for roaming,
And what the sea is said to be and isn't.
Where the dim lamplight fell the wet deck glistened.
Si said the Horn was still some weeks away,
"But tell me, Dauber, where d'you hail from? Eh?"

The rain blew past and let the stars appear;
The seas grew larger as the moonlight grew;
For half an hour the ring of heaven was clear,

Dusty with moonlight, grey rather than blue;
In that great moon the showing stars were few.
The sleepy time-boy's feet passed overhead.
"I come from out past Gloucester," Dauber said;

"Not far from Pauntley, if you know those parts;
The place is Spital Farm, near Silver Hill,
Above a trap-hatch where a mill-stream starts.
We had the mill once, but we've stopped the mill;
My dad and sister keep the farm on still.
We're only tenants, but we've rented there,
Father and son, for over eighty year.

"Father has worked the farm since grandfer went;
It means the world to him; I can't think why.
They bleed him to the last half-crown for rent,
And this and that have almost milked him dry.
The land's all starved; if he'd put money by,
And corn was up, and rent was down two-thirds. . . .
But then they aren't, so what's the use of words.

"Yet still he couldn't bear to see it pass
To strangers, or to think a time would come
When other men than us would mow the grass,
And other names than ours have the home.
Some sorrows come from evil thought, but some
Comes when two men are near, and both are blind
To what is generous in the other's mind.

"I was the only boy, and father thought
I'd farm the Spital after he was dead,
And many a time he took me out and taught

About manures and seed-corn white and red,
And soils and hops, but I'd an empty head;
Harvest or seed, I would not do a turn—
I loathed the farm, I didn't want to learn.

"He did not mind at first, he thought it youth
Feeling the collar, and that I should change.
Then time gave him some inklings of the truth,
And that I loathed the farm, and wished to range.
Truth to a man of fifty's always strange;
It was most strange and terrible to him
That I, his heir, should be the devil's limb.

"Yet still he hoped the Lord might change my mind.
I'd see him bridle-in his wrath and hate,
And almost break my heart he was so kind,
Biting his lips sore with resolve to wait.
And then I'd try awhile; but it was Fate:
I didn't want to learn; the farm to me
Was mire and hopeless work and misery.

"Though there were things I loved about it, too—
The beasts, the apple-trees, and going haying.
And then I tried; but no, it wouldn't do,
The farm was prison, and my thoughts were straying.
And there'd come father, with his grey head, praying,
'O, my dear son, don't let the Spital pass;
It's my old home, boy, where your grandfer was.

"'And now you won't learn farming; you don't care.
The old home's nought to you. I've tried to teach you;
I've begged Almighty God, boy, all I dare,

To use His hand if word of mine won't reach you.
Boy, for your granfer's sake I do beseech you,
Don't let the Spital pass to strangers.   Squire
Has said he'd give it you if we require.

"'Your mother used to walk here, boy, with me;
It was her favourite walk down to the mill;
And there we'd talk how little death would be,
Knowing our work was going on here still.
You've got the brains, you only want the will—
Don't disappoint your mother and your father.
I'll give you time to travel, if you'd rather.'

"But, no, I'd wander up the brooks to read.
Then sister Jane would start with nagging tongue,
Saying my sin made father's heart to bleed,
And how she feared she'd live to see me hung.
And then she'd read me bits from Dr. Young.
And when we three would sit to supper, Jane
Would fillip dad till dad began again.

"'I've been here all my life, boy.   I was born
Up in the room above—looks on the mead.
I never thought you'd cockle my clean corn,
And leave the old home to a stranger's seed.
Father and I have made here 'thout a weed:
We've give our lives to make that.   Eighty years.
And now I go down to the grave in tears.'

"And then I'd get ashamed and take off coat,
And work maybe a week, ploughing and sowing
And then I'd creep away and sail my boat,

Or watch the water when the mill was going.
That's my delight—to be near water flowing,
Dabbling or sailing boats or jumping stanks,
Or finding moorhens' nests along the banks.

"And one day father found a ship I'd built;
He took the cart-whip to me over that,
And I, half mad with pain, and sick with guilt,
Went up and hid in what we called the flat,
A dusty hole given over to the cat.
She kittened there; the kittens had worn paths
Among the cobwebs, dust, and broken laths.

"And putting down my hand between the beams
I felt a leathery thing, and pulled it clear:
A book with white cocoons stuck in the seams.
Where spiders had had nests for many a year.
It was my mother's sketch-book; hid, I fear,
Lest dad should ever see it. Mother's life
Was not her own while she was father's wife.

"There were her drawings, dated, pencilled faint.
March was the last one, eighteen eighty-three,
Unfinished that, for tears had smeared the paint.
The rest was landscape, not yet brought to be.
That was a holy afternoon to me;
That book a sacred book; the flat a place
Where I could meet my mother face to face.

"She had found peace of spirit, mother had,
Drawing the landscape from the attic there—
Heart-broken, often, after rows with dad,

Hid like a wild thing in a secret lair.
That rotting sketch-book showed me how and where
I, too, could get away; and then I knew
That drawing was the work I longed to do.

"Drawing became my life.   I drew, I toiled,
And every penny I could get I spent
On paints and artist's matters, which I spoiled
Up in the attic to my heart's content,
Till one day father asked me what I meant;
The time had come, he said, to make an end.
Now it must finish: what did I intend?

"Either I took to farming, like his son,
In which case he would teach me, early and late
(Provided that my daubing mood was done),
Or I must go: it must be settled straight.
If I refused to farm, there was the gate.
I was to choose, his patience was all gone,
The present state of things could not go on.

"Sister was there; she eyed me while he spoke.
The kitchen clock ran down and struck the hour,
And something told me father's heart was broke,
For all he stood so set and looked so sour.
Jane took a duster, and began to scour
A pewter on the dresser; she was crying.
I stood stock still a long time, not replying.

"Dad waited, then he snorted and turned round.
'Well, think of it,' he said.   He left the room,
His boots went clop along the stony ground

Out to the orchard and the apple-bloom.
A cloud came past the sun and made a gloom;
I swallowed with dry lips, then sister turned.
She was dead white but for her eyes that burned.

"'You're breaking father's heart, Joe,' she began;
'It's not as if——' she checked, in too much pain.
'O, Joe, don't help to kill so fine a man;
You're giving him our mother over again.
It's wearing him to death, Joe, heart and brain;
You know what store he sets on leaving this
To (it's too cruel)—to a son of his.

"'Yet you go painting all the day. O, Joe,
Couldn't you make an effort? Can't you see
What folly it is of yours? It's not as though
You are a genius or could ever be.
O, Joe, for father's sake, if not for me,
Give up this craze for painting, and be wise
And work with father, where your duty lies.'

"'It goes too deep,' I said; 'I loathe the farm;
I couldn't help, even if I'd the mind.
Even if I helped, I'd only do him harm;
Father would see it, if he were not blind.
I was not built to farm, as he would find.
O, Jane, its bitter hard to stand alone
And spoil my father's life or spoil my own.'

"'Spoil both,' she said, 'the way you're shaping now.
You're only a boy not knowing your own good.
Where will you go, suppose you leave here? How

[273]

Do you propose to earn your daily food?
Draw? Daub the pavements? There's a feckless brood
Goes to the devil daily, Joe, in cities
Only from thinking how divine their wit is.

"'Clouds are they, without water, carried away.
And you'll be one of them, the way you're going,
Daubing at silly pictures all the day,
And praised by silly fools who're always blowing.
And you choose this when you might go a-sowing,
Casting the good corn into chosen mould
That shall in time bring forth a hundred-fold.'

"So we went on, but in the end it ended.
I felt I'd done a murder; I felt sick.
There's much in human minds cannot be mended,
And that, not I, played dad a cruel trick.
There was one mercy: that it ended quick.
I went to join my mother's brother: he
Lived down the Severn. He was kind to me.

"And there I learned house-painting for a living.
I'd have been happy there, but that I knew
I'd sinned before my father past forgiving,
And that they sat at home, that silent two,
Wearing the fire out and the evening through,
Silent, defeated, broken, in despair,
My plate unset, my name gone, and my chair.

"I saw all that; and sister Jane came white—
White as a ghost, with fiery, weeping eyes.
I saw her all day long and half the night,

Bitter as gall, and passionate and wise.
'Joe, you have killed your father: there he lies.
You have done your work—you with our mother's ways.'
She said it plain, and then her eyes would blaze.

"And then one day I had a job to do
Down below bridge, by where the docks begin,
And there I saw a clipper towing through,
Up from the sea that morning, entering in.
Raked to the nines she was, lofty and thin,
Her ensign ruffling red, her bunts in pile,
Beauty and strength together, wonder, style.

"She docked close to the gates, and there she lay
Over the water from me, well in sight;
And as I worked I watched her all the day,
Finding her beauty ever fresh delight.
Her house-flag was bright green with strips of white;
High in the sunny air it rose to shake
Above the skysail poles' most splendid rake.

"And when I felt unhappy I would look
Over the river at her; and her pride,
So calm, so quiet, came as a rebuke
To half the passionate pathways which I tried;
And though the autumn ran its term and died,
And winter fell and cold December came,
She was still splendid there, and still the same.

"Then on a day she sailed; but when she went
My mind was clear on what I had to try:
To see the sea and ships, and what they meant,

[275]

That was the thing I longed to do; so I
Drew and worked hard, and studied and put by,
And thought of nothing else but that one end,
But let all else go hang—love, money, friend.

"And now I've shipped as Dauber I've begun.
It was hard work to find a dauber's berth;
I hadn't any friends to find me one,
Only my skill, for what it may be worth;
But I'm at sea now, going about the earth,
And when the ship's paid off, when we return,
I'll join some Paris studio and learn."

He stopped, the air came moist, Si did not speak;
The Dauber turned his eyes to where he sat,
Pressing the sail-room hinges with his cheeek,
His face half covered with a dropping hat.
Huge dewdrops from the stay-sails dropped and spat.
Si did not stir, the Dauber touched his sleeve;
A little birdlike noise came from a sheave.

Si was asleep, sleeping a calm deep sleep,
Still as a warden of the Egyptian dead
In some old haunted temple buried deep
Under the desert sand, sterile and red.
The Dauber shook his arm; Si jumped and said,
"Good yarn, I swear! I say, you have a brain—
Was that eight bells that went?" He slept again.

Then waking up, "I've had a nap," he cried.
"Was that one bell? What, Dauber, you still here?"
"Si there?" the Mate's voice called. "Sir," he replied.

The order made the lad's thick vision clear;
A something in the Mate's voice made him fear.
"Si," said the Mate, "I hear you've made a friend—
Dauber, in short. That friendship's got to end.

"You're a young gentleman. Your place aboard
Is with the gentlemen abaft the mast.
You're learning to command; you can't afford
To yarn with any man. But there . . . it's past.
You've done it once; let this time be the last.
The Dauber's place is forward. Do it again,
I'll put you bunking forward with the men.

"Dismiss." Si went, but Sam, beside the Mate,
Timekeeper there, walked with him to the rail
And whispered him the menace of "You wait"—
Words which have turned full many a reefer pale.
The watch was changed; the watch on deck trimmed sail.
Sam, going below, called all the reefers down,
Sat in his bunk and eyed them with a frown.

"Si here," he said, "has soiled the half-decks' name
Talking to Dauber—Dauber, the ship's clout.
A reefer takes the Dauber for a flame,
The half-deck take the round-house walking out.
He's soiled the half-deck's honour; now, no doubt,
The Bosun and his mates will come here sneaking,
Asking for smokes, or blocking gangways speaking.

"I'm not a vain man, given to blow or boast;
I'm not a proud man, but I truly feel
That while I've bossed this mess and ruled this roast

[277]

DAUBER

I've kept this hooker's half-deck damned genteel.
Si must ask pardon, or be made to squeal.
Down on your knees, dog; them we love we chasten.
Jao, pasea, my son—in English, Hasten."

Si begged for pardon, meekly kneeling down
Before the reefer's mess assembled grim.
The lamp above them smoked the glass all brown;
Beyond the door the dripping sails were dim.
The Dauber passed the door; none spoke to him.
He sought his berth and slept, or, waking, heard
Rain on the deck-house—rain, no other word.

IV

Out of the air a time of quiet came,
Calm fell upon the heaven like a drouth;
The brass sky watched the brassy water flame.
Drowsed as a snail the clipper loitered south
Slowly, with no white bone across her mouth;
No rushing glory, like a queen made bold,
The Dauber strove to draw her as she rolled.

There the four leaning spires of canvas rose,
Royals and skysails lifting, gently lifting,
White like the brightness that a great fish blows
When billows are at peace and ships are drifting;
With mighty jerks that set the shadows shifting,
The courses tugged their tethers: a blue haze
Drifted like ghosts of flocks come down to graze.

There the great skyline made her perfect round,
Notched now and then by the sea's deeper blue;
A smoke-smutch marked a steamer homeward bound,
The haze wrought all things to intenser hue.
In tingling impotence the Dauber drew
As all men draw, keen to the shaken soul
To give a hint that might suggest the whole.

A naked seaman washing a red shirt
Sat at a tub whistling between his teeth;
Complaining blocks quavered like something hurt.
A sailor cut an old boot for a sheath,
The ship bowed to her shadow-ship beneath,
And little splash of spray came at the roll
On to the deck-planks from the scupper-hole.

He watched it, painting patiently, as paints,
With eyes that pierce behind the blue sky's veil,
The Benedictine in a Book of Saints
Watching the passing of the Holy Grail;
The green dish dripping blood, the trump, the hail,
The spears that pass, the memory and the passion,
The beauty moving under this world's fashion.

But as he painted, slowly, man by man,
The seamen gathered near; the Bosun stood
Behind him, jeering; then the Sails began
Sniggering with comment that it was not good.
Chips flicked his sketch with little scraps of wood,
Saying, "That hit the top-knot," every time.
Cook mocked, "My lovely drawings; it's a crime."

Slowly the men came nearer, till a crowd
Stood at his elbow, muttering as he drew;
The Bosun, turning to them, spoke aloud,
"This is the ship that never got there. You
Look at her here, what Dauber's trying to do.
Look at her! lummy, like a Christmas-tree.
That thing's a ship; he calls this painting. See?"

Seeing the crowd, the Mate came forward; then
"Sir," said the Bosun, "come and see the sight!
Here's Dauber makes a circus for the men.
He calls this thing a ship—this hell's delight!"
"Man," said the Mate, "you'll never get her right
Daubing like that. Look here!" He took a brush.
"Now Dauber, watch; I'll put you to the blush.

"Look here. Look there. Now watch this ship of mine."
He drew her swiftly from a memory stored.
"God, sir," the Bosun said, "you do her fine!"
"Ay," said the Mate, "I do so, by the Lord!
I'll paint a ship with any man aboard."
They hung about his sketch like beasts at bait.
"There now, I taught him painting," said the Mate.

When he had gone, the gathered men dispersed;
Yet two or three still lingered to dispute
What errors made the Dauber's work the worst.
They probed his want of knowledge to the root.
"Bei Gott!" they swore, "der Dauber cannot do 't;
He haf no knolich how to put der pense.
Der Mate's is goot. Der Dauber haf no sense."

"You hear?" the Bosun cried, "you cannot do it!"
"A gospel truth," the Cook said, "true as hell!
And wisdom, Dauber, if you only knew it;
A five year boy would do a ship as well."
"If that's the kind of thing you hope to sell,
God help you," echoed Chips. "I tell you true,
The job's beyond you, Dauber; drop it, do.

"Drop it, in God's name drop it, and have done!
You see you cannot do it. Here's the Mate
Paints you to frazzles before everyone;
Paints you a dandy clipper while you wait.
While you, Lord love us, daub. I tell you straight,
We've had enough of daubing; drop it; quit.
You cannot paint, so make an end of it."

"That's sense," said all; "you cannot, why pretend?"
The Dauber rose and put his easel by.
"You've said enough," he said, "now let it end.
Who cares how bad my painting may be? I
Mean to go on, and, if I fail, to try.
However much I miss of my intent,
If I have done my best I'll be content.

"You cannot understand that. Let it be.
You cannot understand, nor know, nor share.
This is a matter touching only me;
My sketch may be a daub, for aught I care.
You may be right. But even if you were,
Your mocking should not stop this work of mine;
Rot though it be, its prompting is divine.

"You cannot understand that—you, and you,
And you, you Bosun. You can stand and jeer,
That is the task your spirit fits you to,
That you can understand and hold most dear.
Grin, then, like collars, ear to donkey ear,
But let me daub. Try, you, to understand
Which task will bear the light best on God's hand."

V

The wester came as steady as the Trades;
Brightly it blew, and still the ship did shoulder
The brilliance of the water's white cockades
Into the milky green of smoky smoulder.
The sky grew bluer and the air grew colder.
Southward she thundered while the westers held,
Proud, with taut bridles, pawing, but compelled.

And still the Dauber strove, though all men mocked,
To draw the splendour of the passing thing,
And deep inside his heart a something locked,
Long pricking in him, now began to sting—
A fear of the disasters storm might bring;
His rank as painter would be ended then—
He would keep watch and watch like other men.

And go aloft with them to man the yard
When the great ship was rolling scuppers under,
Burying her snout all round the compass card,
While the green water struck at her and stunned her;
When the lee-rigging slacked, when one long thunder

DAUBER

Boomed from the black to windward, when the sail
Booted and spurred the devil in the gale.

For him to ride on men: that was the time
The Dauber dreaded; then lest the test would come,
When seas, half-frozen, slushed the decks with slime,
And all the air was blind with flying scum;
When the drenched sails were furled, when the fierce hum
In weather riggings died into the roar
Of God's eternal never tamed by shore.

Once in the passage he had worked aloft,
Shifting her suits one summer afternoon,
In the bright Trade wind, when the wind was soft,
Shaking the points, making the tackle croon.
But that was child's play to the future: soon
He would be ordered up when sails and spars
Were flying and going mad among the stars.

He had been scared that first time, daunted, thrilled,
Not by the height so much as by the size,
And then the danger to the man unskilled
In standing on a rope that runs through eyes.
"But in a storm," he thought, "the yards will rise
And roll together down, and snap their gear!"
The sweat came cold upon his palms for fear.

Sometimes in Gloucester he had felt a pang
Swinging below the house-eaves on a stage.
But stages carry rails; here he would hang
Upon a jerking rope in a storm's rage,
Ducked that the sheltering oilskin might assuage

The beating of the storm, clutching the jack,
Beating the sail, and being beaten back.

Drenched, frozen, gasping, blinded, beaten dumb,
High in the night, reeling great blinding arcs
As the ship rolled, his chappy fingers numb,
The deck below a narrow blur of marks,
The sea a welter of whiteness shot with sparks,
Now snapping up in bursts, now dying away,
Salting the horizontal snow with spray.

A hundred and fifty feet above the deck,
And there, while the ship rolls, boldly to sit
Upon a foot-rope moving, jerk and check,
While half a dozen seamen work on it;
Held by one hand, straining, by strength and wit
To toss a gasket's coil around the yard,
How could he compass that when blowing hard?

And if he failed in any least degree,
Or faltered for an instant, or showed slack,
He might go drown himself within the sea,
And add a bubble to the clipper's track.
He had signed his name, there was no turning back,
No pardon for default—this must be done.
One iron rule at sea binds everyone.

Till now he had been treated with contempt
As neither man nor thing, a creature borne
On the ship's articles, but left exempt
From all the seamen's life except their scorn.
But he would rank as seaman off the Horn,

Work as a seaman, and be kept or cast
By standards set for men before the mast.

Even now they shifted suits of sails; they bent
The storm-suit ready for the expected time;
The mighty wester that the Plate had lent
Had brought them far into the wintry clime.
At dawn, out of the shadow, there was rime,
The dim Magellan Clouds were frosty clear,
The wind had edge, the testing-time was near.

And then he wondered if the tales were lies
Told by old hands to terrify the new,
For, since the ship left England, only twice
Had there been need to start a sheet or clew,
Then only royals, for an hour or two,
And no seas broke aboard, nor was it cold.
What were these gales of which the stories told?

The thought went by. He had heard the Bosun tell
Too often, and too fiercely, not to know
That being off the Horn in June is Hell:
Hell of continual toil in ice and snow,
Frostbitten hell in which the westers blow
Shrieking for days on end, in which the seas
Gulf the starved seamen till their marrows freeze.

Such was the weather he might look to find,
Such was the work expected: there remained
Firmly to set his teeth, resolve his mind,
And be the first, however much it pained,
And bring his honour round the Horn unstained,

And win his mates' respect; and thence, untainted,
Be ranked as man however much he painted.

He drew deep breath; a gantline swayed aloft
A lower topsail, hard with rope and leather,
Such as men's frozen fingers fight with oft
Below the Ramirez in Cape Horn weather.
The arms upon the yard hove all together,
Lighting the head along; a thought occurred
Within the painter's brain like a bright bird:

That this, and so much like it, of man's toil,
Compassed by naked manhood in strange places,
Was all heroic, but outside the coil
Within which modern art gleams or grimaces;
That if he drew that line of sailor's faces
Sweating the sail, their passionate play and change,
It would be new, and wonderful, and strange.

That that was what his work meant; it would be
A training in new vision—a revealing
Of passionate men in battle with the sea,
High on an unseen stage, shaking and reeling;
And men through him would understand their feeling,
Their might, their misery, their tragic power,
And all by suffering pain a little hour;

High on the yard with them, feeling their pain,
Battling with them; and it had not been done.
He was a door to new worlds in the brain,
A window opening letting in the sun,
A voice saying, "Thus is bread fetched and ports won,

And life lived out at sea where men exist
Solely by man's strong brain and sturdy wrist."

So he decided, as he cleaned his brasses,
Hearing without, aloft, the curse, the shout
Where the taut gantline passes and repasses,
Heaving new topsails to be lighted out.
It was most proud, however self might doubt,
To share man's tragic toil and paint it true.
He took the offered Fate: this he would do.

That night the snow fell between six and seven,
A little feathery fall so light, so dry—
An aimless dust out of a confused heaven,
Upon an air no steadier than a sigh;
The powder dusted down and wandered by
So purposeless, so many, and so cold,
Then died, and the wind ceased and the ship rolled.

Rolled till she clanged—rolled till the brain was tired,
Marking the acme of the heaves, the pause
While the sea-beauty rested and respired,
Drinking great draughts of roller at her hawse.
Flutters of snow came aimless upon flaws.
"Lock up your paints," the Mate said, speaking light:
"This is the Horn; you'll join my watch to-night!"

VI

All through the windless night the clipper rolled
In a great swell with oily gradual heaves
Which rolled her down until her time-bells tolled,

Clang, and the weltering water moaned like beeves.
The thundering rattle of slatting shook the sheaves,
Startles of water made the swing ports gush,
The sea was moaning and sighing and saying "Hush!"

It was all black and starless. Peering down
Into the water, trying to pierce the gloom,
One saw a dim, smooth, oily glitter of brown
Heaving and dying away and leaving room
For yet another. Like the march of doom
Came those great powers of marching silences;
Then fog came down, dead-cold, and hid the seas.

They set the Dauber to the foghorn. There
He stood upon the poop, making to sound
Out of the pump the sailor's nasal blare,
Listening lest ice should make the note resound.
She bayed there like a solitary hound
Lost in a covert; all the watch she bayed.
The fog, come closelier down, no answer made.

Denser it grew, until the ship was lost.
The elemental hid her; she was merged
In mufflings of dark death, like a man's ghost,
New to the change of death, yet thither urged.
Then from the hidden waters something surged—
Mournful, despairing, great, greater than speech,
A noise like one slow wave on a still beach.

Mournful, and then again mournful, and still
Out of the night that mighty voice arose;
The Dauber at his foghorn felt the thrill.

DAUBER

Who rode that desolate sea? What forms were those?
Mournful, from things defeated, in the throes
Of memory of some conquered hunting-ground,
Out of the night of death arose the sound.

"Whales!" said the Mate. They stayed there all night long
Answering the horn. Out of the night they spoke,
Defeated creatures who had suffered wrong,
But were still noble underneath the stroke.
They filled the darkness when the Dauber woke;
The men came peering to the rail to hear,
And the sea sighed, and the fog rose up sheer.

A wall of nothing at the world's last edge,
Where no life came except defeated life.
The Dauber felt shut in within a hedge,
Behind which form was hidden and thought was rife,
And that a blinding flash, a thrust, a knife
Would sweep the hedge away and make all plain,
Brilliant beyond all words, blinding the brain.

So the night passed, but then no morning broke—
Only a something showed that night was dead.
A sea-bird, cackling like a devil, spoke,
And the fog drew away and hung like lead.
Like mighty cliffs it shaped, sullen and red;
Like glowering gods at watch it did appear,
And sometimes drew away, and then drew near.

Like islands, and like chasms, and like hell,
But always mighty and red, gloomy and ruddy,
Shutting the visible sea in like a well;

[289]

DAUBER

Slow heaving in vast ripples, blank and muddy,
Where the sun should have risen it streaked bloody.
The day was still-born; all the sea-fowl scattering
Splashed the still water, mewing, hovering, clattering.

Then Polar snow came down little and light,
Till all the sky was hidden by the small,
Most multitudinous drift of dirty white
Tumbling and wavering down and covering all—
Covering the sky, the sea, the clipper tall,
Furring the ropes with white, casing the mast,
Coming on no known air, but blowing past.

And all the air seemed full of gradual moan,
As though in those cloud-chasms the horns were blowing
The mort for gods cast out and overthrown,
Or for the eyeless sun plucked out and going.
Slow the low gradual moan came in the snowing;
The Dauber felt the prelude had begun.
The snowstorm fluttered by; he saw the sun

Show and pass by, gleam from one towering prison
Into another, vaster and more grim,
Which in dull crags of darkness had arisen
To muffle-to a final door on him.
The gods upon the dull crags lowered dim,
The pigeons chattered, quarrelling in the track.
In the south-west the dimness dulled to black.

Then came the cry of "Call all hands on deck!"
The Dauber knew its meaning; it was come:
Cape Horn, that tramples beauty into wreck,

And crumples steel and smites the strong man dumb.
Down clattered flying kites and staysails: some
Sang out in quick, high calls: the fair-leads skirled,
And from the south-west came the end of the world.

"Caught in her ball-dress," said the Bosun, hauling;
"Lee-ay, lee-ay!" quick, high, come the men's call;
It was all wallop of sails and startled calling.
"Let fly!" "Let go!" "Clew up!" and "Let go all!"
"Now up and make them fast!" "Here, give us a haul!"
"Now up and stow them! Quick! By God! we're done!"
The blackness crunched all memory of the sun.

"Up!" said the Mate. "Mizen top-gallants. Hurry!"
The Dauber ran, the others ran, the sails
Slatted and shook; out of the black a flurry
Whirled in fine lines, tattering the edge to trails.
Painting and art and England were old tales
Told in some other life to that pale man,
Who struggled with white fear and gulped and ran.

He struck a ringbolt in his haste and fell—
Rose, sick with pain, half-lamed in his left knee;
He reached the shrouds where clambering men pell-mell
Hustled each other up and cursed him; he
Hurried aloft with them: then from the sea
Came a cold, sudden breath that made the hair
Stiff on the neck, as though Death whispered there.

A man below him punched him in the side.
"Get up, you Dauber, or let me get past."
He saw the belly of the skysail skied,

Gulped, and clutched tight, and tried to go more fast.
Sometimes he missed his ratline and was grassed,
Scraped his shin raw against the rigid line
The clamberers reached the futtock-shrouds' incline.

Cursing they came; one, kicking out behind,
Kicked Dauber in the mouth, and one below
Punched at his calves; the futtock-shrouds inclined
It was a perilous path for one to go.
"Up, Dauber, up!" A curse followed a blow.
He reached the top and gasped, then on, then on.
And one voice yelled "Let go!" and one "All gone!"

Fierce clamberers, some in oilskins, some in rags,
Hustling and hurrying up, up the steep stairs.
Before the windless sails were blown to flags,
And whirled like dirty birds athwart great airs,
Ten men in all, to get this mast of theirs
Snugged to the gale in time. "Up! Damn you, run!"
The mizen topmast head was safely won.

"Lay out!" the Bosun yelled. The Dauber laid
Out on the yard, gripping the yard and feeling
Sick at the mighty space of air displayed
Below his feet, where mewing birds were wheeling.
A giddy fear was on him; he was reeling.
He bit his lip half through, clutching the jack.
A cold sweat glued the shirt upon his back.

The yard was shaking, for a brace was loose.
He felt that he would fall; he clutched, he bent,
Clammy with natural terror to the shoes

While idiotic promptings came and went.
Snow fluttered on a wind-flaw and was spent;
He saw the water darken. Someone yelled,
"Frap it; don't stay to furl! Hold on!" He held.

Darkness came down—half darkness—in a whirl;
The sky went out, the waters disappeared.
He felt a shocking pressure of blowing hurl
The ship upon her side. The darkness speared
At her with wind; she staggered, she careered,
Then down she lay. The Dauber felt her go;
He saw his yard tilt downwards. Then the snow

Whirled all about—dense, multitudinous, cold—
Mixed with the wind's one devilish thrust and shriek,
Which whiffled out men's tears, deafened, took hold,
Flattening the flying drift against the cheek.
The yards buckled and bent, man could not speak.
The ship lay on her broadside; the wind's sound
Had devilish malice at having got her downed

　　　*　　　*　　　*　　　*　　　*

How long the gale had blown he could not tell,
Only the world had changed, his life had died.
A moment now was everlasting hell.
Nature an onslaught from the weather side,
A withering rush of death, a frost that cried,
Shrieked, till he withered at the heart; a hail
Plastered his oilskins with an icy mail.

"Cut!" yelled his mate. He looked—the sail was gone,
Blown into rags in the first furious squall;
The tatters drummed the devil's tattoo. On

The buckling yard a block thumped like a mall.
The ship lay—the sea smote her, the wind's bawl
Came, "loo, loo, loo!"   The devil cried his hounds
On to the poor spent stag strayed in his bounds.

"Cut! Ease her!" yelled his mate; the Dauber heard.
His mate wormed up the tilted yard and slashed,
A rag of canvas skimmed like a darting bird.
The snow whirled, the ship bowed to it, the gear lashed,
The sea-tops were cut off and flung down smashed;
Tatters of shouts were flung, the rags of yells—
And clang, clang, clang, below beat the two bells.

"O God!" the Dauber moaned. A roaring rang,
Blasting the royals like a cannonade;
The backstays parted with a crackling clang,
The upper spars were snapped like twigs decayed—
Snapped at their heels, their jagged splinters splayed,
Like white and ghastly hairs erect with fear.
The Mate yelled, "Gone, by God, and pitched them clear!"

"Up!" yelled the Bosun; "up and clear the wreck!"
The Dauber followed where he led: below
He caught one giddy glimpsing of the deck
Filled with white water, as though heaped with snow.
He saw the streamers of the rigging blow
Straight out like pennons from the splintered mast,
Then, all sense dimmed, all was an icy blast

Roaring from nether hell and filled with ice,
Roaring and crashing on the jerking stage,
An utter bridle given to utter vice,

Limitless power mad with endless rage
Withering the soul; a minute seemed an age.
He clutched and hacked at ropes, at rags of sail.
Thinking that comfort was a fairy-tale

Told long ago— long, long ago— long since
Heard of in other lives—imagined, dreamed—
There where the basest beggar was a prince
To him in torment where the tempest screamed,
Comfort and warmth and ease no longer seemed
Things that a man could know: soul, body, brain,
Knew nothing but the wind, the cold, the pain.

"Leave that!" the Bosun shouted; "Crojick save!"
The splitting crojick, not yet gone to rags,
Thundered below, beating till something gave,
Bellying between its buntlines into bags.
Some birds were blown past, shrieking: dark, like shags,
Their backs seemed, looking down. "Leu, leu!" they cried.
The ship lay, the seas thumped her; she had died.

They reached the crojick yard, which buckled, buckled
Like a thin whalebone to the topsail's strain.
They laid upon the yard and heaved and knuckled,
Pounding the sail, which jangled and leapt again.
It was quite hard with ice, its rope like chain,
Its strength like seven devils; it shook the mast.
They cursed and toiled and froze: a long time passed.

Two hours passed, then a dim lightening came.
Those frozen ones upon the yard could see
The mainsail and the foresail still the same,

Still battling with the hands and blowing free,
Rags tattered where the staysails used to be.
The lower topsails stood; the ship's lee deck
Seethed with four feet of water filled with wreck.

An hour more went by; the Dauber lost
All sense of hands and feet, all sense of all
But of a wind that cut him to the ghost,
And of a frozen fold he had to haul,
Of heavens that fell and never ceased to fall,
And ran in smoky snatches along the sea,
Leaping from crest to wave-crest, yelling.   He

Lost sense of time; no bells went, but he felt
Ages go over him.   At last, at last
They frapped the cringled crojick's icy pelt;
In frozen bulge and bunt they made it fast.
Then, scarcely live, they laid in to the mast.
The Captain's speaking trumpet gave a blare,
"Make fast the topsail, Mister, while you're there."

Some seamen cursed, but up they had to go—
Up to the topsail yard to spend an hour
Stowing a topsail in a blinding snow,
Which made the strongest man among them cower.
More men came up, the fresh hands gave them power,
They stowed the sail; then with a rattle of chain
One half the crojick burst its bonds again.

*   *   *   *   *

They stowed the sail, frapping it round with rope,
Leaving no surface for the wind, no fold,
Then down the weather shrouds, half dead, they grope;

That struggle with the sail had made them old.
They wondered if the crojick furl would hold.
"Lucky," said one, "it didn't spring the spar."
"Lucky!" the Bosun said, "Lucky! We are!"

She came within two shakes of turning top
Or stripping all her shroud-screws, that first quiff.
Now fish those wash-deck buckets out of the slop.
Here's Dauber says he doesn't like Cape Stiff.
This isn't wind, man, this is only a whiff.
Hold on, all hands, hold on!" a sea, half seen,
Paused, mounted, burst, and filled the main-deck green,

The Dauber felt a mountain of water fall.
It covered him deep, deep, he felt it fill,
Over his head, the deck, the fife-rails, all,
Quieting the ship, she trembled and lay still.
Then with a rush and shatter and clanging shrill
Over she went; he saw the water cream
Over the bitts; he saw the half-deck stream.

Then in the rush he swirled, over she went;
Her lee-rail dipped, he struck, and something gave;
His legs went through a port as the roll spent;
She paused, then rolled, and back the water drave.
He drifted with it as a part of the wave,
Drowning, half-stunned, exhausted, partly frozen,
He struck the booby hatchway; then the Bosun

Leaped, seeing his chance, before the next sea burst,
And caught him as he drifted, seized him, held,
Up-ended him against the bitts, and cursed.

DAUBER

"This ain't the George's Swimming Baths," he yelled;
"Keep on your feet!" Another grey-back felled
The two together, and the Bose, half-blind,
Spat: "One's a joke," he cursed, "but two's unkind."

"Now, damn it, Dauber!" said the Mate. "Look out,
Or you'll be over the side!" The water freed;
Each clanging freeing-port became a spout.
The men cleared up the decks as there was need.
The Dauber's head was cut, he felt it bleed
Into his oilskins as he clutched and coiled.
Water and sky were devil's brews which boiled,

Boiled, shrieked, and glowered; but the ship was saved.
Snugged safely down, though fourteen sails were split.
Out of the dark a fiercer fury raved.
The grey-backs died and mounted, each crest lit
With a white toppling gleam that hissed from it
And slid, or leaped, or ran with whirls of cloud,
Mad with inhuman life that shrieked aloud.

The watch was called; Dauber might go below.
"Splice the main brace!" the Mate called. All laid aft
To get a gulp of momentary glow
As some reward for having saved the craft.
The steward ladled mugs, from which each quaff'd
Whisky, with water, sugar, and lime-juice, hot,
A quarter of a pint each made the tot.

Beside the lamp-room door the steward stood
Ladling it out, and each man came in turn,
Tipped his sou'-wester, drank it, grunted "Good!"

And shambled forward, letting it slowly burn:
When all were gone the Dauber lagged astern,
Torn by his frozen body's lust for heat,
The liquor's pleasant smell, so warm, so sweet,

And by a promise long since made at home
Never to taste strong liquor. Now he knew
The worth of liquor; now he wanted some.
His frozen body urged him to the brew;
Yet it seemed wrong, an evil thing to do
To break that promise. "Dauber," said the Mate,
"Drink, and turn in, man; why the hell d'ye wait?"

"Please, sir, I'm temperance." "Temperance are you, hey?
That's all the more for me! So you're for slops?
I thought you'd had enough slops for to-day.
Go to your bunk and ease her when she drops.
And—damme, steward! you brew with too much hops!
Stir up the sugar, man!—and tell your girl
How kind the Mate was teaching you to furl."

Then the Mate drank the remnants, six men's share,
And ramped into his cabin, where he stripped
And danced unclad, and was uproarious there.
In waltzes with the cabin cat he tripped.
Singing in tenor clear that he was pipped—
That "he who strove the tempest to disarm,
Must never first embrail the lee yard-arm."

And that his name was Ginger. Dauber crept
Back to the round-house, gripping by the rail.
The wind howled by; the passionate water leapt;

The night was all one roaring with the gale.
Then at the door he stopped, uttering a wail;
His hands were perished numb and blue as veins,
He could not turn the knob for both the Spains.

A hand came shuffling aft, dodging the seas,
Singing "her nut-brown hair" between his teeth;
Taking the ocean's tumult at his ease
Even when the wash about his thighs did seethe.
His soul was happy in its happy sheath;
"What, Dauber, won't it open?   Fingers cold?
You'll talk of this time, Dauber, when you're old."

He flung the door half open, and a sea
Washed them both in, over the splashboard, down;
"You silly, salt miscarriage!" sputtered he.
"Dauber, pull out the plug before we drown!
That's spoiled my laces and my velvet gown.
Where is the plug?"   Groping in pitch dark water,
He sang between his teeth "The Farmer's Daughter."

It was pitch dark within there; at each roll
The chests slid to the slant; the water rushed,
Making full many a clanging tin pan bowl
Into the black below-bunks as it gushed.
The dog-tired men slept through it; they were hushed.
The water drained, and then with matches damp
The man struck heads off till he lit the lamp.

"Thank you," the Dauber said; the seaman grinned.
"This is your first foul weather?"   "Yes."   "I thought
Up on the yard you hadn't seen much wind.

DAUBER

Them's rotten sea-boots, Dauber, that you brought.
Now I must cut on deck before I'm caught."
He went; the lamp-flame smoked; he slammed the door;
A film of water loitered across the floor.

The Dauber watched it come and watched it go;
He had had revelation of the lies
Cloaking the truth men never choose to know;
He could bear witness now and cleanse their eyes.
He had beheld in suffering; he was wise;
This was the sea, this searcher of the soul—
This never-dying shriek fresh from the Pole.

He shook with cold; his hands could not undo
His oilskin buttons, so he shook and sat,
Watching his dirty fingers, dirty blue,
Hearing without the hammering tackle slat,
Within, the drops from dripping clothes went pat,
Running in little patters, gentle, sweet,
And "Ai, ai!" went the wind, and the seas beat.

His bunk was sopping wet; he clambered in,
None of his clothes were dry; his fear recurred.
Cramps bunched the muscles underneath his skin.
The great ship rolled until the lamp was blurred.
He took his Bible and tried to read a word;
Trembled at going aloft again, and then
Resolved to fight it out and show it to men.

Faces recurred, fierce memories of the yard,
The frozen sail, the savage eyes, the jests,
The oaths of one great seaman, syphilis-scarred,

DAUBER

The tug of leeches jammed beneath their chests,
The buntliness bellying bunts out into breasts.
The deck so desolate-grey, the sky so wild,
He fell asleep, and slept like a young child.

But not for long; the cold awoke him soon,
The hot-ache and the skin-cracks and the cramp,
The seas thundering without, the gale's wild tune,
The sopping misery of the blankets damp.
A speaking-trumpet roared; a sea-boot's stamp
Clogged at the door. A man entered to shout:
"All hands on deck! Arouse here! Tumble out!"

The caller raised the lamp; his oilskins clicked
As the thin ice upon them cracked and fell.
"Rouse out!" he said. "This lamp is frozen wick'd.
Rouse out!" His accent deepened to a yell.
"We're among ice; it's blowing up like hell.
We're going to hand both topsails. Time, I guess,
We're sheeted up. Rouse out! Don't stay to dress!"

"Is it cold on deck?" said Dauber. Is it cold?
We're sheeted up, I tell you, inches thick!
The fo'c'sle's like a wedding-cake, I'm told.
Now tumble out, my sons; on deck here, quick!
Rouse out, away, and come and climb the stick.
I'm going to call the half-deck. Bosun! Hey!
Both topsails coming in. Heave out! Away!"

He went; the Dauber tumbled from his bunk,
Clutching the side. He heard the wind go past,
Making the great ship wallow as if drunk.

There was a shocking tumult up the mast.
"This is the end," he muttered, "come at last!
I've got to go aloft, facing this cold.
I can't.   I can't.   I'll never keep my hold.

"I cannot face the topsail yard again.
I never guessed what misery it would be."
The cramps and hot-ache made him sick with pain.
The ship stopped suddenly from a devilish sea,
Then, with a triumph of wash, a rush of glee,
The door burst in, and in the water rolled,
Filling the lower bunks, black, creaming, cold.

The lamp sucked out.   "Wash!" went the water back,
Then in again, flooding; the Bosun swore.
"You useless thing!   You Dauber!   You lee slack!
Get out, you heekapoota!   Shut the door!
You coo-ilyaira, what are you waiting for?
Out of my way, you thing—you useless thing!"
He slammed the door indignant, clanging the ring.

And then he lit the lamp, drowned to the waist;
"Here's a fine house!   Get at the scupper-holes"—
He bent against it as the water raced—
"And pull them out to leeward when she rolls.
They say some kinds of landsmen don't have souls.
I well believe.   A Port Mahon baboon
Would make more soul than you got with a spoon."

Down in the icy water Dauber groped
To find the plug; the racing water sluiced
Over his head and shoulders as she sloped.

Without, judged by the sound, all hell was loosed.
He felt cold Death about him tightly noosed.
That Death was better than the misery there
Iced on the quaking foothold high in air.

And then the thought came: "I'm a failure. All
My life has been a failure. They were right.
It will not matter if I go and fall;
I should be free then from this hell's delight.
I'll never paint. Best let it end to-night.
I'll slip over the side. I've tried and failed."
So in the ice-cold in the night he quailed.

Death would be better, death, than this long hell
Of mockery and surrender and dismay—
This long defeat of doing nothing well,
Playing the part too high for him to play.
"O Death! who hides the sorry thing away,
Take me; I've failed. I cannot play these cards."
There came a thundering from the topsail yards.

And then he bit his lips, clenching his mind,
And staggered out to muster, beating back
The coward frozen self of him that whined.
Come what cards might he meant to play the pack.
"Ai!" screamed the wind; the topsail sheet went clack;
Ice filled the air with spikes; the grey-backs burst.
"Here's Dauber," said the Mate, "on deck the first.

"Why, holy sailor, Dauber, you're a man!
I took you for a soldier. Up now, come!"
Up on the yards already they began

That battle with a gale which strikes men dumb.
The leaping topsail thundered like a drum.
The frozen snow beat in the face like shots.
The wind spun whipping wave-crests into clots.

So up upon the topsail yard again,
In the great tempest's fiercest hour, began
Probation to the Dauber's soul, of pain
Which crowds a century's torment in a span.
For the next month the ocean taught this man,
And he, in that month's torment, while she wested,
Was never warm nor dry, nor full nor rested.

But still it blew, or, if it lulled, it rose
Within the hour and blew again; and still
The water as it burst aboard her froze.
The wind blew off an ice-field, raw and chill,
Daunting man's body, tampering with his will;
But after thirty days a ghostly sun
Gave sickly promise that the storms were done.

VII

A great grey sea was running up the sky,
Desolate birds flew past; their mewings came
As that lone water's spiritual cry,
Its forlorn voice, its essence, its soul's name.
The ship limped in the water as if lame.
Then in the forenoon watch to a great shout
More sail was made, the reefs were shaken out.

A slant came from the south; the singers stood
Clapped to the halliards, hauling to a tune,
Old as the sea, a fillip to the blood.

DAUBER

The upper topsail rose like a balloon.
"So long, Cape Stiff.   In Valparaiso soon,"
Said one to other, as the ship lay over,
Making her course again—again a rover.

Slowly the sea went down as the wind fell.
Clear rang the songs, "Hurrah! Cape Horn is bet!"
The combless seas were lumping into swell;
The leaking fo'c'sles were no longer wet.
More sail was made; the watch on deck was set
To cleaning up the ruin broken bare
Below, aloft, about her, everywhere.

The Dauber, scrubbing out the roundhouse, found
Old pantiles pulped among the mouldy gear,
Washed underneath the bunks and long since drowned
During the agony of the Cape Horn year.
He sang in scrubbing, for he had done with fear—
Fronted the worst and looked it in the face;
He had got manhood at the testing-place.

Singing he scrubbed, passing his watch below,
Making the round-house fair; the Bosun watched,
Bringing his knitting slowly to the toe.
Sails stretched a mizen skysail which he patched;
They thought the Dauber was a bad egg hatched.
"Daubs," said the Bosun cheerly, "can you knit?
I've made a Barney's bull of this last bit."

Then, while the Dauber counted, Bosun took
Some marline from his pocket.   "Here," he said,
"You want to know square sennit?   So fash.   Look!

Eight foxes take, and stop the ends with thread.
I've known an engineer would give his head
To know square sennit." As the Bose began,
The Dauber felt promoted into man.

It was his warrant that he had not failed—
That the most hard part in his difficult climb
Had not been past attainment; it was scaled:
Safe footing showed above the slippery slime.
He had emerged out of the iron time,
And knew that he could compass his life's scheme;
He had the power sufficient to his dream.

Then dinner came, and now the sky was blue.
The ship was standing north, the Horn was rounded;
She made a thundering as she weltered through.
The mighty grey-backs glittered as she bounded.
More sail was piled upon her; she was hounded
North, while the wind came; like a stag she ran
Over grey hills and hollows of seas wan.

She had a white bone in her mouth: she sped;
Those in the round-house watched her as they ate
Their meal of pork-fat fried with broken bread.
"Good old!" they cried. "She's off; she's gathering gait!"
Her track was whitening like a Lammas spate.
"Good old!" they cried. "Oh, give her cloth! Hurray!
For three weeks more to Valparaiso Bay!

"She smells old Vallipo," the Bosun cried.
"We'll be inside the tier in three weeks more,
Lying at double-moorings where they ride

DAUBER

Off of the market, half a mile from shore,
And bumboat pan, my sons, and figs galore,
And girls in black mantillas fit to make a
Poor seaman frantic when they dance the cueca."

Eight bells were made, the watch was changed, and now
The Mate spoke to the Dauber: "This is better.
We'll soon be getting mudhooks over the bow.
She'll make her passage still if this'll let her.
Oh, run, you drogher! dip your fo'c'sle wetter.
Well, Dauber, this is better than Cape Horn.
Them topsails made you wish you'd not been born."

"Yes, sir," the Dauber said. "Now," said the Mate,
"We've got to smart her up. Them Cape Horn seas
Have made her paint-work like a rusty grate.
Oh, didn't them topsails make your fishhooks freeze?
A topsail don't pay heed to 'Won't you, please?'
Well, you have seen Cape Horn, my son; you've learned.
You've dipped your hand and had your fingers burned.

"And now you'll stow that folly, trying to paint.
You've had your lesson; you're a sailor now.
You come on board a female ripe to faint.
All sorts of slush you'd learned, the Lord knows how.
Cape Horn has sent you wisdom over the bow
If you've got sense to take it. You're a sailor.
My God! before you were a woman's tailor.

"So throw your paints to blazes and have done.
Words can't describe the silly things you did
Sitting before your easel in the sun,

[308]

DAUBER

With all your colours on the paint-box lid.
I blushed for you . . . and then the daubs you hid.
My God! you'll have more sense now, eh? You've quit?"
"No sir." "You've not?" "No, sir." "God give you wit.

"I thought you'd come to wisdom." Thus they talked,
While the great clipper took her bit and rushed
Like a skin-glistening stallion not yet baulked,
Till fire-bright water at her swing ports gushed;
Poising and bowing down her fore-foot crushed
Bubble on glittering bubble; on she went
The Dauber watched her, wondering what it meant.

To come, after long months, at rosy dawn,
Into the placid blue of some great bay.
Treading the quiet water like a fawn
Ere yet the morning haze was blown away.
A rose-flushed figure putting by the grey,
And anchoring there before the city smoke
Rose, or the church-bells rang, or men awoke.

And then, in the first light, to see grow clear
That long-expected haven filled with strangers—
Alive with men and women; see and hear
Its clattering market and its money-changers;
And hear the surf beat, and be free from dangers,
And watch the crinkled ocean blue with calm
Drowsing beneath the Trade, beneath the palm.

Hungry for that he worked; the hour went by,
And still the wind grew, still the clipper strode,
And now a darkness hid the western sky,

And sprays came flicking off at the wind's goad.
She stumbled now, feeling her sail a load.
The Mate gazed hard to windward, eyed his sail,
And said the Horn was going to flick her tail.

Boldly he kept it on her till she staggered,
But still the wind increased; it grew, it grew,
Darkening the sky, making the water haggard;
Full of small snow the mighty wester blew.
"More fun for little fish-hooks," sighed the crew.
They eyed the taut topgallants stiff like steel;
A second hand was ordered to the wheel.

The Captain eyed her aft, sucking his lip,
Feeling the sail too much, but yet refraining
From putting hobbles on the leaping ship,
The glad sea-shattering stallion, halter-straining,
Wing-musical, uproarious, and complaining;
But, in a gust, he cocked his finger, so:
"You'd better take them off, before they go."

All saw. They ran at once without the word
"Lee-ay! Lee-ay!" Loud rang the clewline cries;
Sam in his bunk within the half-deck heard,
Stirred in his sleep, and rubbed his drowsy eyes.
"There go the lower to'gallants." Against the skies
Rose the thin bellying strips of leaping sail.
The Dauber was the first man over the rail.

Three to a mast they ran; it was a race.
"God!" said the Mate; "that Dauber, he can go."
He watched the runners with an upturned face

DAUBER

Over the futtocks, struggling heel to toe,
Up to the topmast cross-trees into the blow
Where the three sails were leaping. "Dauber wins!"
The yards were reached, and now the race begins.

Which three will furl their sail first and come down?
Out to the yard-arm for the leech goes one,
His hair blown flagwise from a hatless crown,
His hands at work like fever to be done.
Out of the gale a fiercer fury spun.
The three sails leaped together, yanking high,
Like talons darting up to clutch the sky.

The Dauber on the fore-topgallant yard
Out at the weather yard-arm was the first
To lay his hand upon the buntline-barred
Topgallant yanking to the wester's burst;
He craned to catch the leech; his comrades cursed;
One at the buntlines, one with oaths observed,
"The eye of the outer jib-stay isn't served."

"No," said the Dauber. "No," the man replied.
They heaved, stowing the sail, not looking round,
Panting, but full of life and eager-eyed;
The gale roared at them with its iron sound.
"That's you," the Dauber said. His gasket wound
Swift round the yard, binding the sail in bands;
There came a gust, the sail leaped from his hands,

So that he saw it high above him, grey,
And there his mate was falling; quick he clutched
An arm in oilskins swiftly snatched away.

A voice said "Christ!" a quick shape stooped and touched,
Chain struck his hands, ropes shot, the sky was smutched
With vast black fires that ran, that fell, that furled,
And then he saw the mast, the small snow hurled,

The fore-topgallant yard far, far aloft,
And blankness settling on him and great pain;
And snow beneath his fingers wet and soft,
And topsail sheet-blocks shaking at the chain.
He knew it was he who had fallen; then his brain
Swirled in a circle while he watched the sky.
Infinite multitudes of snow blew by.

"I thought it was Tom who fell," his brain's voice said.
"Down on the bloody deck!" the Captain screamed.
The multitudinous little snow-flakes sped.
His pain was real enough, but all else seemed.
Si with a bucket ran, the water gleamed
Tilting upon him; others came, the Mate . . .
They knelt with eager eyes like things that wait

For other things to come. He saw them there.
"It will go on," he murmured, watching Si.
Colours and sounds seemed mixing in the air,
The pain was stunning him, and the wind went by.
"More water," said the Mate. "Here, Bosun, try.
Ask if he's got a message. Hell, he's gone!
Here, Dauber, paints." He said, "It will go on."

Not knowing his meaning rightly, but he spoke
With the intenseness of a fading soul
Whose share of Nature's fire turns to smoke,

Whose hand on Nature's wheel loses control.
The eager faces glowered red like coal.
They glowed, the great storm glowed, the sails, the mast.
"It will go on," he cried aloud, and passed.

Those from the yard came down to tell the tale.
"He almost had me off," said Tom. "He slipped.
There come one hell of a jump-like from the sail. . .
He clutched at me and almost had me pipped.
He caught my 'ris'band, but the oilskin ripped. . .
It tore clean off. Look here. I was near gone.
I made a grab to catch him; so did John.

"I caught his arm. My God! I was near done.
He almost had me over; it was near.
He hit the ropes and grabbed at every one."
"Well," said the Mate, "we cannot leave him here.
Run, Si, and get the half-deck table clear.
We'll lay him there. Catch hold there, you, and you,
He's dead, poor son; there's nothing more to do."

Night fell, and all night long the Dauber lay
Covered upon the table; all night long
The pitiless storm exulted at her prey,
Huddling the waters with her icy thong.
But to the covered shape she did no wrong.
He lay beneath the sailcloth. Bell by bell
The night wore through; the stars rose, the stars fell.

Blowing most pitiless cold out of clear sky
The wind roared all night long; and all night through
The green seas on the deck went washing by,

Flooding the half-deck; bitter hard it blew.
But little of it all the Dauber knew—
The sopping bunks, the floating chests, the wet,
The darkness, and the misery, and the sweat.

He was off duty.   So it blew all night,
And when the watches changed the men would come
Dripping within the door to strike a light
And stare upon the Dauber lying dumb,
And say, "He come a cruel thump, poor chum."
Or, "He'd a-been a fine big man;" or, "He . . .
A smart young seaman he was getting to be."

Or, "Damn it all, it's what we've all to face! . . .
I knew another fellow one time . . . ." then
Came a strange tale of death in a strange place
Out on the sea, in ships, with wandering men.
In many ways Death puts us into pen.
The reefers came down tired and looked and slept.
Below the skylight little dribbles crept

Along the painted woodwork, glistening, slow,
Following the roll and dripping, never fast,
But dripping on the quiet form below,
Like passing time talking to time long past.
And all night long "Ai, ai!" went the wind's blast,
And creaming water swished below the pale,
Unheeding body stretched beneath the sail.

At dawn they sewed him up, and at eight bells
They bore him to the gangway, wading deep,
Through the green-clutching, white-toothed water-hells

[314]

That flung his carriers over in their sweep.
They laid an old red ensign on the heap,
And all hands stood bare-headed, stooping, swaying,
Washed by the sea while the old man was praying

Out of a borrowed prayer-book. At a sign
They twitched the ensign back and tipped the grating
A creamier bubbling broke the bubbling brine.
The muffled figure tilted to the weighting;
It dwindled slowly down, slowly gyrating.
Some craned to see; it dimmed, it disappeared;
The last green milky bubble blinked and cleared.

"Mister, shake out your reefs," the Captain called.
"Out topsail reefs!" the Mate cried; then all hands
Hurried, the great sails shook, and all hands hauled,
Singing that desolate song of lonely lands,
Of how a lover came in dripping bands,
Green with the wet and cold, to tell his lover
That Death was in the sea, and all was over.

Fair came the falling wind; a seaman said
The Dauber was a Jonah; once again
The clipper held her course, showing red lead,
Shattering the sea-tops into golden rain.
The waves bowed down before her like blown grain;
Onwards she thundered, on; her voyage was short,
Before the tier's bells rang her into port.

Cheerly they rang her in, those beating bells,
The new-come beauty stately from the sea,
Whitening the blue heave of the drowsy swells,

Treading the bubbles down.   With three times three
They cheered her moving beauty in, and she
Came to her berth so noble, so superb;
Swayed like a queen, and answered to the curb.

Then in the sunset's flush they went aloft,
And unbent sails in that most lovely hour,
When the light gentles and the wind is soft,
And beauty in the heart breaks like a flower.
Working aloft they saw the mountain tower,
Snow to the peak; they heard the launch-men shout;
And bright along the bay the lights came out.

And then the night fell dark, and all night long
The pointed mountain pointed at the stars,
Frozen, alert, austere; the eagle's song
Screamed from her desolate screes and splintered scars.
On her intense crags where the air is sparse
The stars looked down; their many golden eyes
Watched her and burned, burned out, and came to rise.

Silent the finger of the summit stood,
Icy in pure, thin air, glittering with snows.
Then the sun's coming turned the peak to blood,
And in the rest-house the muleteers arose.
And all day long, where only the eagle goes,
Stones, loosened by the sun, fall; the stones falling
Fill empty gorge on gorge with echoes calling.

EXPLANATIONS OF SOME OF THE SEA TERMS USED IN THE POEM

Backstays.—Wire ropes which support the masts against lateral and after strains.

Barney's bull.—A figure in marine proverb. A jewel in marine repartee.

Bells.—Two bells (one forward, one aft) which are struck every half-hour in a certain manner to mark the passage of the watches.

Bitts.—Strong wooden structures (built round each mast) upon which running rigging is secured.

Block.—A sheaved pulley.

Boatswain.—A supernumerary or idler, generally attached to the mate's watch, and holding considerable authority over the crew.

Bouilli tin.—Any tin that contains, or has contained, preserved meat.

Bows.—The forward extremity of a ship.

Brace-blocks.—Pulleys through which the braces travel.

Braces.—Ropes by which the yards are inclined forward or aft.

Bumboat pan.—Soft bread sold by the bumboat man, a kind of sea costermonger who trades with ships in port.

Bunt.—Those cloths of a square sail which are nearest to the mast when the sail is set. The central portion of a furled square sail. The human abdomen (figuratively).

Buntlines.—Ropes which help to confine square sails to the yards in the operation of furling.

Chocks.—Wooden stands on which the boats rest.

Cleats.—Iron or wooden contrivances to which ropes may be secured.

Clew-lines.—Ropes by which the lower corners of square sails are lifted.

Clews.—The lower corners of square sails.

Clipper.—A title of honour given to ships of more than usual speed and beauty.

Coaming.—The raised rim of a hatchway; a barrier at a doorway to keep water from entering.

Courses.—The large square sails set upon the lower yards of sailing ships. The mizen course is called the "crojick."

Cringled.—Fitted with iron rings or cringles, many of which are let into sails or sail-roping for various purposes.

Crojick (or cross-jack).—A square sail set upon the lower yard of the mizen mast.

[317]

Dungarees.—Thin blue or khaki-coloured overalls made from cocoanut fibre.

Fairleads.—Rings of wood or iron by means of which running rigging is led in any direction.

Fife-rails.—Strong wooden shelves fitted with iron pins, to which ropes may be secured.

Fish-hooks.—I.e., fingers.

Foot-ropes.—Ropes on which men stand when working aloft.

Fo'c'sle.—The cabin or cabins in which the men are berthed. It is usually an iron deck-house divided through the middle into two compartments for the two watches, and fitted with wooden bunks. Sometimes it is even fitted with lockers and an iron water-tank.

Foxes.—Strands, yarns, or arrangements of yarns of rope.

Freeing-ports.—Iron doors in the ship's side which open outwards to free the decks of water.

Frap.—To wrap round with rope.

Futtock-shrouds.—Iron bars to which the topmast rigging is secured. As they project outward and upward from the masts they are difficult to clamber over.

Galley.—The ship's kitchen.

Gantline (girtline).—A rope used for the sending of sails up and down from aloft.

Gaskets.—Ropes by which the sails are secured in furling.

Half-deck.—A cabin or apartment in which the apprentices are berthed. Its situation is usually the ship's waist; but it is sometimes further aft, and occasionally it is under the poop or even right forward under the top-gallant fo'c'sle.

Halliards.—Ropes by which sails are hoisted.

Harness-room.—An office or room from which the salt meat is issued, and in which it is sometimes stored.

Hawse.—The bows or forward end of a ship.

Head.—The forward part of a ship. That upper edge of a square sail which is attached to the yard.

House-flag.—The special flag of the firm to which a ship belongs.

Idlers.—The members of the round-house mess, generally consisting of the carpenter, cook, sailmaker, boatswain, painter, etc., are known as the idlers.

EXPLANATIONS OF SOME OF THE SEA TERMS

Jack (or jackstay).—An iron bar (fitted along all yards in sailing ships) to which the head of a square sail is secured when bent.

Kites.—Light upper sails.

Leeches.—The outer edges of square sails. In furling some square sails the leech is dragged inwards till it lies level with the head upon the surface of the yard. This is done by the first man who gets upon the yard, beginning at the weather side.

Logship.—A contrivance by which a ship's speed is measured.

Lower topsail.—The second sail from the deck on square rigged masts. It is a very strong, important sail.

Marline.—Tarry line or coarse string made of rope-yarns twisted together.

Mate.—The First or Chief Mate is generally called the Mate.

Mizen-topmast-head.—The summit of the second of the three or four spars which make the complete mizen-mast.

Mudhooks.—Anchors.

Pins.—Iron or wooden bars to which running rigging is secured.

Pointing.—A kind of neat plait with which ropes are sometimes ended off or decorated.

Poop-break.—The forward end of the after superstructure.

Ratlines.—The rope steps placed across the shrouds to enable the seamen to go aloft.

Reefers.—Apprentices.

Reef-points.—Ropes by which the area of some sails may be reduced in the operation of reefing. Reef-points are securely fixed to the sails fitted with them, and when not in use their ends patter continually upon the canvas with a gentle drumming noise.

Reel.—A part of the machinery used with a logship.

Round-house.—A cabin (of all shapes except round) in which the idlers are berthed.

Royals.—Light upper square sails; the fourth, fifth, or sixth sails from the deck according to the mast's rig.

Sail-room.—A large room or compartment in which the ship's sails are stored.

"Sails."—The sailmaker is meant.

Scuttle-butt.—A cask containing fresh water.

Shackles.—Rope handles for a sea-chest.

Sheet-blocks.—Iron blocks, by means of which sails are sheeted home. In any violent wind they beat upon the mast with great rapidity and force.

Sheets.—Ropes or chains which extend the lower corners of square sails in the operation of sheeting home.

Shifting suits (of sails).—The operation of removing a ship's sails, and replacing them with others.

Shrouds.—Wire ropes of great strength, which support lateral strains on masts.

Shroud-screws.—Iron contrivances by which shrouds are hove taut.

Sidelights.—A sailing ship carries two of these between sunset and sunrise: one green, to starboard; one red, to port.

Sights.—Observations to help in the finding of a ship's position.

Skid.—A wooden contrivance on which ship's boats rest.

Skysails.—The uppermost square sails; the fifth, sixth, or seventh sails from the deck according to the mast's rig.

Slatting.—The noise made by sails flogging in the wind.

Slush.—Grease, melted fat.

South-wester.—A kind of oilskin hat. A gale from the south-west.

Spit brown.—To chew tobacco.

Square sennit.—A cunning plait which makes a four-square bar.

Staysails.—Fore and aft sails set upon the stays between the masts.

Stow.—To furl.

Strop (the, putting on).—A strop is a grument or rope ring. The two players kneel down facing each other, the strop is placed over their heads, and the men then try to pull each other over by the strength of their neck-muscles.

Swing ports.—Iron doors in the ship's side which open outwards to free the decks from water.

Tackle (pronounced "taykel").—Blocks, ropes, pulleys, etc.

Take a caulk.—To sleep upon the deck.

Topsails.—The second and third sails from the deck on the masts of a modern square-rigged ship are known as the lower and upper topsails.

Trucks.—The summits of the masts.

Upper topsail.—The third square sail from the deck on the masts of square-rigged ships.

Yards.—The steel or wooden spars (placed across masts) from which square sails are set.

THE DAFFODIL FIELDS

THE DAFFODIL FIELDS

I

Between the barren pasture and the wood
There is a patch of poultry-stricken grass,
Where, in old time, Ryemeadows' Farmhouse stood,
And human fate brought tragic things to pass.
A spring comes bubbling up there, cold as glass,
It bubbles down, crusting the leaves with lime,
Babbling the self-same song that it has sung through time.

Ducks gobble at the selvage of the brook,
But still it slips away, the cold hill-spring,
Past the Ryemeadows' lonely woodland nook
Where many a stubble gray-goose preens her wing,
On, by the woodland side.   You hear it sing
Past the lone copse where poachers set their wires,
Past the green hill once grim with sacrificial fires.

Another water joins it; then it turns,
Runs through the Ponton Wood, still turning west,
Past foxgloves, Canterbury bells, and ferns,
And many a blackbird's, many a thrush's nest;
The cattle tread it there; then, with a zest
It sparkles out, babbling its pretty chatter
Through Foxholes Farm, where it gives white-faced cattle water.

Under the road it runs, and now it slips
Past the great ploughland, babbling, drop and linn,
To the moss'd stumps of elm trees which it lips,

And blackberry-bramble-trails where eddies spin.
Then, on its left, some short-grassed fields begin,
Red-clayed and pleasant, which the young spring fills
With the never-quiet joy of dancing daffodils.

There are three fields where daffodils are found;
The grass is dotted blue-gray with their leaves;
Their nodding beauty shakes along the ground
Up to a fir-clump shutting out the eaves
Of an old farm where always the wind grieves
High in the fir boughs, moaning; people call
This farm The Roughs, but some call it the Poor Maid's Hall.

There, when the first green shoots of tender corn
Show on the plough; when the first drift of white
Stars the black branches of the spiky thorn,
And afternoons are warm and evenings light,
The shivering daffodils do take delight,
Shaking beside the brook, and grass comes green,
And blue dog-violets come and glistening celandine.

And there the pickers come, picking for town
Those dancing daffodils; all day they pick;
Hard-featured women, weather-beaten brown,
Or swarthy-red, the colour of old brick.
At noon they break their meats under the rick.
The smoke of all three farms lifts blue in air
As though man's passionate mind had never suffered there.

And sometimes as they rest an old man comes,
Shepherd or carter, to the hedgerow-side,
And looks upon their gangrel tribe, and hums,

And thinks all gone to wreck since master died;
And sighs over a passionate harvest-tide
Which Death's red sickle reaped under those hills,
There, in the quiet fields among the daffodils.

When this most tragic fate had time and place,
And human hearts and minds to show it by,
Ryemeadows' Farmhouse was in evil case:
Its master, Nicholas Gray, was like to die.
He lay in bed, watching the windy sky,
Where all the rooks were homing on slow wings,
Cawing, or blackly circling in enormous rings.

With a sick brain he watched them; then he took
Paper and pen, and wrote in straggling hand
(Like spider's legs, so much his fingers shook)
Word to the friends who held the adjoining land,
Bidding them come; no more he could command
His fingers twitching to the feebling blood;
He watched his last day's sun dip down behind the wood,

While all his life's thoughts surged about his brain:
Memories and pictures clear, and faces known—
Long dead, perhaps; he was a child again,
Treading a threshold in the dark alone.
Then back the present surged, making him moan.
He asked if Keir had come yet. "No," they said.
'Nor Occleve?" "No." He moaned: "Come soon or I'll be
    dead."

The names like live things wandered in his mind:
"Charles Occleve of The Roughs," and "Rowland Keir—
Keir of Foxholes"; but his brain was blind,

[325]

A blind old alley in the storm of the year,
Baffling the traveller life with "No way here,"
For all his lantern raised; life would not tread
Within that brain again, along those pathways red.

Soon all was dimmed but in the heaven one star.
"I'll hold to that," he said then footsteps stirred.
Down in the court a voice said, "Here they are,"
And one, "He's almost gone."   The sick man heard.
"Oh God, be quick," he moaned.   "Only one word.
Keir! Occleve! Let them come. Why don't they come?
Why stop to tell them that?—the devil strike you dumb.

"I'm neither doll nor dead; come in, come in.
Curse you, you women, quick," the sick man flamed.
"I shall be dead before I can begin.
A sick man's womaned-mad, and nursed and damed."
Death had him by the throat; his wrath was tamed.
"Come in," he fumed; "stop muttering at the door."
The friends came in; a creaking ran across the floor.

"Now, Nick, how goes it, man?" said Occleve.   "Oh,"
The dying man replied, "I am dying; past;
Mercy of God, I die, I'm going to go.
But I have much to tell you if I last.
Come near me, Occleve, Keir. I am sinking fast,
And all my kin are coming; there, look there.
All the old, long dead Grays are moving in the air.

"It is my Michael that I called you for:
My son, abroad, at school still, over sea.
See if that hag is listening at the door.

No? Shut the door; don't lock it, let it be.
No faith is kept to dying men like me.
I am dipped deep and dying, bankrupt, done;
I leave not even a farthing to my lovely son.

"Neighbours, these many years our children played,
Down in the fields together, down the brook;
Your Mary, Keir, the girl, the bonny maid,
And Occleve's Lion, always at his book;
Them and my Michael: dear, what joy they took
Picking the daffodils; such friends they've been—
My boy and Occleve's boy and Mary Keir for queen.

"I had made plans; but I am done with, I.
Give me the wine. I have to ask you this:
I can leave Michael nothing, and I die.
By all our friendship used to be and is,
Help him, old friends. Don't let my Michael miss
The schooling I've begun. Give him his chance.
He does not know I am ill; I kept him there in France.

"Saving expense; each penny counts. Oh, friends,
Help him another year; help him to take
His full diploma when the training ends,
So that my ruin won't be his. Oh, make
This sacrifice for our old friendship's sake,
And God will pay you; for I see God's hand
Pass in most marvellous ways on souls: I understand

"How just rewards are given for man's deeds
And judgment strikes the soul. The wine there, wine.
Life is the daily thing man never heeds.

It is ablaze with sign and countersign.
Michael will not forget: that son of mine
Is a rare son, my friends; he will go far.
I shall behold his course from where the blessed are."

"Why, Nick," said Occleve, "come, man. Gather hold.
Rouse up. You've given way. If times are bad,
Times must be bettering, master; so be bold;
Lift up your spirit, Nicholas, and be glad.
Michael's as much to me as my dear lad.
I'll see he takes his school." "And I," said Keir.
 "Set you no keep by that, but be at rest, my dear.

"We'll see your Michael started on the road."
"But there," said Occleve, "Nick's not going to die.
Out of the ruts, good nag, now; zook the load.
Pull up, man. Death! Death and the fiend defy.
We'll bring the farm round for you, Keir and I.
Put heart at rest and get your health." "Ah, no,"
The sick man faintly answered. "I have got to go."

Still troubled in his mind, the sick man tossed.
"Old friends," he said, "I once had hoped to see
Mary and Michael wed, but fates are crossed,
And Michael starts with nothing left by me.
Still, if he loves her, will you let it be?
So in the grave, maybe, when I am gone,
I'll know my hope fulfilled, and see the plan go on."

"I judge by hearts, not money," answered Keir.
"If Michael suits in that and suits my maid,
I promise you, let Occleve witness here

He shall be free for me to drive his trade.
Free, ay, and welcome, too. Be not afraid,
I'll stand by Michael as I hope some friend
Will stand beside my girl in case my own life end."

"And I," said Occleve; but the sick man seemed
Still ill at ease. "My friends," he said, "my friends,
Michael may come to all that I have dreamed,
But he's a wild yarn full of broken ends.
So far his life in France has made amends.
God grant he steady so; but girls and drink
Once brought him near to hell, aye, to the very brink.

"There is a running vein of wildness in him:
Wildness and looseness both, which vices make
That woman's task a hard one who would win him:
His life depends upon the course you take.
He is a fiery-mettled colt to break,
And one to curb, one to be curbed, remember."
The dying voice died down, the fire left the ember.

But once again it flamed. "Ah me," he cried;
'Our secret sins take body in our sons,
To haunt our age with what we put aside.
I was a devil for the women once.
He is as I was. Beauty like the sun's;
Within, all water; minded like the moon.
Go now. I sinned. I die. I shall be punished soon."

The two friends tiptoed to the room below.
There, till the woman came to them, they told
Of brave adventures in the long ago,

Ere Nick and they had thought of growing old;
Snipe-shooting in the marshlands in the cold,
Old soldiering days as yeomen, days at fairs,
Days that had sent Nick tired to those self-same chairs.

They vowed to pay the schooling for his son.
They talked of Michael, testing men's report,
How the young student was a lively one,
Handsome and passionate both, and fond of sport,
Eager for fun, quick-witted in retort.
The girls' hearts quick to see him cocking by,
Young April on a blood horse, with a roving eye.

And, as they talked about the lad, Keir asked
If Occleve's son had not, at one time, been
Heartsick for Mary, though with passion masked.
"Ay," Occleve said: "Time was.   At seventeen.
It took him hard, it ran his ribs all lean,
All of a summer; but it passed, it died.
Her fancying Michael better touched my Lion's pride."

Mice flickered from the wainscot to the press,
Nibbling at crumbs, rattling to shelter, squeaking.
Each ticking in the clock's womb made life less;
Oil slowly dropped from where the lamp was leaking.
At times the old nurse set the staircase creaking,
Harked to the sleeper's breath, made sure, returned,
Answered the questioning eyes, then wept. The great stars
    burned.

"Listen," said Occleve, "listen, Rowland. Hark."
"It's Mary, come with Lion," answered Keir:
"They said they'd come together after dark."

He went to door and called "Come in, my dear."
The burning wood log blazed with sudden cheer,
So that a glowing lighted all the room.
His daughter Mary entered from the outer gloom.

The wind had brought the blood into her cheek,
Heightening her beauty, but her great grey eyes
Were troubled with a fear she could not speak.
Firm, scarlet lips she had, not made for lies.
Gentle she seemed, pure-natured, thoughtful, wise,
And when she asked what turn the sickness took,
Her voice's passing pureness on a low note shook.

Young Lion Occleve entered at her side,
A well-built, clever man, unduly grave,
One whose repute already travelled wide
For skill in breeding beasts. His features gave
Promise of brilliant mind, far-seeing, brave,
One who would travel far. His manly grace
Grew wistful when his eyes were turned on Mary's face.

"Tell me," said Mary, "what did doctor say?
How ill is he? What chance of life has he?
The cowman said he couldn't last the day,
And only yesterday he joked with me."
"We must be meek," the nurse said; "such things be."
"There's little hope," said Keir; "he's dying, sinking."
"Dying without his son," the young girl's heart was thinking.

"Does Michael know?" she asked. "Has he been called?"
A slow confusion reddened on the faces,
As when one light neglect leaves friends appalled.

[331]

"No time to think," said nurse, "in such like cases."
Old Occleve stooped and fumbled with his laces.
"Let be," he said; "there's always time for sorrow.
He could not come in time; he shall be called to-morrow."

"There is a chance," she cried, "there always is.
Poor Mr. Gray might rally, might live on.
Oh, I must telegraph to tell him this.
Would it were day still and the message gone."
She rose, her breath came fast, her grey eyes shone.
She said, "Come Lion; see me through the wood.
Michael must know." Keir sighed. "Girl, it will do no good.

"Our friend is on the brink and almost passed."
"All the more need," she said, "for word to go;
Michael could well arrive before the last.
He'd see his father's face at least. I know
The office may be closed; but even so,
Father, I must. Come, Lion." Out they went,
Into the roaring woodland where the saplings bent.

Like breakers of the sea the leafless branches
Swished, bowing down, rolling like water, roaring
Like the sea's welcome when the clipper launches
And full affronted tideways call to warring.
Daffodils glimmered underfoot, the flooring
Of the earthy woodland smelt like torn-up moss;
Stones in the path showed white, and rabbits ran across.

They climbed the rise and struck into the ride,
Talking of death, while Lion, sick at heart,
Thought of the woman walking at his side,

And as he talked his spirit stood apart,
Old passion for her made his being smart,
Rankling within. Her thought for Michael ran
Like glory and like poison through his inner man.

"This will break Michael's heart," he said at length.
"Poor Michael," she replied; "they wasted hours.
He loved his father so. God give him strength.
This is a cruel thing this life of ours."
The windy woodland glimmered with shut flowers,
White wood anemones that the wind blew down.
The valley opened wide beyond the starry town.

"Ten," clanged out of the belfry. Lion stayed
One hand upon a many-carven bole.
"Mary," he said. "Dear, my beloved maid,
I love you, dear one, from my very soul."
Her beauty in the dusk destroyed control.
"Mary, my dear, I've loved you all these years."
"Oh, Lion, no," she murmured, choking back her tears.

"I love you," he repeated. "Five years since
This thing began between us: every day
Oh sweet, the thought of you has made me wince;
The thought of you, my sweet, the look, the way.
It's only you, whether I work or pray,
You and the hope of you, sweet you, dear you.
I never spoke before; now it has broken through.

"Oh, my belovéd, can you care for me?"
She shook her head. "O, hush, oh, Lion dear,
Don't speak of love, for it can never be

[333]

Between us two, never, however near.
Come on, my friend, we must not linger here."
White to the lips she spoke; he saw her face
White in the darkness by him in the windy place.

"Mary, in time you could, perhaps," he pleaded.
"No," she replied, "no, Lion; never, no."
Over the stars the boughs burst and receded.
The nobleness of Love comes in Love's woe.
"God bless you then, belovéd, let us go.
Come on," he said, "and if I gave you pain,
Forget it, dear; be sure I never will again."

They stepped together down the ride, their feet
Slipped on loose stones. Little was said; his fate,
Staked on a kingly cast, had met defeat.
Nothing remained but to endure and wait.
She was still wonderful, and life still great.
Great in that bitter instant side by side,
Hallowed by thoughts of death there in the blinded ride.

He heard her breathing by him, saw her face
Dim, looking straight ahead; her feet by his
Kept time beside him, giving life a grace;
Night made the moment full of mysteries.
"You are beautiful," he thought; "and life is this:
Walking a windy night while men are dying,
To cry for one to come, and none to heed our crying."

"Mary," he said, "are you in love with him,
With Michael? Tell me. We are friends, we three."
They paused to face each other in the dim.

"Tell me," he urged. "Yes, Lion," answered she;
"I love him, but he does not care for me.
I trust your generous mind, dear; now you know,
You, who have been my brother, how our fortunes go.

"Now come; the message waits." The heavens cleared,
Cleared, and were starry as they trod the ride.
Chequered by tossing boughs the moon appeared;
A whistling reached them from the Hall House side;
Climbing, the whistler came. A brown owl cried.
The whistler paused to answer, sending far
That haunting, hunting note. The echoes laughed Aha!

Something about the calling made them start.
Again the owl note laughed; the ringing cry
Made the blood quicken within Mary's heart.
Like a dead leaf a brown owl floated by.
"Michael?" said Lion. "Hush." An owl's reply
Came down the wind; they waited; then the man,
Content, resumed his walk, a merry song began.

"Michael," they cried together. "Michael, you?"
"Who calls?" the singer answered. "Where away?
Is that you, Mary?" Then with glad halloo
The singer ran to meet them on the way.
It was their Michael; in the moonlight grey,
They made warm welcome; under tossing boughs,
They met and told the fate darkening Ryemeadows' House.

As they returned at speed their comrade spoke
Strangely and lightly of his coming home,
Saying that leaving France had been a joke,

But that events now proved him wise to come.
Down the steep 'scarpment to the house they clomb,
And Michael faltered in his pace; they heard
How dumb rebellion in the much-wronged cattle stirred.

And as they came, high, from the sick man's room,
Old Gray burst out a-singing of the light
Streaming upon him from the outer gloom,
As his eyes dying gave him mental sight.
"Triumphing swords," he carolled, "in the bright;
Oh fire, Oh beauty fire," and fell back dead.
Occleve took Michael up to kneel beside the bed.

So the night passed; the noisy wind went down;
The half-burnt moon her starry trackway rode.
Then the first fire was lighted in the town,
And the first carter stacked his early load.
Upon the farm's drawn blinds the morning glowed;
And down the valley, with little clucks and trills,
The dancing waters danced by dancing daffodils.

II

They buried Gray; his gear was sold; his farm
Passed to another tenant.   Thus men go;
The dropped sword passes to another arm,
And different waters in the river flow.
His two old faithful friends let Michael know
His father's ruin and their promise.   Keir
Brought him to stay at Foxholes till a path was clear.

There, when the sale was over, all three met
To talk about the future, and to find
Upon what project Michael's heart was set.

Gentle the two old men were, thoughtful, kind.
They urged the youth to speak his inmost mind,
For they would compass what he chose; they told
How he might end his training; they would find the gold.

"Thanks, but I cannot," Michael said. He smiled.
"Cannot. They've kicked me out. I've been expelled;
Kicked out for good and all for being wild.
They stopped our evening leave, and I rebelled.
I am a gentle soul until compelled,
And then I put my ears back. The old fool
Said that my longer presence might inflame the school.

"And I am glad, for I have had my fill
Of farming by the book with those old fools,
Exhausted talkatives whose blood is still,
Who strive to bind a living man with rules.
This fettered kind of life, these laws, these schools,
These codes, these checks, what are they but the clogs
Made by collected sheep to mortify the dogs?

"And I have had enough of them; and now
I make an end of them. I want to go
Somewhere where man has never used a plough,
Nor ever read a book; where clean winds blow,
And passionate blood is not its owner's foe,
And land is for the asking for it. There
Man can create a life and have the open air.

"The River Plate's the country. There, I know,
A man like me can thrive. There, on the range,
The cattle pass like tides; they ebb and flow,

And life is changeless in unending change,
And one can ride all day, and all day strange,
Strange, never trodden, fenceless, waiting there,
To feed unending cattle for the men who dare.

"There I should have a chance; this land's too old."
Old Occleve grunted at the young man's mood;
Keir, who was losing money, thought him bold,
And thought the scheme for emigration good.
He said that, if he wished to go, he should.
South to the pampas, there to learn the trade.
Old Occleve thought it mad, but no objection made.

So it was settled that the lad should start,
A place was found for him, a berth was taken;
And Michael's beauty plucked at Mary's heart,
And now the fabric of their lives was shaken:
For now the hour's nearness made love waken
In Michael's heart for Mary. Now Time's guile
Granted her passionate prayer, nor let her see his smile.

Granted his greatest gifts; a night time came
When the two walking down the water learned
That life till then had only been a name;
Love had unsealed their spirits: they discerned.
Mutely, at moth time there, their spirits yearned.
"I shall be gone three years, dear soul," he said.
"Dear, will you wait for me?" "I will," replied the maid.

So troth was pledged between them. Keir received
Michael as Mary's suitor, feeling sure
That the lad's fortunes would be soon retrieved,

Having a woman's promise as a lure.
The three years' wait would teach them to endure.
He bade them love and prosper and be glad.
And fast the day drew near that was to take the lad.

Cowslips had come along the bubbling brook,
Cowslips and oxlips rare, and in the wood
The many-blossomed stalks of bluebells shook;
The outward beauty fed their mental mood.
Thought of the parting stabbed her as he wooed,
Walking the brook with her, and day by day,
The precious fortnight's grace dropped, wasted, slipped away.

Till only one clear day remained to her:
One whole clear, precious day, before he sailed.
Some forty hours, no more, to minister
To months of bleakness before which she quailed.
Mist rose along the brook; the corncrake railed;
Dim red the sunset burned. He bade her come
Into the wood with him; they went, the night came dumb.

Still as high June, the very water's noise
Seemed but a breathing of the earth; the flowers
Stood in the dim like souls without a voice.
The wood's conspiracy of occult powers
Drew all about them, and for hours on hours
No murmur shook the oaks, the stars did house
Their lights like lamps upon those never-moving boughs.

Under their feet the woodland sloped away
Down to the valley, where the farmhouse lights
Were sparks in the expanse the moon made grey.

June's very breast was bare this night of nights.
Moths blundered up against them, greys and whites
Moved on the darkness where the moths were out,
Nosing for sticky sweet with trembling uncurled snout.

But all this beauty was but music played,
While the high pageant of their hearts prepared.
A spirit thrilled between them, man to maid,
Mind flowed in mind, the inner heart was bared,
They needed not to tell how much each cared;
All the soul's strength was at the other's soul.
Flesh was away awhile, a glory made them whole.

Nothing was said by them; they understood,
They searched each other's eyes without a sound.
Alone with moonlight in the heart of the wood,
Knowing the stars and all the soul of the ground.
"Mary," he murmured. "Come." His arms went round,
A white moth glimmered by, the woods were hushed;
The rose at Mary's bosom dropped its petals, crushed.

No word profaned the peace of that glad giving,
But the warm dimness of the night stood still,
Drawing all beauty to the point of living,
There in the beech-tree's shadow on the hill.
Spirit to spirit murmured; mingling will
Made them one being; Time's decaying thought
Fell from them like a rag; it was the soul they sought.

The moonlight found an opening in the boughs;
It entered in, it filled that sacred place
With consecration on the throbbing brows;

It came with benediction and with grace.
A whispering came from face to yearning face:
"Beloved, will you wait for me?" "My own."
"I shall be gone three years, you will be left alone;

"You'll trust and wait for me?" "Yes, yes," she sighed;
She would wait any term of years, all time—
So faithful to first love these souls abide,
Carrying a man's soul with them as they climb.
Life was all flower to them; the church bells' chime
Rang out the burning hour ere they had sealed
Love's charter there below the June sky's starry field.

Sweetly the church bells' music reached the wood,
Chiming an old slow tune of some old hymn,
Calling them back to life from where they stood
Under the moonlit beech-tree grey and dim.
"Mary," he murmured; pressing close to him,
Her kiss came on the gift he gave her there,
A silken scarf that bore her name worked in his hair.

But still the two affixed their hands and seals
To a life compact witnessed by the sky,
Where the great planets drove their glittering wheels,
Bringing conflicting fate, making men die.
They loved, and she would wait, and he would try.
"Oh, beauty of my love," "My lovely man."
So beauty made them noble for their little span.

Time cannot pause, however dear the wooer;
The moon declined, the sunrise came, the hours,
Left to the lovers, dwindled swiftly fewer,

Even as the seeds from dandelion-flowers
Blow, one by one, until the bare stalk cowers,
And the June grass grows over; even so
Daffodil-picker Time took from their lives the glow,

Stole their last walk along the three green fields,
Their latest hour together; he took, he stole
The white contentment that a true love yields;
He took the triumph out of Mary's soul.
Now she must lie awake and blow the coal
Of sorrow of heart.   The parting hour came;
They kissed their last good-bye, murmuring the other's name.

Then the flag waved, the engine snorted, then
Slowly the couplings tautened, and the train
Moved, bearing off from her her man of men;
She looked towards its going blind with pain.
Her father turned and drove her home again.
It was a different home.   Awhile she tried
To cook the dinner there, but flung her down and cried.

Then in the dusk she wandered down the brook,
Treading again the trackway trod of old,
When she could hold her loved one in a look.
The night was all unlike those nights of gold.
Michael was gone, and all the April old,
Withered and hidden.   Life was full of ills;
She flung her down and cried i' the withered daffodils.

III

The steaming river loitered like old blood
On which the tugboat bearing Michael beat,
Past whitened horse bones sticking in the mud.

THE DAFFODIL FIELDS

The reed stems looked like metal in the heat.
Then the banks fell away, and there were neat,
Red herds of sullen cattle drifting slow.
A fish leaped, making rings, making the dead blood flow.

Wormed hard-wood piles were driv'n in the river bank,
The steamer threshed alongside with sick screws
Churning the mud below her till its tank;
Big gassy butcher-bubbles burst on the ooze.
There Michael went ashore; as glad to lose
One not a native there, the Gauchos flung
His broken gear ashore, one waved, a bell was rung.

The bowfast was cast off, the screw revolved,
Making a bloodier bubbling; rattling rope
Fell to the hatch, the engine's tune resolved
Into its steadier beat of rise and slope;
The steamer went her way; and Michael's hope
Died as she lessened; he was there alone.
The lowing of the cattle made a gradual moan.

He thought of Mary, but the thought was dim;
That was another life, lived long before.
His mind was in new worlds which altered him.
The startling present left no room for more.
The sullen river lipped, the sky, the shore
Were vaster than of old, and lonely, lonely.
Sky and low hills of grass and moaning cattle only.

But for a hut bestrewn with skulls of beeves,
Round which the flies danced, where an Indian girl
Bleared at him from her eyes' ophthalmic eaves,

Grinning a welcome; with a throaty skirl,
She offered him herself; but he, the churl,
Stared till she thought him fool; she turned, she sat,
Scratched in her short, black hair, chewed a cigar-end, spat.

Up, on the rise, the cattle bunched; the bulls
Drew to the front with menace, pawing bold,
Snatching the grass-roots out with sudden pulls,
The distant cattle raised their heads; the wold
Grew dusty at the top; a waggon rolled,
Drawn by a bickering team of mules whose eyes
Were yellow like their teeth and bared and full of vice.

Down to the jetty came the jingling team,
An Irish cowboy driving, while a Greek
Beside him urged the mules with blow and scream.
They cheered the Indian girl and stopped to speak.
Then lifting her aloft they kissed her cheek,
Calling to Michael to be quick aboard,
Or they (they said) would fall from virtue, by the Lord.

So Michael climbed aboard, and all day long
He drove the cattle range, rise after rise,
Dotted with limber shorthorns grazing strong,
Cropping sweet-tasted pasture, switching flies;
Dull trouble brooded in their smoky eyes.
Some horsemen watched them. As the sun went down,
The waggon reached the estancia builded like a town.

With wide corráles where the horses squealed,
Biting and lashing out; some half-wild hounds
Gnawed at the cowbones littered on the field,

Or made the stallions stretch their picket bounds.
Some hides were drying; horsemen came from rounds,
Unsaddled stiff, and turned their mounts to feed,
And then brewed bitter drink and sucked it through a reed.

The Irishman removed his pipe and spoke:
"You take a fool's advice," he said. "Return.
Go back where you belong before you're broke;
You'll spoil more clothes at this job than you'll earn;
It's living death, and when you die you'll burn:
Body and soul it takes you. Quit it. No?
Don't say I never told you, then. Amigos. Ho.

"Here comes a Gringo; make him pay his shot.
Pay up your footing, Michael; rum's the word,
It suits my genius, and I need a lot."
So the great cauldron full was mixed and stirred.
And all night long the startled cattle heard
Shouting and shooting, and the moon beheld
Mobs of dim, struggling men, who fired guns and yelled

That they were Abel Brown just come to town,
Michael among them. By a bonfire some
Betted on red and black for money down,
Snatching their clinking winnings, eager, dumb.
Some danced unclad, rubbing their heads with rum.
The grey dawn, bringing beauty to the skies,
Saw Michael stretched among them, far too drunk to rise.

His footing paid, he joined the living-shed,
Lined with rude bunks and set with trestles: there
He, like the other ranchers, slept and fed,

Save when the staff encamped in open air,
Rounding the herd for branding. Rude and bare
That barrack was; men littered it about
With saddles, blankets blue, old headstalls, many a clout

Torn off to wipe a knife or clean a gun,
Tin dishes, sailors' hookpots, all the mess
Made where the outdoor work is never done
And every cleaning makes the sleeping less.
Men came from work too tired to undress,
And slept all standing like the trooper's horse;
Then with the sun they rose to ride the burning course,

Whacking the shipment cattle into pen,
Where, in the dust, among the stink of burning,
The half-mad heifers bolted from the men,
And tossing horns arose and hoofs were churning,
A lover there had little time for yearning;
But all day long, cursing the flies and heat,
Michael was handling steers on horseback till his feet

Gave on dismounting. All day long he rode,
Then, when the darkness came, his mates and he
Entered dog-tired to the rude abode
And ate their meat and sucked their bitter tea,
And rolled themselves in rugs and slept. The sea
Could not make men more drowsy; like the dead,
They lay under the lamp while the mosquitos fed.

There was no time to think of Mary, none;
For when the work relaxed, the time for thought
Was broken up by men demanding fun:

Cards, or a well-kept ring while someone fought,
Or songs and dancing; or a case was bought
Of white Brazilian rum, and songs and cheers
And shots and oaths rang loud upon the twitching ears

Of the hobbled horses hopping to their feed.
So violent images displaced the rose
In Michael's spirit: soon he took the lead;
None was more apt than he for games or blows.
Even as the battle-seeking bantam crows,
So crowed the cockerel of his mind to feel
Life's bonds removed and blood quick in him toe to heel.

But sometimes when her letters came to him,
Full of wise tenderness and maiden mind,
He felt that he had let his clearness dim;
The riot with the cowboys seemed unkind
To that far faithful heart; he could not find
Peace in the thought of her; he found no spur
To instant upright action in his love for her.

She faded to the memory of a kiss,
There in the rough life among foreign faces;
Love cannot live where leisure never is;
He could not write to her from savage places,
Where drunken mates were betting on the aces,
And rum went round and smutty songs were lifted.
He would not raise her banner against that; he drifted,

Ceasing, in time, to write, ceasing to think,
But happy in the wild life to the bone;
The riding in vast space, the songs, the drink,

Some careless heart beside him like his own,
The racing and the fights, the ease unknown
In older, soberer lands; his young blood thrilled.
The pampas seemed his own, his cup of joy was filled.

And one day, riding far after strayed horses,
He rode beyond the ranges to a land
Broken and made most green by watercourses,
Which served as strayline to the neighbouring brand.
A house stood near the brook; he stayed his hand,
Seeing a woman there, whose great eyes burned,
So that he could not choose but follow when she turned.

After that day he often rode to see
That woman at the peach farm near the brook,
And passionate love between them came to be
Ere many days. Their fill of love they took;
And even as the blank leaves of a book
The days went over Mary, day by day,
Blank as the last, was turned, endured, passed, turned away.

Spring came again greening the hawthorn buds;
The shaking flowers, new-blossomed, seemed the same,
And April put her riot in young bloods;
The jays flapped in the larch clump like blue flame.
She did not care; his letter never came.
Silent she went, nursing the grief that kills,
And Lion watched her pass among the daffodils.

IV

Time passed, but still no letter came; she ceased,
Almost, to hope, but never to expect.
The June moon came which had beheld love's feast,

Then waned, like it; the meadow-grass was flecked
With moon-daisies, which died; little she recked
Of change in outward things, she did not change;
Her heart still knew one star, one hope, it did not range,

Like to the watery hearts of tidal men,
Swayed by all moons of beauty; she was firm,
When most convinced of misery firmest then.
She held a light not subject to the worm.
The pageant of the summer ran its term,
The last stack came to staddle from the wain;
The snow fell, the snow thawed, the year began again.

With the wet glistening gold of celandines,
And snowdrops pushing from the withered grass,
Before the bud upon the hawthorn greens,
Or blackbirds go to building; but, alas!
No spring within her bosom came to pass.
"You're going like a ghost," her father said.
"Now put him out of mind, and be my prudent maid."

It was an April morning brisk with wind,
She wandered out along the brook sick-hearted,
Picking the daffodils where the water dinned,
While overhead the first-come swallow darted.
There, at the place where all the passion started,
Where love first knocked about her maiden heart,
Young Lion Occleve hailed her, calling her apart

To see his tulips at the Roughs, and take
A spray of flowering currant; so she went.
It is a bitter moment, when hearts ache,

To see the loved unhappy; his intent
Was but to try comfort her; he meant
To show her that he knew her heart's despair,
And that his own heart bled to see her wretched there.

So, as they talked, he asked her, had she heard
From Michael lately? No, she had not; she
Had been a great while now, without a word.
"No news is always good news," answered he.
"You know," he said, "how much you mean to me;
You've always been the queen. Oh, if I could
Do anything to help, my dear, you know I would."

"Nothing," she said, much touched. "But you believe—
You still believe in him?" "Why, yes," he said.
Lie though it was he did not dare deceive
The all too cruel faith within the maid.
"That ranching is a wild and lonely trade,
Far from all posts; it may be hard to send;
All puzzling things like this prove simple in the end.

"We should have heard if he were ill or dead.
Keep a good heart. Now come"; he led the way
Beyond the barton to the calving-shed,
Where, on a strawy litter topped with hay,
A double-pedigree prize bull-calf lay.
"Near three weeks old," he said, "the Wrekin's pet;
Come up, now, son, come up; you haven't seen him yet.

"We have done well," he added, "with the stock,
But this one, if he lives, will make a name."
The bull-calf gambolled with his tail acock,

[350]

Then shyly nosed towards them, scared but tame;
His troublous eyes were sulky with blue flame.
Softly he tip-toed, shying at a touch;
He nosed, his breath came sweet, his pale tongue curled to clutch.

They rubbed his head, and Mary went her way,
Counting the dreary time, the dreary beat
Of dreary minutes dragging through the day;
Time crawled across her life with leaden feet;
There still remained a year before her sweet
Would come to claim her; surely he would come;
Meanwhile there was the year, her weakening father, home.

Home with its deadly round, with all its setting,
Things, rooms, and fields and flowers to sting, to burn
With memories of the love time past forgetting
Ere absence made her very being yearn.
"My love, be quick," she moaned, "return, return;
Come when the three years end, oh, my dear soul,
It's bitter, wanting you." The lonely nights took toll,

Putting a sadness where the beauty was,
Taking a lustre from the hair; the days
Saw each a sadder image in the glass.
And when December came, fouling the ways,
And ashless beech-logs made a Christmas blaze,
Some talk of Michael came; a rumour ran,
Someone had called him "wild" to some returning man,

Who, travelling through that cattle-range, had heard
Nothing more sure than this; but this he told
At second-hand upon a cowboy's word.

It struck on Mary's heart and turned her cold.
That winter was an age which made her old.
"But soon," she thought, "soon the third year will end;
March, April, May, and June, then I shall see my friend.

"He promised he would come; he will not fail.
Oh, Michael, my beloved man, come soon;
Stay not to make a home for me, but sail.
Love and the hour will put the world in tune.
You in my life for always is the boon
I ask from life—we two, together, lovers."
So leaden time went by who eats things and discovers.

Then, in the winds of March, her father rode,
Hunting the Welland country on Black Ned;
The tenor cry gave tongue past Clencher's Lode,
And on he galloped, giving the nag his head;
Then, at the brook, he fell, was picked up dead.
Hounds were whipped off; men muttered with one breath,
"We knew that hard-mouthed brute would some day be his
    death."

They bore his body on a hurdle home;
Then came the burial, then the sadder day
When the peaked lawyer entered like a gnome,
With word to quit and lists of debts to pay.
There was a sale; the Foxholes passed away
To strangers, who discussed the points of cows,
Where love had put such glory on the lovers' brows.

Kind Lion Occleve helped the maid's affairs.
Her sorrow brought him much beside her; he
Caused her to settle, having stilled her cares,

THE DAFFODIL FIELDS

In the long cottage under Spital Gree.
He had no hope that she would love him; she
Still waited for her lover, but her eyes
Thanked Lion to the soul; he made the look suffice.

By this the yearling bull-calf had so grown
That all men talked of him; mighty he grew,
Huge-shouldered, scaled above a hundred stone,
With deep chest many-wrinkled with great thew,
Plain-loined and playful-eyed; the Occleves knew
That he surpassed his pasture; breeders came
From far to see this bull; he brought the Occleves fame.

Till a meat-breeding rancher on the plains
Where Michael wasted, sent to buy the beast,
Meaning to cross his cows with heavier strains
Until his yield of meat and bone increased.
He paid a mighty price; the yearling ceased
To be the wonder of the countryside.
He sailed in Lion's charge, south, to the Plate's red tide.

There Lion landed with the bull, and there
The great beast raised his head and bellowed loud,
Challenging that expanse and that new air;
Trembling, but full of wrath and thunder-browed,
Far from the daffodil fields and friends, but proud,
His wild eye kindled at the great expanse.
Two scraps of Shropshire life they stood there; their advance

Was slow along the well-grassed cattle land,
But at the last an end was made; the brute
Ate his last bread crust from his master's hand,

And snuffed the foreign herd and stamped his foot;
Steers on the swelling ranges gave salute.
The great bull bellowed back and Lion turned;
His task was now to find where Michael lived; he learned

The farm's direction, and with heavy mind,
Thinking of Mary and her sorrow, rode,
Leaving the offspring of his fields behind.
A last time in his ears the great bull lowed.
Then, shaking up his horse, the young man glowed
To see the unfenced pampas opening out
Grass that makes old earth sing and all the valleys shout.

At sunset on the second day he came
To that white cabin in the peach-tree plot
Where Michael lived; they met, the Shropshire name
Rang trebly dear in that outlandish spot.
Old memories swam up dear, old joys forgot,
Old friends were real again; but Mary's woe
Came into Lion's mind, and Michael vexed him so,

Talking with careless freshness, side by side
With that dark Spanish beauty who had won,
As though no heart-broke woman, heavy-eyed,
Mourned for him over sea, as though the sun
Shone but to light his steps to love and fun,
While she, that golden and beloved soul,
Worth ten of him, lay wasting like an unlit coal.

So supper passed; the meat in Lion's gorge
Stuck at the last, he could not bide that face.
The idle laughter on it plied the forge

Where hate was smithying tools; the jokes, the place,
Wrought him to wrath; he could not stay for grace.
The tin mug full of red wine spilled and fell.
He kicked his stool aside with "Michael, this is hell.

"Come out into the night and talk to me."
The young man lit a cigarette and followed;
The stars seemed trembling at a brink to see;
A little ghostly white-owl stooped and holloed.
Beside the stake-fence Lion stopped and swallowed,
While all the wrath within him made him grey.
Michael stood still and smoked, and flicked his ash away.

"Well, Lion," Michael said, "men make mistakes,
And then regret them; and an early flame
Is frequently the worst mistakes man makes.
I did not seek this passion, but it came.
Love happens so in life. Well? Who's to blame?
You'll say I've broken Mary's heart; the heart
Is not the whole of life, but an inferior part,

"Useful for some few years and then a curse.
Nerves should be stronger. You have come to say
The three-year term is up; so much the worse.
I cannot meet the bill; I cannot pay.
I would not if I could. Men change. To-day
I know that that first choice, however sweet,
Was wrong and a mistake; it would have meant defeat,

"Ruin and misery to us both. Let be.
You say I should have told her this? Perhaps.
You try to make a loving woman see

That the warm link which holds you to her snaps.
Neglect is deadlier than the thunder-claps.
Yet she is bright and I am water. Well,
I did not make myself; this life is often hell.

"Judge if you must, but understand it first.
We are old friends, and townsmen, Shropshire born,
Under the Wrekin. You believe the worst.
You have no knowledge how the heart is torn,
Trying for duty up against the thorn.
Now say I've broken Mary's heart: begin.
Break hers, or hers and mine, which were the greater sin?"

"Michael," said Lion, "I have heard you. Now
Listen to me. Three years ago you made
With a most noble soul a certain vow.
Now you reject it, saying that you played.
She did not think so, Michael, she has stayed,
Eating her heart out for a line, a word,
News that you were not dead; news that she never heard.

"Not once, after the first. She has held firm
To what you counted pastime; she has wept
Life, day by weary day throughout the term,
While her heart sickened, and the clock-hand crept.
While you, you with your woman here, have kept
Holiday, feasting; you are fat; you smile.
You have had love and laughter all the ghastly while.

"I shall be back in England six weeks hence,
Standing with your poor Mary face to face;
Far from a pleasant moment, but intense.

THE DAFFODIL FIELDS

I shall be asked to tell her of this place.
And she will eye me hard and hope for grace,
Some little crumb of comfort while I tell;
And every word will burn like a red spark from hell,

"That you have done with her, that you are living
Here with another woman; that you care
Nought for the pain you've given and are giving;
That all your lover's vows were empty air.
This I must tell: thus I shall burn her bare,
Burn out all hope, all comfort, every crumb,
End it, and watch her whiten, hopeless, tearless, dumb.

"Or do I judge you wrongly?" He was still.
The cigarette-end glowed and dimmed with ash;
A preying night bird whimpered on the hill.
Michael said "Ah!" and fingered with his sash,
Then stilled. The night was still; there came no flash
Of sudden passion bursting. All was still;
A lonely water gurgled like a whip-poor-will.

"Now I must go," said Lion; "where's the horse?"
"There," said his friend; "I'll set you on your way."
They caught and rode, both silent, while remorse
Worked in each heart, though neither would betray
What he was feeling, and the moon came grey,
Then burned into an opal white and great,
Silvering the downs of grass where these two travelled late,

Thinking of English fields which that moon saw,
Fields full of quiet beauty lying hushed
At midnight in the moment full of awe,

When the red fox comes creeping, dewy-brushed.
But neither spoke; they rode; the horses rushed,
Scattering the great clods skywards with such thrills
As colts in April feel there in the daffodils.

V

The river brimming full was silvered over
By moonlight at the ford; the river bank
Smelt of bruised clote buds and of yellow clover.
Nosing the gleaming dark the horses drank,
Drooping and dripping as the reins fell lank;
The men drooped too; the stars in heaven drooped;
Rank after hurrying rank the silver water trooped

In ceaseless bright procession past the shallows,
Talking its quick inconsequence. The friends,
Warmed by the gallop on the unfenced fallows,
Felt it a kindlier thing to make amends.
"A jolly burst," said Michael; "here it ends.
Your way lies straight beyond the water. There.
Watch for the lights, and keep those two stars as they bear."

Something august was quick in all that sky,
Wheeling in multitudinous march with fire;
The falling of the wind brought it more nigh,
They felt the earth take solace and respire;
The horses shifted foothold in the mire,
Splashing and making eddies. Lion spoke:
"Do you remember riding past the haunted oak

"That Christmas Eve, when all the bells were ringing,
So that we picked out seven churches' bells,
Ringing the night, and people carol-singing?

It hummed and died away and rose in swells
Like a sea breaking. We have been through hells
Since then, we two, and now this being here
Brings all that Christmas back, and makes it strangely near."

"Yes," Michael answered, "they were happy times,
Riding beyond there; but a man needs a change;
I know what they connote, those Christmas chimes,
Fudge in the heart, and pudding in the grange.
It stifles me all that; I need the range,
Like this before us, open to the sky;
There every wing is clipped, but here a man can fly."

"Ah," said his friend, "man only flies in youth,
A few short years at most, until he finds
That even quiet is a form of truth,
And all the rest a coloured rag that blinds.
Life offers nothing but contented minds.
Some day you'll know it, Michael. I am grieved
That Mary's heart will pay until I am believed."

There was a silence while the water dripped
From the raised muzzles champing on the steel.
Flogging the crannied banks the water lipped.
Night up above them turned her starry wheel;
And each man feared to let the other feel
How much he felt; they fenced; they put up bars.
The moon made heaven pale among the withering stars.

"Michael," said Lion, "why should we two part?
Ride on with me; or shall we both return,
Make preparation, and to-morrow start,

And travel home together? You would learn
How much the people long to see you; turn.
We will ride back and say good-bye, and then
Sail, and see home again, and see the Shropshire men,

"And see the old Shropshire mountain and the fair,
Full of drunk Welshmen bringing mountain ewes;
And partridge shooting would be starting there."
Michael hung down his head and seemed to choose.
The horses churned fresh footing in the ooze.
Then Michael asked if Tom were still alive,
Old Tom, who fought the Welshman under Upton Drive,

For nineteen rounds, on grass, with the bare hands?
"Shaky," said Lion, "living still, but weak;
Almost past speaking, but he understands."
"And old Shon Shones we teased so with the leek?"
"Dead." "When?" "December." Michael did not speak,
But muttered "Old Jones dead." A minute passed.
"What came to little Sue, his girl?" he said at last.

"Got into trouble with a man and died;
Her sister keeps the child." His hearer stirred.
"Dead, too? She was a pretty girl," he sighed,
"A graceful pretty creature, like a bird.
What is the child?" "A boy. Her sister heard
Too late to help; poor Susan died; the man
None knew who he could be, but many rumours ran."

"Ah," Michael said. The horses tossed their heads;
A little wind arising struck in chill;
"Time," he began, "that we were in our beds."

THE DAFFODIL FIELDS

A distant heifer challenged from the hill,
Scraped at the earth with 's forefoot and was still.
"Come with me," Lion pleaded. Michael grinned;
He turned his splashing horse, and prophesied a wind.

"So long," he said, and "Kind of you to call.
Straight on, and watch the stars"; his horse's feet
Trampled the firmer foothold, ending all.
He flung behind no message to his sweet,
No other word to Lion; the dull beat
Of his horse's trample drummed upon the trail;
Lion could watch him drooping in the moonlight pale,

Drooping and lessening; half expectant still
That he would turn and greet him; but no sound
Came, save the lonely water's whip-poor-will
And the going horse hoofs dying on the ground.
"Michael," he cried, "Michael!" A lonely mound
Beyond the water gave him back the cry.
"That's at an end," he said, "and I have failed her—I."

Soon the far hoof-beats died, save for a stir
Half heard, then lost, then still, then heard again.
A quickening rhythm showed he plied the spur.
Then a vast breathing silence took the plain.
The moon was like a soul within the brain
Of the great sleeping world; silent she rode
The water talked, talked, talked; it trembled as it flowed.

A moment Lion thought to ride in chase.
He turned, then turned again, knowing his friend.
He forded through with death upon his face,

And rode the plain that seemed never to end.
Clumps of pale cattle nosed the thing unkenned,
Riding the night; out of the night they rose,
Snuffing with outstretched heads, stamping with surly lows,

Till he was threading through a crowd, a sea
Of curious shorthorns backing as he came,
Barring his path, but shifting warily;
He slapped the flanks of the more tame.
Unreal the ghostly cattle lumbered lame.
His horse kept at an even pace; the cows
Broke right and left like waves before advancing bows.

Lonely the pampas seemed amid that herd.
The thought of Mary's sorrow pricked him sore;
He brought no comfort for her, not a word;
He would not ease her pain, but bring her more.
The long miles dropped behind; lights rose before,
Lights and the seaport and the briny air;
And so he sailed for home to comfort Mary there.

*　　　*　　　*　　　*　　　*

When Mary knew the worst she only sighed,
Looked hard at Lion's face, and sat quite still,
White to the lips, but stern and stony-eyed,
Beaten by life in all things but the will.
Though the blow struck her hard it did not kill.
She rallied on herself, a new life bloomed
Out of the ashy heart where Michael lay entombed.

And more than this: for Lion touched a sense
That he, the honest humdrum man, was more
Than he by whom the glory and the offence

THE DAFFODIL FIELDS

Came to her life three bitter years before.
This was a treason in her being's core;
It smouldered there; meanwhile as two good friends
They met at autumn dusks and winter daylight-ends.

And once, after long twilight talk, he broke
His strong restraint upon his passion for her,
And burningly, most like a man he spoke,
Until her pity almost overbore her.
It could not be, she said; her pity tore her;
But still it could not be, though this was pain.
Then on a frosty night they met and spoke again.

And then he wooed again, clutching her hands,
Calling the maid his mind, his heart, his soul,
Saying that God had linked their lives in bands
When the worm Life first started from the goal;
That they were linked together, past control,
Linked from all time, could she but pity; she
Pitied from the soul, but said it could not be.

"Mary," he asked, "you cannot love me? No?"
"No," she replied; "would God I could, my dear."
"God bless you, then," he answered, "I must go,
Go over sea to get away from here,
I cannot think of work when you are near;
My whole life falls to pieces; it must end.
This meeting now must be 'good-bye,' beloved friend."

White-lipped she listened, then with failing breath,
She asked for yet a little time; her face
Was even as that of one condemned to death.

She asked for yet another three months' grace,
Asked it, as Lion inly knew, in case
Michael should still return; and "Yes" said he,
"I'll wait three months for you, beloved; let it be."

Slowly the three months dragged: no Michael came.
March brought the daffodils and set them shaking.
April was quick in Nature like green flame;
May came with dog-rose buds, and corncrakes craking,
Then dwindled like her blossom; June was breaking.
"Mary," said Lion, "can you answer now?"
White like a ghost she stood, he long remembered how.

Wild-eyed and white, and trembling like a leaf,
She gave her answer, "Yes"; she gave her lips,
Cold as a corpse's to the kiss of grief,
Shuddering at him as if his touch were whips.
Then her best nature, struggling to eclipse
This shrinking self, made speech; she jested there;
They searched each other's eyes, and both souls saw despair.

So the first passed, and after that began
A happier time: she could not choose but praise
That recognition of her in the man
Stiving to salve her pride in myriad ways;
He was a gentle lover: gentle days
Passed like a music after tragic scenes;
Her heart gave thanks for that; but still the might-have-beens

Haunted her inner spirit day and night,
And often in his kiss the memory came
Of Michael's face above her, passionate, white,

His lips at her lips murmuring her name,
Then she would suffer sleepless, sick with shame,
And struggle with her weakness. She had vowed
To give herself to Lion; she was true and proud.

He should not have a woman sick with ghosts,
But one firm-minded to be his; so time
Passed one by one the summer's marking posts,
The dog-rose and the foxglove and the lime.
Then on a day the church-bells rang a chime.
Men fired the bells till all the valley filled
With bell-noise from the belfry where the jackdaws build.

Lion and she were married; home they went,
Home to The Roughs as man and wife; the news
Was printed in the paper. Mary sent
A copy out to Michael. Now we lose
Sight of her for a time, and the great dews
Fall, and the harvest-moon grows red and fills
Over the barren fields where March brings daffodils.

VI

The rider lingered at the fence a moment,
Tossed out the pack to Michael, whistling low,
Then rode, waving his hand, without more comment,
Down the vast grey-green pampas sloping slow.
Michael's last news had come so long ago,
He wondered who had written now; the hand
Thrilled him with vague alarm, it brought him to a stand.

He opened it with one eye on the hut,
Lest she within were watching him, but she
Was combing out her hair, the door was shut,

[365]

The green sun-shutters closed, she could not see.
Out fell the love-tryst handkerchief which he
Had had embroidered with his name for her;
It had been dearly kept, it smelt of lavender.

Something remained: a paper, crossed with blue,
Where he should read; he stood there in the sun,
Reading of Mary's wedding till he knew
What he had cast away, what he had done.
He was rejected, Lion was the one.
Lion, the godly and the upright, he.
The black lines in the paper showed how it could be.

He pocketed the love gift and took horse,
And rode out to the pay-shed for his savings.
Then turned, and rode a lonely water-course,
Alone with bitter thoughts and bitter cravings.
Sun-shadows on the reeds made twinkling wavings;
An orange-bellied turtle scooped the mud;
Mary had married Lion, and the news drew blood.

And with the bitterness, the outcast felt
A passion for those old kind Shropshire places,
The ruined chancel where the nuns had knelt;
High Ercall and the Chase End and the Chases,
The glimmering mere, the burr, the well-known faces,
By Wrekin and by Zine and country town.
The orange-bellied turtle burrowed further down.

He could remember Mary now; her crying
Night after night alone through weary years,
Had touched him now and set the cords replying;

He knew her misery now, her ache, her tears,
The lonely nights, the ceaseless hope, the fears,
The arm stretched out for one not there, the slow
Loss of the lover's faith, the letting comfort go.

"Now I will ride," he said. Beyond the ford
He caught a fresh horse and rode on. The night
Found him a guest at Pepe Blanco's board,
Moody and drinking rum and ripe for fight;
Drawing his gun, he shot away the light,
And parried Pepe's knife and caught his horse,
And all night long he rode bedevilled by remorse.

At dawn he caught an eastward-going ferry,
And all day long he steamed between great banks
Which smelt of yellow thorn and loganberry.
Then wharves appeared, and chimneys rose in ranks,
Mast upon mast arose; the river's flanks
Were filled with English ships, and one he found
Needing another stoker, being homeward bound.

And all the time the trouble in his head
Ran like a whirlwind moving him; he knew
Since she was lost that he was better dead.
He had no project outlined, what to do,
Beyond go home; he joined the steamer's crew.
She sailed that night: he dulled his maddened soul,
Plying the iron coal-slice on the bunker coal.

Work did not clear the turmoil in his mind;
Passion takes colour from the nature's core;
His misery was as his nature, blind.

[367]

Life was still turmoil when he went ashore.
To see his old love married lay before;
To see another have her, drink the gall,
Kicked like a dog without, while he within had all.

   *   *   *   *   *

Soon he was at the Foxholes, at the place
Whither, from over sea, his heart had turned
Often at evening-ends in times of grace.
But little outward change his eye discerned;
A red rose at her bedroom window burned,
Just as before. Even as of old the wasps
Poised at the yellow plums: the gate creaked on its hasps,

And the white fantails sidled on the roof
Just as before; their pink feet, even as of old,
Printed the frosty morning's rime with proof.
Still the zew-tallat's thatch was green with mould;
The apples on the withered boughs were gold.
Men and the times were changed: "And I," said he,
"Will go and not return, since she is not for me.

"I'll go, for it would be a scurvy thing
To spoil her marriage, and besides, she cares
For that half-priest she married with the ring.
Small joy for me in seeing how she wears,
Or seeing what he takes and what he shares.
That beauty and those ways: she had such ways,
There in the daffodils in those old April days."

So with an impulse of good will he turned,
Leaving that place of daffodils; the road
Was paven sharp with memories which burned;

[368]

THE DAFFODIL FIELDS

He trod them strongly under as he strode.
At the Green Turning's forge the furnace glowed;
Red dithying sparks flew from the crumpled soft
Fold from the fire's heart; down clanged the hammers oft.

That was a bitter place to pass, for there
Mary and he had often, often stayed
To watch the horseshoe growing in the glare.
It was a tryst in childhood when they strayed.
There was a stile beside the forge; he laid
His elbows on it, leaning, looking down
The river-valley stretched with great trees turning brown.

Infinite, too, because it reached the sky,
And distant spires arose and distant smoke;
The whiteness on the blue went stilly by;
Only the clinking forge the stillness broke.
Ryemeadows brook was there; The Roughs, the oak
Where the White Woman walked; the black firs showed
Around the Occleve homestead Mary's new abode.

A long, long time he gazed at that fair place,
So well remembered from of old; he sighed.
"I will go down and look upon her face,
See her again, whatever may betide.
Hell is my future; I shall soon have died,
But I will take to hell one memory more;
She shall not see nor know; I shall be gone before;

"Before they turn the dogs upon me, even.
I do not mean to speak; but only see.
Even the devil gets a peep at heaven;

One peep at her shall come to hell with me;
One peep at her, no matter what may be."
He crossed the stile and hurried down the slope.
Remembered trees and hedges gave a zest to hope.

     *   *   *   *   *

A low brick wall with privet shrubs beyond
Ringed in The Roughs upon the side he neared.
Eastward some bramble bushes cloaked the pond;
Westward was barley-stubble not yet cleared.
He thrust aside the privet boughs and peered.
The drooping fir trees let their darkness trail
Black like a pirate's masts bound under easy sail.

The garden with its autumn flowers was there;
Few that his wayward memory linked with her.
Summer had burnt the summer flowers bare,
But honey-hunting bees still made a stir.
Sprigs were still bluish on the lavender,
And bluish daisies budded, bright flies poised;
The wren upon the tree-stump carolled cheery-voiced.

He could not see her there. Windows were wide,
Late wasps were cruising, and the curtains shook.
Smoke, like the house's breathing, floated, sighed,
Among the trembling firs strange ways it took.
But still no Mary's presence blessed his look;
The house was still as if deserted, hushed.
Faint fragrance hung about it as if herbs were crushed.

Fragrance that gave his memory's guard a hint
Of times long past, of reapers in the corn,
Bruising with heavy boots the stalks of mint,

[370]

When first the berry reddens on the thorn.
Memories of her that fragrance brought. Forlorn
That vigil of the watching outcast grew;
He crept towards the kitchen, sheltered by a yew.

The windows of the kitchen opened wide.
Again the fragrance came; a woman spoke;
Old Mrs. Occleve talked to one inside.
A smell of cooking filled a gust of smoke.
Then fragrance once again, for herbs were broke;
Pourri was being made; the listener heard
Things lifted and laid down, bruised into sweetness, stirred.

While an old woman made remarks to one
Who was not the beloved: Michael learned
That Roger's wife at Upton had a son,
And that the red geraniums should be turned;
A hen was missing, and a rick was burned;
Our Lord commanded patience; here it broke;
The window closed, it made the kitchen chimney smoke.

Steps clacked on flagstones to the outer door;
A dairy-maid, whom he remembered well,
Lined, now, with age, and greyer than before,
Rang a cracked cow-bell for the dinner-bell.
He saw the dining-room; he could not tell
If Mary were within: inly he knew
That she was coming now, that she would be in blue,

Blue with a silver locket at the throat,
And that she would be there, within there, near,
With the little blushes that he knew by rote,

[371]

And the grey eyes so steadfast and so dear,
The voice, pure like the nature, true and clear,
Speaking to her belov'd within the room.
The gate clicked, Lion came: the outcast hugged the gloom,

Watching intently from below the boughs,
While Lion cleared his riding-boots of clay,
Eyed the high clouds and went within the house.
His eyes looked troubled, and his hair looked grey.
Dinner began within with much to say.
Old Occleve roared aloud at his own joke.
Mary, it seemed, was gone; the loved voice never spoke.

Nor could her lover see her from the yew;
She was not there at table; she was ill,
Ill, or away perhaps—he wished he knew.
Away, perhaps, for Occleve bellowed still.
"If sick," he thought, "the maid or Lion will
Take food to her." He watched; the dinner ended.
The staircase was not used; none climbed it, none descended.

"Not here," he thought; but wishing to be sure,
He waited till the Occleves went to field,
Then followed, round the house, another lure,
Using the well-known privet as his shield.
He meant to run a risk; his heart was steeled.
He knew of old which bedroom would be hers;
He crouched upon the north front in among the firs.

The house stared at him with its red-brick blank,
Its vacant window-eyes; its open door,
With old wrought bridle ring-hooks at each flank,

Swayed on a creaking hinge as the wind bore.
Nothing had changed; the house was as before,
The dull red brick, the windows sealed or wide:
"I will go in," he said. He rose and stepped inside.

None could have seen him coming; all was still;
He listened in the doorway for a sign.
Above, a rafter creaked, a stir, a thrill
Moved, till the frames clacked on the picture line.
"Old Mother Occleve sleeps, the servants dine,"
He muttered, listening. "Hush." A silence brooded.
Far off the kitchen dinner clattered; he intruded.

Still, to his right, the best room door was locked.
Another door was at his left; he stayed.
Within, a stately timepiece ticked and tocked,
To one who slumbered breathing deep; it made
An image of Time's going and man's trade.
He looked: Old Mother Occleve lay asleep,
Hands crossed upon her knitting, rosy, breathing deep.

He tiptoed up the stairs which creaked and cracked.
The landing creaked; the shut doors, painted gray,
Loomed, as if shutting in some dreadful act.
The nodding frames seemed ready to betray.
The east room had been closed in Michael's day,
Being the best; but now he guessed it hers;
The fields of daffodils lay next it, past the firs.

Just as he reached the landing, Lion cried,
Somewhere below, "I'll get it." Lion's feet
Struck on the flagstones with a hasty stride.

"He's coming up," thought Michael, "we shall meet."
He snatched the nearest door for his retreat,
Opened with thieves' swift silence, dared not close,
But stood within, behind it. Lion's footsteps rose,

Running two steps at once, while Michael stood,
Not breathing, only knowing that the room
Was someone's bedroom smelling of old wood,
Hung with engravings of the day of doom.
The footsteps stopped; and Lion called, to whom?
A gentle question, tapping at a door,
And Michael shifted feet, and creakings took the floor.

The footsteps recommenced, a door-catch clacked;
Within an eastern room the footsteps passed.
Drawers were pulled loudly open and ransacked,
Chattels were thrust aside and overcast.
What could the thing be that he sought. At last
His voice said, "Here it is." The wormèd floor
Creaked with returning footsteps down the corridor.

The footsteps came as though the walker read,
Or added rows of figures by the way;
There was much hesitation in the tread;
Lion seemed pondering which, to go or stay;
Then, seeing the door, which covered Michael, sway,
He swiftly crossed and shut it. "Always one
For order," Michael muttered. "Now be swift, my son."

The action seemed to break the walker's mood;
The footsteps passed downstairs, along the hall,
Out at the door and off towards the wood.

THE DAFFODIL FIELDS

"Gone," Michael muttered. "Now to hazard all."
Outside, the frames still nodded on the wall.
Michael stepped swiftly up the floor to try
The door where Lion tapped and waited for reply.

It was the eastmost of the rooms which look
Over the fields of daffodils; the bound
Scanned from its windows is Ryemeadows brook,
Banked by gnarled apple trees and rising ground.
Most gently Michael tapped; he heard no sound,
Only the blind-pull tapping with the wind;
The kitchen-door was opened; kitchen-clatter dinned.

A woman walked along the hall below,
Humming; a maid, he judged; the footsteps died,
Listening intently still, he heard them go,
Then swiftly turned the knob and went inside.
The blind-pull at the window volleyed wide;
The curtains streamed out like a waterfall;
The pictures of the fox-hunt clacked along the wall.

No one was there; no one; the room was hers.
A book of praise lay open on the bed;
The clothes-press smelt of many lavenders,
Her spirit stamped the room; herself was fled.
Here she found peace of soul like daily bread,
Here, with her lover Lion; Michael gazed;
He would have been the sharer had he not been crazed.

He took the love-gift handkerchief again;
He laid it on her table, near the glass,
So opened that the broidered name was plain;

[375]

"Plain," he exclaimed, "she cannot let it pass.
It stands and speaks for me as bold as brass.
My answer, my heart's cry, to tell her this,
That she is still my darling: all she was she is.

"So she will know at least that she was wrong,
That underneath the blindness I was true.
Fate is the strongest thing, though men are strong;
Out from beyond life I was sealed to you.
But my blind ways destroyed the cords that drew;
And now, the evil done, I know my need;
Fate has his way with those who mar what is decreed.

"And now, goodbye." He closed the door behind him,
Then stept, with firm swift footstep down the stair,
Meaning to go where she would never find him;
He would go down through darkness to despair.
Out at the door he stept; the autumn air
Came fresh upon his face; none saw him go.
"Goodbye, my love," he muttered; "it is better so."

Soon he was on the high road, out of sight
Of valley and farm; soon he could see no more
The oast-house pointing finger take the light
As tumbling pigeons glittered over; nor
Could he behold the wind-vane gilded o'er,
Swinging above the church; the road swung round.
"Now, the last look," he cried: he saw that holy ground.

"Goodbye," he cried; he could behold it all,
Spread out as in a picture; but so clear
That the gold apple stood out from the wall;

[376]

Like a red jewel stood the grazing steer.
Precise, intensely coloured, all brought near,
As in a vision, lay that holy ground.
"Mary is there," he moaned, "and I am outward bound.

"I never saw this place so beautiful,
Never like this. I never saw it glow.
Spirit is on this place; it fills it full.
So let the die be cast; I will not go.
But I will see her face to face and know
From her own lips what thoughts she has of me;
And if disaster come: right; let disaster be."

Back, by another way, he turned. The sun
Fired the yew-tops in the Roman woods.
Lights in the valley twinkled one by one,
The starlings whirled in dropping multitudes.
Dusk fingered into one earth's many moods,
Back to The Roughs he walked; he neared the brook;
A lamp burned in the farm; he saw; his fingers shook.

He had to cross the brook, to cross a field,
Where daffodils were thick when years were young.
Then, were she there, his fortunes should be sealed.
Down the mud trackway to the brook he swung;
Then while the passion trembled on his tongue,
Dim, by the dim bridge-stile, he seemed to see
A figure standing mute; a woman—it was she.

She stood quite stilly, waiting for him there.
She did not seem surprised; the meeting seemed
Planned from all time by powers in the air

To change their human fates; he even deemed
That in another life this thing had gleamed,
This meeting by the bridge.   He said, "It's you."
"Yes, I," she said, "who else?   You must have known; you
  knew

"That I should come here to the brook to see,
After your message."   "You were out," he said.
"Gone, and I did not know where you could be.
Where were you, Mary, when the thing was laid?"
"Old Mrs. Cale is dying, and I stayed
Longer than usual, while I read the Word.
You could have hardly gone."   She paused, her bosom stirred.

"Mary, I sinned," he said.   "Not that, dear, no,"
She said; "but, oh, you were unkind, unkind,
Never to write a word and leave me so,
But out of sight with you is out of mind."
"Mary, I sinned," he said, "and I was blind.
Oh, my beloved, are you Lion's wife?"
"Belov'd sounds strange," she answered, "in my present life.

"But it is sweet to hear it, all the same.
It is a language little heard by me
Alone, in that man's keeping, with my shame.
I never thought such miseries could be.
I was so happy in you, Michael.   He
Came when I felt you changed from what I thought you.
Even now it is not love, but jealousy that brought you."

"That is untrue," he said.   "I am in hell.
You are my heart's beloved, Mary, you.
By God, I know your beauty now too well.

We are each other's, flesh and soul, we two."
"That was sweet knowledge once," she said; "we knew
That truth of old.   Now, in a strange man's bed,
I read it in my soul, and find it written red."

"Is he a brute?" he asked.   "No," she replied.
"I did not understand what it would mean.
And now that you are back, would I had died;
Died, and the misery of it not have been.
Lion would not be wrecked, nor I unclean.
I was a proud one once, and now I'm tame;
Oh, Michael, say some word to take away my shame."

She sobbed; his arms went round her; the night heard
Intense fierce whispering passing, soul to soul,
Love running hot on many a murmured word,
Love's passionate giving into new control.
Their present misery did but blow the coal,
Did but entangle deeper their two wills,
While the brown brook ran on by buried daffodils.

VII

Upon a light gust came a waft of bells,
Ringing the chimes for nine; a broken sweet,
Like waters bubbling out of hidden wells,
Dully upon those lovers' ears it beat,
Their time was at an end.   Her tottering feet
Trod the dim field for home; he sought an inn.
"Oh, I have sinned," she cried, "but not a secret sin."

Inside The Roughs they waited for her coming;
Eyeing the ticking clock the household sat.
"Nine," the clock struck; the clock-weights ran down drumming;

Old Mother Occleve stretched her sewing flat.
"It's nine," she said. Old Occleve stroked the cat.
"Ah, cat," he said, "hast had good go at mouse?"
Lion sat listening tense to all within the house.

"Mary is late to-night," the gammer said.
"The times have changed," her merry husband roared.
"Young married couples now like lonely trade,
Don't think of bed at all, they think of board.
No multiplying left in people. Lord!
When I was Lion's age I'd had my five.
There was some go in folk when us two took to wive."

Lion arose and stalked and bit his lip.
"Or was it six?" the old man muttered, "six.
Us had so many I've alost the tip.
Us were two right good souls at getting chicks.
Two births of twins, then Johnny's birth, then Dick's". . .
"Now give a young man time," the mother cried.
Mary came swiftly in and flung the room door wide.

Lion was by the window when she came,
Old Occleve and his wife were by the fire;
Big shadows leapt the ceiling from the flame.
She fronted the three figures and came nigher.
"Lion," she whispered, "I return my hire."
She dropped her marriage-ring upon the table.
Then, in a louder voice, "I bore what I was able,

"And Time and marriage might have worn me down,
Perhaps, to be a good wife and a blest,
With little children clinging to my gown,

[380]

And little blind mouths fumbling for my breast,
And this place would have been a place of rest
For you and me; we could have come to know
The depth; but that is over; I have got to go.

"He has come back, and I have got to go.
Our marriage ends." She stood there white and breathed.
Old Occleve got upon his feet with "So."
Blazing with wrath upon the hearth he seethed.
A log fell from the bars; blue spirals wreathed
Across the still old woman's startled face;
The cat arose and yawned. Lion was still a space.

Old Occleve turned to Lion. Lion moved
Nearer to Mary, picking up the ring.
His was grim physic from the soul beloved;
His face was white and twitching with the sting.
"You are my wife, you cannot do this thing,"
He said at last. "I can respect your pride.
This thing affects your soul; my judgment must decide.

"You are unsettled, shaken from the shock."
"Not so," she said. She stretched a hand to him,
White, large and noble, steady as a rock,
Cunning with many powers, curving, slim.
The smoke, drawn by the door-draught, made it dim.
"Right," Lion answered. "You are steady. Then
There is but one world, Mary; this, the world of men.

"And there's another world, without its bounds,
Peopled by streaked and spotted souls who prize
The flashiness that comes from marshy grounds

Above plain daylight.   In their blinkered eyes
Nothing is bright but sentimental lies,
Such as are offered you, dear, here and now;
Lies which betray the strongest, God alone knows how.

"You, in your beauty and your whiteness, turn
Your strong, white mind, your faith, your fearless truth,
All for these rotten fires that so burn.
A sentimental clutch at perished youth.
I am too sick for wisdom, sick with ruth,
And this comes suddenly; the unripe man
Misses the hour, oh God.   But you, what is your plan?

"What do you mean to do, how act, how live?
What warrant have you for your life? What trust?
You are for going sailing in a sieve.
This brightness is too mortal not to rust.
So our beginning marriage ends in dust.
I have not failed you, Mary.   Let me know
What you intend to do, and whither you will go."

"Go from this place; it chokes me," she replied.
"This place has branded me; I must regain
My truth that I have soiled, my faith, my pride,
It is all poison and it leaves a stain.
I cannot stay nor be your wife again.
Never.   You did your best, though; you were kind.
I have grown old to-night and left all that behind.

"Goodbye."   She turned.   Old Occleve faced his son.
Wrath at the woman's impudence was blent,
Upon his face, with wrath that such an one

Should stand unthrashed until her words were spent.
He stayed for Lion's wrath; but Mary went
Unchecked; he did not stir. Her footsteps ground
The gravel to the gate; the gate-hinge made a sound

Like to a cry of pain after a shot.
Swinging, it clicked, it clicked again, it swung
Until the iron latch bar hit the slot.
Mary had gone, and Lion held his tongue.
Old Mother Occleve sobbed; her white head hung
Over her sewing while the tears ran down
Her worn, blood-threaded cheeks and splashed upon her gown.

"Yes, it is true," said Lion, "she must go.
Michael is back. Michael was always first,
I did but take his place. You did not know.
Now it has happened, and you know the worst.
So passion makes the passionate soul accurst
And crucifies his darling. Michael comes
And the savage truth appears and rips my life to thrums."

Upon Old Occleve's face the fury changed
First to contempt, and then to terror lest
Lion, beneath the shock, should be deranged.
But Lion's eyes were steady, though distressed.
"Father, good-night," he said, "I'm going to rest.
Good-night, I cannot talk. Mother, good-night."
He kissed her brow and went; they heard him strike a light,

And go with slow depressed step up the stairs,
Up to the door of her deserted bower;
They heard him above them, moving chairs;

The memory of his paleness made them cower.
They did not know their son; they had no power
To help, they only saw the new-won bride
Defy their child, and faith and custom put aside.

  *   *   *   *   *

After a time men learned where Mary was:
Over the hills, not many miles away,
Renting a cottage and a patch of grass
Where Michael came to see her. Every day
Taught her what fevers can inhabit clay,
Shaking this body that so soon must die.
The time made Lion old: the winter dwindled by.

Till the long misery had to end or kill:
And "I must go to see her," Lion cried;
"I am her standby, and she needs me still;
If not to love she needs me to decide.
Dear, I will set you free. Oh, my bright bride,
Lost in such piteous ways, come back." He rode
Over the wintry hills to Mary's new abode.

And as he topped the pass between the hills,
Towards him, up the swerving road, there came
Michael, the happy cause of all his ills;
Walking as though repentance were the shame,
Sucking a grass, unbuttoned, still the same,
Humming a tune; his careless beauty wild
Drawing the women's eyes; he wandered with a child.

Who heard, wide-eyed, the scraps of tales which fell
Between the fragments of the tune; they seemed
A cherub bringing up a soul from hell.

Meeting unlike the meeting long since dreamed.
Lion dismounted; the great valley gleamed
With waters far below; his teeth were set
His heart thumped at his throat; he stopped; the two men met.

The child well knew that fatal issues joined;
He stood round-eyed to watch them, even as Fate
Stood with his pennypiece of causes coined
Ready to throw for issue; the bright hate
Throbbed, that the heavy reckoning need not wait.
Lion stepped forward, watching Michael's eyes.
"We are old friends," he said. "Now, Michael, you be wise,

"And let the harm already done suffice;
Go, before Mary's name is wholly gone.
Spare her the misery of desertion twice,
There's only ruin in the road you're on—
Ruin for both, whatever promise shone
In sentimental shrinkings from the fact.
So, Michael, play the man, and do the generous act.

"And go; if not for my sake, go for hers.
You only want her with your sentiment.
You are water roughed by every wind that stirs,
One little gust will alter your intent
All ways, to every wind, and nothing meant,
Is your life's habit. Man, one takes a wife,
Not for a three months' fancy, but the whole of life.

"We have been friends, so I speak you fair.
How will you bear her ill, or cross, or tired?
Sentiment sighing will not help you there.

You call a half life's volume not desired.
I know your love for her. I saw it mired,
Mired, past going, by your first sharp taste
Of life and work; it stopped; you let her whole life waste,

"Rather than have the trouble of such love,
You will again; but if you do it now,
It will mean death, not sorrow. But enough.
You know too well you cannot keep a vow.
There are grey hairs already on her brow.
You brought them there. Death is the next step. Go,
Before you take the step." "No," Michael answered, "No.

"As for my past, I was a dog, a cur,
And I have paid blood-money, and still pay.
But all my being is ablaze with her;
There is no talk of giving up to-day.
I will not give her up. You used to say
Bodies are earth. I heard you say it. Liar!
You never loved her, you. She turned the earth to fire."

"Michael," said Lion, "you have said such things
Of other women; less than six miles hence
You and another woman felt love's wings
Rosy and fair, and so took leave of sense.
She's dead, that other woman, dead, with pence
Pressed on her big brown eyes, under the ground;
She that was merry once, feeling the world go round.

"Her child (and yours) is with her sister now,
Out there, behind us, living as they can;
Pinched by the poverty that you allow.

All a long autumn many rumours ran
About Sue Jones that was: you were the man.
The lad is like you. Think about his mother,
Before you turn the earth to fire with another."

"That is enough," said Michael, "you shall know
Soon, to your marrow, what my answer is;
Know to your lying heart; now kindly go.
The neighbours smell that something is amiss.
We two will keep a dignity in this,
Such as we can.   No quarrelling with me here.
Mary might see; now go; but recollect, my dear,

"That if you twit me with your wife, you lie;
And that your further insult waits a day
When God permits that Mary is not by;
I keep the record of it, and shall pay.
And as for Mary; listen: we betray
No one. We keep our troth-plight as we meant.
Now go, the neighbours gather." Lion bowed and went.

Home to his memories for a month of pain,
Each moment like a devil with a tongue,
Urging him, "Set her free," or "Try again,"
Or "Kill that man and stamp him into dung."
"See her," he cried. He took his horse and swung
Out on the road to her; the rain was falling;
Her dropping house-eaves splashed him when he knocked there,
    calling.

Drowned yellow jasmine dripped; his horse's flanks
Steamed, and dark runnels on his yellow hair
Streaked the groomed surface into blotchy ranks.

[387]

The noise of water dropping filled the air.
He knocked again; but there was no one there;
No one within, the door was locked, no smoke
Came from the chimney stacks, no clock ticked, no one spoke.

Only the water dripped and dribble-dripped,
And gurgled through the rain-pipe to the butt;
Drops, trickling down the windows paused or slipped;
A wet twig scraked as though the glass were cut.
The blinds were all drawn down, the windows shut.
No one was there. Across the road a shawl
Showed at a door a space; a woman gave a call.

"They're gone away," she cried. "They're gone away.
Been gone a matter of a week." Where to?
The woman thought to Wales, but could not say,
Nor if she planned returning; no one knew.
She looked at Lion sharply; then she drew
The half-door to its place and passed within,
Saying she hoped the rain would stop and spring begin.

Lion rode home. A month went by, and now
Winter was gone; the myriad shoots of green
Bent to the wind, like hair, upon the plough,
And up from withered leaves came celandine.
And sunlight came, though still the air was keen,
So that the first March market was most fair,
And Lion rode to market, having business there.

And in the afternoon, when all was done,
While Lion waited idly near the inn,
Watching the pigeons sidling in the sun,

As Jim the ostler put his gelding in,
He heard a noise of rioting begin
Outside the yard, with catcalls; there were shouts
Of "Occleve. Lion Occleve," from a pack of louts,

Who hung about the courtyard-arch, and cried,
"Yah, Occleve, of The Roughs, the married man,
Occleve, who had the bed and not the bride."
At first without the arch; but some began
To sidle in, still calling; children ran
To watch the baiting; they were farmer's leavings
Who shouted thus, men cast for drunkenness and thievings.

Lion knew most of them of old; he paid
No heed to them, but turned his back and talked
To Jim, of through-pin in his master's jade,
And how no horse-wounds should be stuped or caulked.
The rabble in the archway, not yet baulked,
Came crowding nearer, and the boys began,
"Who was it took your mistress, master married man?"

"Who was it, master, took your wife away?"
"I wouldn't let another man take mine."
"She had two husbands on her wedding day."
"See at a blush: he blushed as red as wine."
"She'd ought a had a cart-whip laid on fine."
The farmers in the courtyard watched the baiting,
Grinning, the barmaids grinned above the window grating.

Then through the mob of brawlers Michael stepped
Straight to where Lion stood. "I come," he said,
"To give you back some words which I have kept

Safe in my heart till I could see them paid.
You lied about Sue Jones; she died a maid
As far as I'm concerned, and there's your lie,
Full in your throat, and there, and there, and in your eye.

"And there's for stealing Mary". . . as he struck,
He slipped upon a piece of peel and dropped
Souse in a puddle of the courtyard muck;
Loud laughter followed when he rose up sopped.
Friends rushed to intervene, the fight was stopped.
The two were hurried out by different ways.
Men said, "'Tis stopped for now, but not for many days."

*　　　*　　　*　　　*　　　*

April appeared, the green earth's impulse came,
Pushing the singing sap until each bud
Trembled with delicate life as soft as flame,
Filled by the mighty heart-beat as with blood;
Death was at ebb, and Life in brimming flood.
But little joy in life could Lion see,
Striving to gird his will to set his loved one free,

While in his heart a hope still struggled dim
That the mad hour would pass, the darkness break,
The fever die, and she return to him,
The routed nightmare let the sleeper wake.
"Then we could go abroad," he cried, "and make
A new life, soul to soul; oh, love! return."
"Too late," his heart replied.　At last he rode to learn.

Bowed, but alive with hope, he topped the pass,
And saw, below, her cottage by the way,
White, in a garden green with springing grass,

And smoke against the blue sky going grey.
"God make us all the happier for to-day,"
He muttered humbly; then, below, he spied,
Mary and Michael entering, walking side by side.

Arm within arm, like lovers, like dear lovers
Matched by the happy stars and newly wed,
Over whose lives a rosy presence hovers.
Lion dismounted, seeing hope was dead.
A child was by the road, he stroked his head,
And "Little one," he said, "who lives below
There, in the cottage there, where those two people go?"

"They do," the child said, pointing: "Mrs. Gray
Lives in the cottage there, and he does, too.
They've been back near a week since being away."
It was but seal to what he inly knew.
He thanked the child and rode. The Spring was blue,
Bluer than ever, and the birds were glad;
Such rapture in the hedges all the blackbirds had.

He was not dancing to that pipe of the Spring.
He reached The Roughs, and there, within her room,
Bowed for a time above her wedding ring,
Which had so chained him to unhappy doom;
All his dead marriage haunted in the gloom
Of that deserted chamber; all her things
Lay still as she had left them when her love took wings.

He kept a bitter vigil through the night,
Knowing his loss, his ten years' passion wasted,
His life all blasted, even at its height,

His cup of life's fulfilment hardly tasted.
Grey on the budding woods the morning hasted,
And looking out he saw the dawn come chill
Over the shaking acre pale with daffodil.

Birds were beginning in the meadows; soon
The blackbirds and the thrushes with their singing
Piped down the withered husk that was the moon,
And up the sky the ruddy sun came winging.
Cows plodded past, yokes clanked, the men were bringing
Milk from the barton. Someone shouted "Hup.
Dog, drive them dangy red ones down away on up."

Some heavy hours went by before he rose.
He went out of the house into the grass,
Down which the wind flowed much as water flows;
The daffodils bowed down to let it pass.
At the brook's edge a boggy bit there was,
Right at the field's north corner, near the bridge,
Fenced by a ridge of earth; he sat upon the ridge,

Watching the water running to the sea,
Watching the bridge, the stile, the path beyond,
Where the white violet's sweetness brought the bee.
He paid the price of being overfond.
The water babbled always from the pond
Over the pretty shallows, chattering, tinkling,
With trembles from the sunlight in its clearness wrinkling.

So gazing, like one stunned, it reached his mind,
That the hedge-brambles overhung the brook
More than was right, making the selvage blind;

The dragging brambles too much flotsam took.
Dully he thought to mend. He fetched a hook,
And standing in the shallow stream he slashed,
For hours, it seemed; the thorns, the twigs, the dead leaves
    splashed,

Splashed and were bobbed away across the shallows;
Pale grasses with the sap gone from them fell,
Sank, or were carried down beyond the sallows.
The bruised ground-ivy gave out earthy smell.
"I must be dead," he thought, "and this is hell."
Fiercely he slashed, till, glancing at the stile,
He saw that Michael stood there, watching, with a smile,

His old contemptuous smile of careless ease,
As though the world with all its myriad pain
Sufficed, but only just sufficed, to please.
Michael was there, the robber come again.
A tumult ran like flame in Lion's brain;
Then, looking down, he saw the flowers shake:
Gold, trembling daffodils; he turned, he plucked a stake

Out of the hedge that he had come to mend,
And flung his hook to Michael, crying, "Take;
We two will settle our accounts, my friend,
Once and for ever. May the Lord God make
You see your sins in time." He whirled his stake
And struck at Michael's head; again he struck;
While Michael dodged and laughed, "Why, man, I bring you
    luck.

"Don't kill a bringer of good news. You fool,
Stop it and listen. I have come to say:
Lion, for God's sake, listen and be cool.

You silly hothead, put that stake away.
Listen, I tell you." But he could not stay
The anger flaming in that passionate soul.
Blows rained upon him thick; they stung; he lost control.

Till, "If you want to fight," he cried, "let be.
Let me get off the bridge and we will fight.
That firm bit by the quag will do for me.
So. Be on guard, and God defend the right.
You foaming madman, with your hell's delight,
Smashing a man with stakes before he speaks:
On guard. I'll make you humbler for the next few weeks."

The ground was level there; the daffodils
Glimmered and danced beneath their cautious feet,
Quartering for openings for the blow that kills.
Beyond the bubbling brook a thrush was sweet.
Quickly the footsteps slid; with feint and cheat,
The weapons poised and darted and withdrew.
"Now stop it," Michael said, "I want to talk to you."

"We do not stop till one of us is dead,"
Said Lion, rushing in. A short blow fell
Dizzily, through all guard, on Michael's head.
His hedging-hook slashed blindly but too well:
It struck in Lion's side. Then, for a spell,
Both, sorely stricken, staggered, while their eyes
Dimmed under mists of blood; they fell, they tried to rise,—

Tried hard to rise, but could not, so they lay,
Watching the clouds go sailing on the sky,
Touched with a redness from the end of day.

There was all April in the blackbird's cry.
And lying there they felt they had to die,
Die and go under mould and feel no more
April's green fire of life go running in earth's core.

"There was no need to hit me," Michael said;
"You quiet thinking fellows lose control.
This fighting business is a foolish trade.
And now we join the grave-worm and the mole.
I tried to stop you. You're a crazy soul;
You always were hot-headed. Well, let be:
You deep and passionate souls have always puzzled me.

"I'm sorry that I struck you. I was hit,
And lashed out blindly at you; you were mad.
It would be different if you'd stopped a bit.
You are too blind when you are angry, lad.
Oh, I am giddy, Lion; dying, bad.
Dying." He raised himself, he sat, his look
Grew greedy for the water bubbling in the brook.

And as he watched it, Lion raised his head
Out of a bloodied clump of daffodil.
"Michael," he moaned, "I, too, am dying: dead.
You're nearer to the water. Could you fill
Your hat and give me drink? Or would it spill?
Spill, I expect." "I'll try," said Michael, "try—
I may as well die trying, since I have to die."

Slowly he forced his body's failing life
Down to the water; there he stooped and filled;
And as his back turned Lion drew his knife,

And hid it close, while all his being thrilled
To see, as Michael came, the water spilled,
Nearer and ever nearer, bright, so bright.
"Drink," muttered Michael, "drink. We two shall sleep to-
    night."

He tilted up the hat, and Lion drank.
Lion lay still a moment, gathering power,
Then rose, as Michael gave him more, and sank.
Then, like a dying bird whom death makes tower,
He raised himself above the bloodied flower
And struck with all his force in Michael's side.
"You should not have done that," his stricken comrade cried.

"No; for I meant to tell you, Lion; meant
To tell you; but I cannot now; I die.
That hit me to the heart and I am spent.
Mary and I have parted; she and I
Agreed she must return, lad. That is why
I came to see you. She is coming here,
Back to your home to-night. Oh, my beloved dear,

"You come to tread a bloody path of flowers.
All the gold flowers are covered up with blood,
And the bright bugles blow along the towers;
The bugles triumph like the Plate in flood."
His spilled life trickled down upon the mud
Between weak, clutching fingers. "Oh," he cried,
"This isn't what we planned here years ago." He died.

Lion lay still while the cold tides of death
Came brimming up his channels. With one hand
He groped to know if Michael still drew breath.

His little hour was running out its sand.
Then, in a mist, he saw his Mary stand
Above. He cried aloud, "He was my brother.
I was his comrade sworn, and we have killed each other.

"Oh desolate grief, belovèd, and through me.
We wise who try to change. Oh, you wild birds,
Help my unhappy spirit to the sea.
The golden bowl is scattered into sherds."
And Mary knelt and murmured passionate words
To that poor body on the dabbled flowers:
"Oh, beauty, oh, sweet soul, oh, little love of ours—

"Michael, my own heart's darling, speak; it's me,
Mary. You know my voice. I'm here, dear, here.
Oh, little golden-haired one, listen. See,
It's Mary, Michael. Speak to Mary, dear.
Oh, Michael, little love, he cannot hear;
And you have killed him, Lion; he is dead.
My little friend, my love, my Michael, golden head.

"We had such fun together, such sweet fun,
My love and I, my merry love and I.
Oh, love, you shone upon me like the sun.
Oh, Michael, say some little last good-bye."
Then in a great voice Lion called, "I die.
Go home and tell my people. Mary. Hear.
Though I have wrought this ruin, I have loved you, dear.

"Better than he; not better, dear, as well.
If you could kiss me, dearest, at this last.
We have made bloody doorways from our hell,

Cutting our tangle.   Now, the murder past,
We are but pitiful poor souls; and fast
The darkness and the cold come.   Kiss me, sweet;
I loved you all my life; but some lives never meet

"Though they go wandering side by side through Time.
Kiss me," he cried.   She bent, she kissed his brow:
"Oh, friend," she said, "you're lying in the slime."
"Three blind ones, dear," he murmured, "in the slough,
Caught fast for death; but never mind that now;
Go home and tell my people.   I am dying,
Dying, dear, dying now."   He died; she left him lying,

And kissed her dead one's head and crossed the field.
"They have been killed," she called, in a great crying.
"Killed, and our spirits' eyes are all unsealed.
The blood is scattered on the flowers drying."
It was the hush of dusk, and owls were flying;
They hooted as the Occleves ran to bring
That sorry harvest home from Death's red harvesting.

They laid the bodies on the bed together.
And "You were beautiful," she said, "and you
Were my own darling in the April weather.
You knew my very soul, you knew, you knew.
Oh, my sweet, piteous love, I was not true.
Fetch me fair water and the flowers of spring;
My love is dead, and I must deck his burying."

They left her with her dead; they could not choose
But grant the spirit burning in her face
Rights that their pity urged them to refuse.

They did her sorrow and the dead a grace.
All night they heard her passing footsteps trace
Down to the garden from the room of death.
They heard her singing there, lowly, with gentle breath,

To the cool darkness full of sleeping flowers,
Then back, still singing soft, with quiet tread,
But at the dawn her singing gathered powers
Like to the dying swan who lifts his head
On Eastnor, lifts it, singing, dabbled red,
Singing the glory in his tumbling mind,
Before the doors burst in, before death strikes him blind.

So triumphing her song of love began,
Ringing across the meadows like old woe
Sweetened by poets to the help of man
Unconquered in eternal overthrow;
Like a great trumpet from the long ago
Her singing towered; all the valley heard.
Men jingling down to meadow stopped their teams and stirred.

And they, the Occleves, hurried to the door,
And burst it, fearing; there the singer lay
Drooped at her lover's bedside on the floor,
Singing her passionate last of life away.
White flowers had fallen from a blackthorn spray
Over her loosened hair. Pale flowers of spring
Filled the white room of death; they covered everything.

Primroses, daffodils, and cuckoo-flowers.
She bowed her singing head on Michael's breast.
"Oh, it was sweet," she cried, "that love of ours.

You were the dearest, sweet; I loved you best.
Beloved, my beloved, let me rest
By you forever, little Michael mine.
Now the great hour is stricken, and the bread and wine

"Broken and spilt; and now the homing birds
Draw to a covert, Michael; I to you.
Bury us two together," came her words.
The dropping petals fell about the two.
Her heart had broken; she was dead. They drew
Her gentle head aside; they found it pressed
Against the broidered 'kerchief spread on Michael's breast,

The one that bore her name in Michael's hair,
Given so long before. They let her lie,
While the dim moon died out upon the air,
And happy sunlight coloured all the sky.
The last cock crowed for morning; carts went by;
Smoke rose from cottage chimneys; from the byre
The yokes went clanking by, to dairy, through the mire.

In the day's noise the water's noise was stilled,
But still it slipped along, the cold hill-spring,
Dropping from leafy hollows, which it filled,
On to the pebbly shelves which made it sing;
Glints glittered on it from the 'fisher's wing;
It saw the moorhen nesting; then it stayed
In a great space of reeds where merry otters played.

Slowly it loitered past the shivering reeds
Into a mightier water; thence its course
Becomes a pasture where the salmon feeds,

Wherein no bubble tells its humble source;
But the great waves go rolling, and the horse
Snorts at the bursting waves and will not drink,
And the great ships go outward, bubbling to the brink,

Outward, with men upon them, stretched in line,
Handling the halliards to the ocean's gates,
Where flicking windflaws fill the air with brine,
And all the ocean opens.   Then the mates
Cry, and the sunburnt crew no longer waits,
But sing triumphant and the topsail fills
To this old tale of woe among the daffodils.

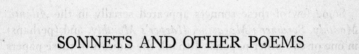

SONNETS AND OTHER POEMS

Some few of these sonnets appeared serially in the *Atlantic Monthly*, *Scribner's Magazine*, *Harper's Monthly*, and (perhaps) in one or two other papers. I thank the Editors of these papers for permission to reprint them here.

JOHN MASEFIELD.

London, 16th Dec. 1915.

SONNETS

Long long ago, when all the glittering earth
Was heaven itself, when drunkards in the street
Were like mazed kings shaking at giving birth
To acts of war that sickle men like wheat,
When the white clover opened Paradise
And God lived in a cottage up the brook,
Beauty, you lifted up my sleeping eyes
And filled my heart with longing with a look;
And all the day I searched but could not find
The beautiful dark-eyed who touched me there,
Delight in her made trouble in my mind,
She was within all Nature, everywhere,
The breath I breathed, the brook, the flower, the grass,
Were her, her word, her beauty, all she was.

Night came again, but now I could not sleep.
The owls were watching in the yew, the mice
Gnawed at the wainscot; the mid dark was deep,
The death-watch knocked the dead man's summons thrice.
The cats upon the pointed housetops peered
About the chimneys, with lit eyes which saw
Things in the darkness, moving, which they feared.
The midnight filled the quiet house with awe.
So, creeping down the stair, I drew the bolt
And passed into the darkness, and I knew
That Beauty was brought near by my revolt.
Beauty was in the moonlight, in the dew,
But more within myself whose venturous tread
Walked the dark house where death ticks called the dead.

Even after all these years there comes the dream
Of lovelier life than this in some new earth,
In the full summer of that unearthly gleam
Which lights the spirit when the brain gives birth,
Of a perfected I, in happy hours,
Treading above the sea that trembles there,
A path through thickets of immortal flowers
That only grow where sorrows never were.
And, at a turn, of coming face to face
With Beauty's self, that Beauty I have sought
In women's hearts, in friends, in many a place,
In barren hours passed at grips with thought,
Beauty of woman, comrade, earth and sea,
Incarnate thought come face to face with me.

If I could come again to that dear place
Where once I came, where Beauty lived and moved,
Where, by the sea, I saw her face to face,
That soul alive by which the world has loved;
If, as I stood at gaze among the leaves,
She would appear again, as once before,
While the red herdsman gathered up his sheaves
And brimming waters trembled up the shore;
If, as I gazed, her Beauty that was dumb,
In that old time, before I learned to speak,
Would lean to me and revelation come,
Words to the lips and color to the cheek,
Joy with its searing-iron would burn me wise,
I should know all; all powers, all mysteries.

Men are made human by the mighty fall
The mighty passion led to, these remain.

[406]

The despot, at the last assaulted wall,
By long disaster is made man again,
The faithful fool who follows the torn flag,
The woman marching by the beaten man,
Make with their truth atonement for the brag,
And earn a pity for the too proud plan.
For in disaster, in the ruined will,
In the soiled shreds of what the brain conceived,
Something above the wreck is steady still,
Bright above all that cannot be retrieved,
Grandeur of soul, a touching of the star
That good days cover but by which we are.

Here in the self is all that man can know
Of Beauty, all the wonder, all the power,
All the unearthly color, all the glow,
Here in the self which withers like a flower;
Here in the self which fades as hours pass,
And droops and dies and rots and is forgotten,
Sooner, by ages, than the mirroring glass
In which it sees its glory still unrotten.
Here in the flesh, within the flesh, behind,
Swift in the blood and throbbing on the bone,
Beauty herself, the universal mind,
Eternal April wandering alone.
The god, the holy ghost, the atoning lord,
Here in the flesh, the never yet explored.

Flesh, I have knocked at many a dusty door,
Gone down full many a windy midnight lane,
Probed in old walls and felt along the floor,
Pressed in blind hope the lighted window-pane.

But useless all, though sometimes, when the moon
Was full in heaven and the sea was full,
Along my body's alleys came a tune
Played in the tavern by the Beautiful.
Then for an instant I have felt at point
To find and seize her, whosoe'er she be,
Whether some saint whose glory does not anoint
Those whom she loves, or but a part of me,
Or something that the things not understood
Make for their uses out of flesh and blood.

But all has passed, the tune has died away,
The glamour gone, the glory; is it chance?
Is the unfeeling mud stabbed by a ray
Cast by an unseen splendor's great advance?
Or does the glory gather crumb by crumb
Unseen, within, as coral islands rise,
Till suddenly the apparitions come
Above the surface, looking at the skies?
Or does sweet Beauty dwell in lovely things,
Scattering the holy hintings of her name
In women, in dear friends, in flowers, in springs,
In the brook's voice, for us to catch the same?
Or is it we who are Beauty, we who ask,
We by whose gleams the world fulfils its task?

These myriad days, these many thousand hours,
A man's long life, so choked with dusty things,
How little perfect poise with perfect powers,
Joy at the heart and Beauty at the springs.
One hour, or two, or three, in long years scattered,
Sparks from a smithy that have fired a thatch,

Are all that life has given and all that mattered,
The rest, all heaving at a moveless latch.
For these, so many years of useless toil,
Despair, endeavor, and again despair,
Sweat, that the base machine may have its oil,
Idle delight to tempt one everywhere.
A life upon the cross. To make amends
Three flaming memories that the deathbed ends.

There, on the darkened deathbed, dies the brain
That flared three several times in seventy years;
It cannot lift the silly hand again,
Nor speak, nor sing, it neither sees nor hears.
And muffled mourners put it in the ground
And then go home, and in the earth it lies,
Too dark for vision and too deep for sound,
The million cells that made a good man wise.
Yet for a few short years an influence stirs
A sense or wraith or essence of him dead,
Which makes insensate things its ministers
To those beloved, his spirit's daily bread;
Then that, too, fades; in book or deed a spark
Lingers, then that, too, fades; then all is dark.

So in the empty sky the stars appear,
Are bright in heaven marching through the sky,
Spinning their planets, each one to his year,
Tossing their fiery hair until they die;
Then in the tower afar the watcher sees
The sun, that burned, less noble than it was,
Less noble still, until by dim degrees,
No spark of him is specklike in his glass.

Then blind and dark in heaven the sun proceeds,
Vast, dead and hideous, knocking on his moons,
Till crashing on his like creation breeds,
Striking such life a constellation swoons.
From dead things striking fire a new sun springs,
New fire, new life, new planets with new wings.

It may be so with us, that in the dark,
When we have done with Time and wander Space,
Some meeting of the blind may strike a spark,
And to Death's empty mansion give a grace.
It may be, that the loosened soul may find
Some new delight of living without limbs,
Bodiless joy of flesh-untrammelled mind,
Peace like a sky where starlike spirit swims.
It may be, that the million cells of sense,
Loosed from their seventy years' adhesion, pass
Each to some joy of changed experience,
Weight in the earth or glory in the grass;
It may be that we cease; we cannot tell.
Even if we cease life is a miracle.

Man has his unseen friend, his unseen twin,
His straitened spirit's possibility,
The palace unexplored he thinks an inn,
The glorious garden which he wanders by.
It is beside us while we clutch at clay
To daub ourselves that we may never see.
Like the lame donkey lured by moving hay
We chase the shade but let the real be.
Yet, when confusion in our heaven brings stress,
We thrust on that unseen, get stature from it,

Cast to the devil's challenge the man's yes,
And stream our fiery hour like a comet,
And know for that fierce hour a friend behind,
With sword and shield, the second to the mind.

What am I, Life? A thing of watery salt
Held in cohesion by unresting cells,
Which work they know not why, which never halt,
Myself unwitting where their Master dwells.
I do not bid them, yet they toil, they spin;
A world which uses me as I use them,
Nor do I know which end or which begin
Nor which to praise, which pamper, which condemn.
So, like a marvel in a marvel set,
I answer to the vast, as wave by wave
The sea of air goes over, dry or wet,
Or the full moon comes swimming from her cave,
Or the great sun comes north, this myriad I
Tingles, not knowing how, yet wondering why.

If I could get within this changing I,
This ever altering thing which yet persists,
Keeping the features it is reckoned by,
While each component atom breaks or twists,
If, wandering past strange groups of shifting forms,
Cells at their hidden marvels hard at work,
Pale from much toil, or red from sudden storms,
I might attain to where the Rulers lurk.
If, pressing past the guards in those grey gates,
The brain's most folded intertwisted shell,
I might attain to that which alters fates,
The King, the supreme self, the Master Cell,

Then, on Man's earthly peak, I might behold
The unearthly self beyond, unguessed, untold.

What is this atom which contains the whole,
This miracle which needs adjuncts so strange,
This, which imagined God and is the soul,
The steady star persisting amid change?
What waste, that smallness of such power should need
Such clumsy tools so easy to destroy,
Such wasteful servants difficult to feed,
Such indirect dark avenues to joy.
Why, if its business is not mainly earth,
Should it demand such heavy chains to sense?
A heavenly thing demands a swifter birth,
A quicker hand to act intelligence.
An earthly thing were better like the rose
At peace with clay from which its beauty grows.

Ah, we are neither heaven nor earth, but men;
Something that uses and despises both,
That takes its earth's contentment in the pen,
Then sees the world's injustice and is wroth,
And flinging off youth's happy promise, flies
Up to some breach, despising earthly things,
And, in contempt of hell and heaven, dies,
Rather than bear some yoke of priests or kings.
Our joys are not of heaven nor earth, but man's,
A woman's beauty or a child's delight,
The trembling blood when the discoverer scans
The sought-for world, the guessed-at satellite;
The ringing scene, the stone at point to blush
For unborn men to look at and say "Hush."

Roses are beauty, but I never see
Those blood drops from the burning heart of June
Glowing like thought upon the living tree,
Without a pity that they die so soon,
Die into petals, like those roses old,
Those women, who were summer in men's hearts
Before the smile upon the Sphinx was cold,
Or sand had hid the Syrian and his arts.
O myriad dust of beauty that lies thick
Under our feet that not a single grain
But stirred and moved in beauty and was quick
For one brief moon and died nor lived again;
But when the moon rose lay upon the grass
Pasture to living beauty, life that was.

Over the church's door they moved a stone
And there, unguessed, forgotten, mortared up,
Lay the priest's cell where he had lived alone;
There was his ashy hearth, his drinking cup;
There was the window whence he saw the host,
The god whose beauty quickened bread and wine,
The skeleton of a religion lost,
The ghostless bones of what had been divine.
O many a time the dusty masons come,
Knocking their trowels in the stony brain,
To cells where perished priests had once a home,
Or where devout brows pressed the window pane,
Watching the thing made God, the god whose bones
Bind underground our soul's foundation stones.

I never see the red rose crown the year,
Nor feel the young grass underneath my tread,

Without the thought "This living beauty here
Is earth's remembrance of a beauty dead.
Surely where all this glory is displayed
Love has been quick, like fire, to high ends,
Here, in this grass, an altar has been made
For some white joy, some sacrifice of friends;
Here, where I stand, some leap of human brains
Has touched immortal things and left its trace,
The earth is happy here, the gleam remains;
Beauty is here, the spirit of the place,
I touch the faith which nothing can destroy,
The earth, the living church of ancient joy."

Out of the clouds come torrents, from the earth
Fire and quakings, from the shrieking air
Tempests that harry half the planet's girth.
Death's unseen seeds are scattered everywhere.
Yet in his iron cage the mind of man
Measures and braves the terrors of all these,
The blindest fury and the subtlest plan
He turns, or tames, or shows in their degrees.
Yet it himself are forces of like power,
Untamed, unreckoned; seeds that brain to brain
Pass across oceans bringing thought to flower,
New worlds, new selves, where he can live again,
Eternal beauty's everlasting rose
Which casts this world as shadow as it goes.

O little self, within whose smallness lies
All that man was, and is, and will become,
Atom unseen that comprehends the skies

[414]

And tells the tracks by which the planets roam.
That, without moving, knows the joys of wings,
The tiger's strength, the eagle's secrecy,
And in the hovel can consort with kings,
Or clothe a god with his own mystery.
O with what darkness do we cloak thy light,
What dusty folly gather thee for food,
Thou who alone art knowledge and delight,
The heavenly bread, the beautiful, the good.
O living self, O god, O morning star,
Give us thy light, forgive us what we are.

I went into the fields, but you were there
Waiting for me, so all the summer flowers
Were only glimpses of your starry powers,
Beautiful and inspired dust they were.
I went down by the waters, and a bird
Sang with your voice in all the unknown tones
Of all that self of you I have not heard,
So that my being felt you to the bones.
I went into my house, and shut the door
To be alone, but you were there with me;
All beauty in a little room may be
Though the roof lean and muddy be the floor.
Then in my bed I bound my tired eyes
To make a darkness for my weary brain,
But like a presence you were there again,
Being and real, beautiful and wise,
So that I could not sleep and cried aloud,
"You strange grave thing, what is it you would say?"
The redness of your dear lips dimmed to grey,
The waters ebbed, the moon hid in a cloud.

There are two forms of life, of which one moves,
Seeking its meat in many forms of Death,
On scales, on wings, on all the myriad hooves
Which stamp earth's exultation in quick breath.
It rustles through the reeds in shivering fowl,
Cries over moors in curlew, glitters green
In the lynx' eye, is fearful in the howl
Of winter-bitten wolves whose flanks are lean.
It takes dumb joy in cattle, it is fierce,
It torts the tiger's loin, the eagle's wings,
Its tools are claws to smite and teeth to pierce,
Arms to destroy, and coils, and poison stings;
Wherever earth is quick and life runs red
Its mark is death, its meat is something dead.

Restless and hungry, still it moves and slays
Feeding its beauty on dead beauty's bones,
Most merciless in all its million ways,
Its breath for singing bought by dying groans,
Roving so far with such a zest to kill
(Its strongness adding hunger) that at last
Its cells attain beyond the cruel skill
To where life's earliest impulses are past.
Then this creation of the linkéd lusts,
To move and eat, still under their control,
Hunts for his prey in thought, his thinking thrusts
Through the untrodden jungle of the soul,
Through slip and quag, morasses dripping green,
Seeking the thing supposed but never seen.

How many ways, how many different times
The tiger Mind has clutched at what it sought,

[416]

Only to prove supposéd virtues crimes,
The imagined godhead but a form of thought.
How many restless brains have wrought and schemed,
Padding their cage, or built, or brought to law,
Made in outlasting brass the something dreamed,
Only to prove themselves the things of awe,
Yet, in the happy moment's lightning blink,
Comes scent, or track, or trace, the game goes by,
Some leopard thought is pawing at the brink,
Chaos below, and, up above, the sky.
Then the keen nostrils scent, about, about,
To prove the Thing Within a Thing Without.

The other form of Living does not stir;
Where the seed chances there it roots and grows,
To suck what makes the lily or the fir
Out of the earth and from the air that blows.
Great power of Will that little thing the seed
Has, all alone in earth, to plan the tree,
And, though the mud oppresses, to succeed,
And put out branches where the birds may be.
Then the wind blows it, but the bending boughs
Exult like billows, and their million green
Drink the all-living sunlight in carouse,
Like dainty harts where forest wells are clean.
While it, the central plant, which looks o'er miles,
Draws milk from the earth's breast, and sways, and smiles.

Is there a great green commonwealth of Thought
Which ranks the yearly pageant, and decides
How Summer's royal progress shall be wrought,
By secret stir which in each plant abides?

Does rocking daffodil consent that she,
The snowdrop of wet winters, shall be first?
Does spotted cowslip with the grass agree
To hold her pride before the rattle burst?
And in the hedge what quick agreement goes,
When hawthorn blossoms redden to decay,
That Summer's pride shall come, the Summer's rose,
Before the flower be on the bramble spray?
Or is it, as with us, unresting strife,
And each consent a lucky gasp for life?

Beauty, let be; I cannot see your face,
I shall not know you now, nor touch your feet,
Only within me tremble to your grace
Tasting this crumb vouchsafed which is so sweet.
Even when the full-leaved Summer bore no fruit,
You give me this, this apple of man's tree;
This planet sings when other spheres were mute,
This light begins when darkness covered me.
Now, though I know that I shall never know
All, through my fault, nor blazon with my pen
That path prepared where only I could go,
Still, I have this, not given to other men.
Beauty, this grace, this spring, this given bread,
This life, this dawn, this wakening from the dead.

Here, where we stood together, we three men,
Before the war had swept us to the East
Three thousand miles away, I stand again
And hear the bells, and breathe, and go to feast.
We trod the same path, to the self-same place,
Yet here I stand, having beheld their graves,

Skyros whose shadows the great seas erase,
And Seddul Bahr that ever more blood craves.
So, since we communed here, our bones have been
Nearer, perhaps, than they again will be,
Earth and the world-wide battle lie between,
Death lies between, and friend-destroying sea.
Yet here, a year ago, we talked and stood
As I stand now, with pulses beating blood.

I saw her like a shadow on the sky
In the last light, a blur upon the sea,
Then the gale's darkness put the shadow by,
But from one grave that island talked to me;
And, in the midnight, in the breaking storm,
I saw its blackness and a blinking light,
And thought, "So death obscures your gentle form,
So memory strives to make the darkness bright;
And, in that heap of rocks, your body lies,
Part of the island till the planet ends,
My gentle comrade, beautiful and wise,
Part of this crag this bitter surge offends,
While I, who pass, a little obscure thing,
War with this force, and breathe, and am its king."

Not that the stars are all gone mad in heaven
Plucking the unseen reins upon men's souls,
Not that the law that bound the planets seven
Is discord now; man probes for new controls.
He bends no longer to the circling stars,
New moon and full moon and the living sun,
Love-making Venus, Jove and bloody Mars
Pass from their thrones, their rule of him is done.

And paler gods, made liker men, are past,
Like their sick eras to their funeral urns,
They cannot stand the fire blown by the blast
In which man's soul that measures heaven burns.
Man in his cage of many millioned pain
Burns all to ash to prove if God remain.

There is no God, as I was taught in youth,
Though each, according to his stature, builds
Some covered shrine for what he thinks the truth,
Which day by day his reddest heart-blood gilds.
There is no God; but death, the clasping sea,
In which we move like fish, deep over deep
Made of men's souls that bodies have set free,
Floods to a Justice though it seems asleep.
There is no God, but still, behind the veil,
The hurt thing works, out of its agony.
Still, like a touching of a brimming Grail,
Return the pennies given to passers by.
There is no God, but we, who breathe the air,
Are God ourselves and touch God everywhere.

Beauty retires; the blood out of the earth
Shrinks, the stalk dries, lifeless November still
Drops the brown husk of April's greenest birth.
Through the thinned beech clump I can see the hill.
So withers man, and though his life renews
In Aprils of the soul, an autumn comes
Which gives an end, not respite, to the thews
That bore his soul through the world's martyrdoms.
Then all the beauty will be out of mind,
Part of man's store, that lies outside his brain,

Touch to the dead and vision to the blind,
Drink in the desert, bread, eternal grain;
Part of the untilled field that beauty sows
With flowers untold, where quickened spirit goes.

Wherever beauty has been quick in clay
Some effluence of it lives, a spirit dwells,
Beauty that death can never take away,
Mixed with the air that shakes the flower bells;
So that by waters where the apples fall,
Or in lone glens, or valleys full of flowers,
Or in the streets where bloody tidings call,
The haunting waits the mood that makes it ours.
Then at a turn, a word, an act, a thought,
Such difference comes, the spirit apprehends
That place's glory, for where beauty fought
Under the veil the glory never ends,
But the still grass, the leaves, the trembling flower,
Keep, through dead time, that everlasting hour.

You are more beautiful than women are,
Wiser than men, stronger than ribbéd death,
Juster than Time, more constant than the star,
Dearer than love, more intimate than breath;
Having all art, all science, all control
Over the still unsmithied, even as Time
Cradles the generations of man's soul,
You are the light to guide, the way to climb.
So, having followed beauty, having bowed
To wisdom and to death, to law, to power,
I like a blind man stumble from the crowd
Into the darkness of a deeper hour,

Where in the lonely silence I may wait
The prayed-for gleam—your hand upon the gate.

Out of the barracks to the castle yard
Those Roman soldiers came, buckling their gear;
The word was passed that they were prison guard;
The sergeant proved their dressing with his spear.
Then, as the prisoner came, a wretch who bled
Holding a cross, those nearest cursed his soul:
He might have died some other time, they said,
Not at high noon: the sergeant called the roll.
Then, sloping spears, the files passed from the court
Into the alleys, thrusting back the crowd,
They cursed the bleeding man for stepping short;
The drums beat time: the sergeant hummed aloud;
The rabble closed behind: the soldiers cursed
The prisoner's soul, the flies, their packs, their thirst.

Not for the anguish suffered is the slur,
Not for the women's mocks, the taunts of men,
No, but because you never welcomed her,
Her of whose beauty I am only the pen.
There was a dog, dog-minded, with dog's eyes,
Damned by a dog's brute-nature to be true,
Something within her made his spirit wise,
He licked her hand, he knew her, not so you.
When all adulterate beauty has gone by,
When all inanimate matter has gone down,
We will arise and walk, that dog and I,
The only two who knew her in the town,
We'll range the pleasant mountains side by side,
Seeking the blood-stained flowers where Christs have died.

Beauty was with me once, but now, grown old,
I cannot hear nor see her: thus a king
In the high turret kept him from the cold
Over the fire with his magic ring
Which, as he wrought, made pictures come and go
Of men and times, past, present, and to be,
Now like a smoke, now flame-like, now a glow,
Now dead, now bright, but always fantasy.
While, on the stair without, a faithful slave
Stabbed to the death, crawled bleeding, whispering "Sir,
They come to kill you, fly: I come to save;
O you great gods, have pity, let him hear."
Then, with his last strength tapped and muttered, "Sire,"
While the king smiled and drowsed above the fire.

So beauty comes, so with a failing hand
She knocks and cries, and fails to make me hear,
She who tells futures in the falling sand
And still, by signs, makes hidden meanings clear;
She, who behind this many peopled smoke,
Moves in the light and struggles to direct,
Through the deaf ear and by the baffled stroke,
The wicked man, the honored architect.
Yet at a dawn before the birds begin,
In dreams, as the horse stamps and the hound stirs,
Sleep slips the bolt and beauty enters in
Crying aloud those hurried words of hers,
And I awake and, in the birded dawn,
Know her for Queen and own myself a pawn.

If Beauty be at all, if, beyond sense,
There be a wisdom piercing into brains,

Why should the glory wait on impotence,
Biding its time till blood is in the veins?
There is no beauty, but when thought is quick,
Out of the noisy sickroom of ourselves,
Some flattery comes to try to cheat the sick,
Some drowsy drug is groped for on the shelves,
And, for the rest, we play upon a scene
Beautiful with the blood of living things;
We move and speak and wonder and have been,
Upon the dust as dust, not queens and kings;
We know no beauty, nor does beauty care
For us, this dust, that men make everywhere.

Each greedy self, by consecrating lust,
Desire pricking into sacrifice,
Adds, in his way, some glory to the dust,
Brings, to the light, some haze of Paradise,
Hungers and thirsts for beauty; like the hound
Snaps it, to eat alone; in secret keeps
His miser's patch of consecrated ground
Where beauty's coins are dug down to the deeps.
So when disturbing death digs up our lives,
Some little gleam among the broken soil
May witness for us as the shovel rives
The dirty heap of all our tiny toil;
Some gleam of you may make the digger hold,
Touched for an instant with the thought of gold.

Time being an instant in eternity,
Beauty above man's million years must see
The heaped corrupted mass that had to die,
The husk of man that set the glitter free;

Now from those million bodies in the dark,
Forgotten, rotten, part of fields or roads,
The million gleam united makes a spark
Which Beauty sees among her star abodes.
And, from the bodies, comes a sigh, "Alas,
We hated, fought and killed, as separate men;
Now all is merged and we are in the grass,
Our efforts merged, would we had known it then.
All our lives' battle, all our spirits' dream,
Nought in themselves, a clash which made a gleam."

You will remember me in days to come
With love, or pride, or pity, or contempt;
So will my friends (not many friends, yet some)
When this my life will be a dream out-dreamt;
And one, remembering friendship by the fire,
And one, remembering love time in the dark,
And one, remembering unfulfilled desire,
Will sigh, perhaps, yet be beside the mark;
For this my body with its wandering ghost
Is nothing solely but an empty grange,
Dark in a night that owls inhabit most,
Yet when the king rides by there comes a change;
The windows gleam, the cresset's fiery hair
Blasts the blown branch and beauty lodges there.

They took the bloody body from the cross,
They laid it in its niche and rolled the stone.
One said, "Our blessed Master," one "His loss
Ends us companions, we are left alone."
And one, "I thought that Pilate would acquit
Right to the last;" and one, "The sergeant took

The trenching mall and drove the nails with it."
One who was weeping went apart and shook.
Then one, "He promised that in three short days
He would return, oh God; but He is dead."
And one, "What was it that He meant to raise?
The Temple? No? What was it that He said?
He said that He would build? That He would rise?"
"No," answered one, "but come from Paradise.

"Come to us fiery with the saints of God
To judge the world and take His power and reign."
Then one. "This was the very road we trod
That April day, would it could come again;
The day they flung the flowers." "Let be," said one,
"He was a lovely soul, but what He meant
Passes our wit, for none among us, none,
Had brains enough to fathom His intent.
His mother did not, nor could one of us,
But while He spoke I felt I understood."
And one, "He knew that it would finish thus.
Let His thought be, I know that He was good.
There is the orchard see, the very same
Where we were sleeping when the soldiers came."

So from the cruel cross they buried God;
So, in their desolation, as they went
They dug him deeper with each step they trod,
Their lightless minds distorting what He meant.
Lamenting Him, their leader, who had died,
They heaped the stones, they rolled the heavy door;
They said, "Our glory has been crucified,
Unless He rise our glory will be o'er"

While in the grave the spirit left the corpse
Broken by torture, slowly, line by line,
And saw the dawn come on the eastern thorpes,
And shook his wings and sang in the divine,
Crying "I told the truth, even unto death,
Though I was earth and now am only breath."

If all be governed by the moving stars,
If passing planets bring events to be,
Searing the face of Time with bloody scars,
Drawing men's souls even as the moon the sea;
If as they pass they make a current pass
Across man's life and heap it to a tide,
We are but pawns, ignobler than the grass
Cropped by the beast and crunched and tossed aside.
Is all this beauty that does inhabit heaven
Trail of a planet's fire? Is all this lust
A chymic means by warring stars contriven
To bring the violets out of Cæsar's dust?
Better be grass, or in some hedge unknown
The spilling rose whose beauty is its own.

In emptiest furthest heaven where no stars are
Perhaps some planet of our master sun
Still rolls an unguessed orbit round its star
Unthought, unseen, unknown of any one.
Roving dead space according to its law
Casting our light on burnt-out suns and blind
Singing in the frozen void its word of awe
One wandering thought in all that idiot mind.
And, in some span of many a thousand year,
Passing through heaven, its influence may arouse

Beauty unguessed in those who habit here,
And men may rise with glory on their brows,
And feel new life like fire, and see the old
Fall from them dead, the bronze's broken mould.

Perhaps in chasms of the wasted past,
That planet wandered within hail of ours,
And plucked men's souls to loveliness and cast
The old, that was, away, like husks of flowers;
And made them stand erect and bade them build
Nobler than hovels plaited in the mire,
Gave them an altar and a god to gild,
Bridled the brooks for them and fettered fire;
And, in another coming, forged the steel
Which, on life's scarlet wax, forever set
Longing for beauty bitten as a seal
That blood not clogs nor centuries forget,
That built Atlantis, and, in time will raise
That grander thing whose image haunts our days.

For, like an outcast from the city, I
Wander the desert strewn with traveller's bones,
Having no comrade but the starry sky
Where the tuned planets ride their floating thrones.
I pass old ruins where the kings caroused
In cups long shards from vines long since decayed,
I tread the broken brick where queens were housed
In beauty's time ere beauty was betrayed;
And in the ceaseless pitting of the sand
On monolith and pyle, I see the dawn,
Making those skeletons of beauty grand
By fire that comes as darkness is withdrawn;

[428]

And in that fire the art of men to come
Shines with such glow I bless my martyrdom.

Death lies in wait for you, you wild thing in the wood,
Shy-footed beauty dear, half-seen, half-understood,
Glimpsed in the beech wood dim, and in the dropping fir,
Shy like a fawn and sweet and beauty's minister.
Glimpsed as in flying clouds by night the little moon,
A wonder, a delight, a paleness passing soon.
Only a moment held, only an hour seen,
Only an instant known in all that life has been,
One instant in the sand to drink that gush of grace
The beauty of your way, the marvel of your face.
Death lies in wait for you, but few short hours he gives,
I perish even as you by whom all spirit lives,
Come to me, spirit, come, and fill my hour of breath
With hours of life in life that pay no toll to death.

What are we given, what do we take away?
Five little senses, startling with delight,
That dull to death and perish into clay
And pass from human memory as from sight.
So the new penny glittering from the mint,
Bears the king's head awhile, but Time effaces
The head, the date, the seated queen, the print
Even as a brook the stone in pebbly places.
We bear the stamp, are current, and are prized,
Hoarded or spent, the while the mintage passes,
Then, like light money, challenged or despised,
We join the heap of dross which Time amasses,
Erased, uncurrent discs no more to range
The clanging counters in the great exchange.

They called that broken hedge The Haunted Gate.
Strange fires (they said) burnt there at moonless times.
Evil was there, men never went there late,
The darkness there was quick with threatened crimes.
And then one digging in that bloodied clay
Found, but a foot below, a rotted chest.
Coins of the Romans, tray on rusted tray,
Hurriedly heaped there by a digger prest.
So that one knew how, centuries before,
Some Roman flying from the sack by night,
Digging in terror there to hide his store,
Sweating his pick, by windy lantern light,
Had stamped his anguish on that place's soul,
So that it knew and could rehearse the whole.

There was an evil in the nodding wood
Above the quarry long since overgrown,
Something which stamped it as a place of blood
Where tortured spirit cried from murdered bone.
Then, after years, I saw a rusty knife
Stuck in a woman's skull, just as 'twas found,
Blackt with a centuried crust of clotted life,
In the red clay of that unholy ground.
So that I knew the unhappy thing had spoken,
That tongueless thing for whom the quarry spoke,
The evil seals of murder had been broken
By the red earth, the grass, the rooted oak,
The inarticulate dead had forced the spade,
The hand, the mind, till murder was displayed.

Go, spend your penny, Beauty, when you will,
In the grave's darkness let the stamp be lost.
The water still will bubble from the hill,

And April quick the meadows with her ghost;
Over the grass the daffodils will shiver,
The primroses with their pale beauty abound,
The blackbird be a lover and make quiver
With his glad singing the great soul of the ground;
So that if the body rot, it will not matter;
Up in the earth the great game will go on,
The coming of Spring and the running of the water,
And the young things glad of the womb's darkness gone;
And the joy we felt will be a part of the glory
In the lover's kiss that makes the old couple's story.

Not for your human beauty nor the power
To shake me by your voice or by your touch,
Summer must have its rose, the rose must flower,
Beauty burn deep, I do not yield to such.
No, but because your beauty where it falls
Lays bare the spirits in the crowded streets,
Shatters the lock, destroys the castle walls,
Breaks down the bars till friend with comrade meets,
So that I wander brains where beauty dwelled
In long dead time, and see again the rose
By long dead men for living beauty held,
That Death's knife spares, and Winter with his snows,
And know it bloodied by that pulse of birth
Which greens the grass in Aprils upon earth.

The little robin hopping in the wood
Draws friendship from you, the rapt nightingale
Making the night a marvellous solitude,
Only of you to darkness tells the tale.

Kingfishers are but jewels on your dress,
Dun deer that rove and timid rabbits shy
Are but the hintings of your gentleness.
Upon your wings the eagle climbs the sky.
Fish that are shadows in the water pass
With mystery from you, the purpled moth
Dust from your kirtle on his broidery has,
Out of your bounty every beauty flowth.
For you are all, all fire, all living form,
Marvel in man and glory in the worm.

Though in life's streets the tempting shops have lured,
Because all beauty, howsoever base,
Is vision of you, marred, I have endured
Tempted or fall'n, to look upon your face.
Now through the grinning death's head in the paint,
Within the tavern-song, hid in the wine,
In many kinded man, emperor and saint,
I see you pass, you breath of the divine.
I see you pass, as centuries ago
The long dead men with passionate spirit saw,
O brother man, whom spirit habits so,
Through your red sorrows Beauty keeps her law,
Beauty herself, who takes your dying hand,
To leave through Time the Memnon in the sand.

When all these million cells that are my slaves
Fall from my pourried ribs and leave me lone,
A living speck among a world of graves,
What shall I be, that spot in the unknown?
A glow-worm in a night that floats the sun?
Or deathless dust feeling the passer's foot?

SONNETS

An eye undying mourning things undone?
Or seed for quickening free from prisoning fruit?
Or an eternal jewel on your robe,
Caught to your heart, one with the April fire
That made me yours as man upon the globe,
One with the Spring, a breath in all desire,
One with the primrose, present in all joy?
Or pash that rots, which pismires can destroy?

Let that which is to come be as it may,
Darkness, extinction, justice, life intense
The flies are happy in the summer day,
Flies will be happy many summers hence.
Time with his antique breeds that built the Sphinx
Time with her men to come whose wings will tower,
Poured and will pour, not as the wise man thinks,
But with blind force, to each his little hour.
And when the hour has struck, comes death or change,
Which, whether good or ill, we cannot tell,
But the blind planet will wander through her range
Bearing men like us who will serve as well.
The sun will rise, the winds that ever move
Will blow our dust that once were men in love.

THE MADMAN'S SONG

You have not seen what I have seen,
The town besieged by a million men;
I saw it though, the people starved,
My rib-bones here came through my skin.
Thousands were killed and thousands died,
We ate dead blow-flies from the stalls;
"Help us, O Lord, our King," we cried;
He could not help, for all our calls.
No, but there was a poor mean man,
A skinny man and mad, like me,
He saw: he told the King his plan,
A plan to set our city free.
The King in fury had him bound,
Dragged to the walls with kick and curse,
And flung from off them to the ground;
Daily our agonies grew worse.
And all our sallies came to wreck,
We ate the dead men from the grave,
Our troops were killed or put in check,
"O King," we cried, "in pity, save,
Save us or we shall die," we cried.
He could not save us, so we died.

*   *   *   *   *

But then he called to mind the man
Whose bones the dogs had picked by this,
He murmured, "We will try the plan,
Death would be better than what is.

[434]

THE MADMAN'S SONG

I'll try the madman's plan to-night.
Do I remember it aright?"

*   *   *   *

We did the madman's will, we won,
We left the million rotting there;
Not one remained alive, not one,
The madman's wisdom was most rare.
We laughed, we ate again, we drank,
Rebuilt the city, walls and towers,
We cried "We have the King to thank."
We strewed his royal path with flowers.

*   *   *   *   *

But I who am mad am wiser now,
I wander in the city ditch,
For wisdom grows on the withered bough.
Flowers are fair and fruit is rich,
But wisdom is lovelier than them all.
So when the world is hard at work,
I kneel in the foss below the wall
On the rubble where the lizards lurk.

*   *   *   *   *

The goutweed hides the poor man's bones,
The mint-scent warms in the hot air,
An influence comes out of the stones,
The dead man's spirit quickens there,
Singing, "I trod the piteous way
The world despised me, comrades failed,
But from above an unquenched ray
Burned in my brain: it never quailed;

My body shook, my mind had doubt,
That star within me helped me on,
Man, the walled town which cast me out,
Was powerless like a fever gone.
And now I know that light is like the sea,
I was the rock it girt, it beat on me.
I was the deaf-mute, blinded by a curse,
Outside me was the starry universe
I had but to unlatch to let it in.
Nothing but mental blindness can be sin,
All seeing saves, all hearing, all delight,
I am a star. I wander through the night."

THE "WANDERER"

All day they loitered by the resting ships,
Telling their beauties over, taking stock;
At night the verdict left my messmates' lips,
"The *Wanderer* is the finest ship in dock."

I had not seen her, but a friend, since drowned,
Drew her, with painted ports, low, lovely, lean,
Saying, "The *Wanderer*, clipper, outward bound,
The loveliest ship my eyes have ever seen—

"Perhaps to-morrow you will see her sail.
She sails at sunrise": but the morrow showed
No *Wanderer* setting forth for me to hail;
Far down the stream men pointed where she rode,

Rode the great trackway to the sea, dim, dim,
Already gone before the stars were gone.
I saw her at the sea-line's smoky rim
Grow swiftly vaguer as they towed her on.

Soon even her masts were hidden in the haze
Beyond the city; she was on her course
To trample billows for a hundred days;
That afternoon the norther gathered force,

Blowing a small snow from a point of east.
"Oh, fair for her," we said, "to take her south."
And in our spirits, as the wind increased,
We saw her there, beyond the river mouth,

Setting her side-lights in the wildering dark,
To glint upon mad water, while the gale
Roared like a battle, snapping like a shark,
And drunken seamen struggle with the sail.

While with sick hearts her mates put out of mind
Their little children left astern, ashore,
And the gale's gathering made the darkness blind,
Water and air one intermingled roar.

Then we forgot her, for the fiddlers played,
Dancing and singing held our merry crew;
The old ship moaned a little as she swayed.
It blew all night, oh, bitter hard it blew!

So that at midnight I was called on deck
To keep an anchor-watch: I heard the sea
Roar past in white procession filled with wreck;
Intense bright frosty stars burned over me,

And the Greek brig beside us dipped and dipped,
White to the muzzle like a half-tide rock,
Drowned to the mainmast with the seas she shipped;
Her cable-swivels clanged at every shock.

And like a never-dying force, the wind
Roared till we shouted with it, roared until
Its vast vitality of wrath was thinned,
Had beat its fury breathless and was still.

By dawn the gale had dwindled into flaw,
A glorious morning followed: with my friend
I climbed the fo'c's'le-head to see; we saw
The waters hurrying shorewards without end.

Haze blotted out the river's lowest reach;
Out of the gloom the steamers, passing by,
Called with their sirens, hooting their sea-speech;
Out of the dimness others made reply.

And as we watched, there came a rush of feet
Charging the fo'c's'le till the hatchway shook.
Men all about us thrust their way, or beat,
Crying, "The *Wanderer!* Down the river! Look!"

I looked with them towards the dimness; there
Gleamed like a spirit striding out of night,

[438]

THE "WANDERER"

A full-rigged ship unutterably fair,
Her masts like trees in winter, frosty-bright.

Foam trembled at her bows like wisps of wool;
She trembled as she towed.   I had not dreamed
That work of man could be so beautiful,
In its own presence and in what it seemed.

"So, she is putting back again," I said.
"How white with frost her yards are on the fore."
One of the men about me answer made,
"That is not frost, but all her sails are tore,

"Torn into tatters, youngster, in the gale;
Her best foul-weather suit gone."   It was true,
Her masts were white with rags of tattered sail
Many as gannets when the fish are due.

Beauty in desolation was her pride,
Her crowned array a glory that had been;
She faltered tow'rds us like a swan that died,
But although ruined she was still a queen.

"Put back with all her sails gone," went the word;
Then, from her signals flying, rumour ran,
"The sea that stove her boats in killed her third;
She has been gutted and has lost a man."

So, as though stepping to a funeral march,
She passed defeated homewards whence she came,
Ragged with tattered canvas white as starch,
A wild bird that misfortune had made tame.

She was refitted soon: another took
The dead man's office; then the singers hove
Her capstan till the snapping hawsers shook;
Out, with a bubble at her bows, she drove.

Again they towed her seawards, and again
We, watching, praised her beauty, praised her trim,
Saw her fair house-flag flutter at the main,
And slowly saunter seawards, dwindling dim;

And wished her well, and wondered, as she died,
How, when her canvas had been sheeted home,
Her quivering length would sweep into her stride,
Making the greenness milky with her foam.

But when we rose next morning, we discerned
Her beauty once again a shattered thing;
Towing to dock the *Wanderer* returned,
A wounded sea-bird with a broken wing.

A spar was gone, her rigging's disarray
Told of a worse disaster than the last;
Like draggled hair dishevelled hung the stay,
Drooping and beating on the broken mast.

Half-mast upon her flagstaff hung her flag;
Word went among us how the broken spar
Had gored her captain like an angry stag,
And killed her mate a half-day from the bar.

She passed to dock upon the top of flood.
An old man near me shook his head and swore:

"Like a bad woman, she has tasted blood—
There'll be no trusting in her any more."

We thought it truth, and when we saw her there
Lying in dock, beyond, across the stream,
We would forget that we had called her fair,
We thought her murderess and the past a dream.

And when she sailed again, we watched in awe,
Wondering what bloody act her beauty planned,
What evil lurked behind the thing we saw,
What strength was there that thus annulled man's hand,

How next its triumph would compel man's will
Into compliance with external Fate,
How next the powers would use her to work ill
On suffering men; we had not long to wait.

For soon the outcry of derision rose,
"Here comes the *Wanderer!*" the expected cry.
Guessing the cause, our mockings joined with those
Yelled from the shipping as they towed her by.

She passed us close, her seamen paid no heed
To what was called: they stood, a sullen group,
Smoking and spitting, careless of her need,
Mocking the orders given from the poop.

Her mates and boys were working her; we stared.
What was the reason of this strange return,
This third annulling of the thing prepared?
No outward evil could our eyes discern.

Only like one who having formed a plan
Beyond the pitch of common minds, she sailed,
Mocked and deserted by the common man,
Made half divine to me for having failed.

We learned the reason soon; below the town
A stay had parted like a snapping reed,
"Warning," the men thought, "not to take her down."
They took the omen, they would not proceed.

Days passed before another crew would sign.
The *Wanderer* lay in dock alone, unmanned,
Feared as a thing possessed by powers malign,
Bound under curses not to leave the land.

But under passing Time fear passes too;
That terror passed, the sailors' hearts grew bold.
We learned in time that she had found a crew
And was bound out and southwards as of old.

And in contempt we thought, "A little while
Will bring her back again, dismantled, spoiled.
It is herself; she cannot change her style;
She has the habit now of being foiled."

So when a ship appeared among the haze,
We thought, "The *Wanderer* back again"; but no,
No *Wanderer* showed for many, many days,
Her passing lights made other waters glow.

But we would often think and talk of her,
Tell newer hands her story, wondering, then,

THE "WANDERER"

Upon what ocean she was *Wanderer*,
Bound to the cities built by foreign men.

And one by one our little conclave thinned,
Passed into ships and sailed and so away,
To drown in some great roaring of the wind,
Wanderers themselves, unhappy fortune's prey.

And Time went by me making memory dim,
Yet still I wondered if the *Wanderer* fared
Still pointing to the unreached ocean's rim,
Brightening the water where her breast was bared.

And much in ports abroad I eyed the ships,
Hoping to see her well-remembered form
Come with a curl of bubbles at her lips
Bright to her berth, the sovereign of the storm.

I never did, and many years went by,
Then, near a Southern port, one Christmas Eve,
I watched a gale go roaring through the sky,
Making the caldrons of the clouds upheave.

Then the wrack tattered and the stars appeared,
Millions of stars that seemed to speak in fire;
A byre cock cried aloud that morning neared,
The swinging wind-vane flashed upon the spire.

And soon men looked upon a glittering earth,
Intensely sparkling like a world new-born;
Only to look was spiritual birth,
So bright the raindrops ran along the thorn.

So bright they were, that one could almost pass
Beyond their twinkling to the source, and know
The glory pushing in the blade of grass,
That hidden soul which makes the flowers grow.

That soul was there apparent, not revealed,
Unearthly meanings covered every tree,
That wet grass grew in an immortal field
Those waters fed some never-wrinkled sea.

The scarlet berries in the hedge stood out
Like revelations but the tongue unknown;
Even in the brooks a joy was quick: the trout
Rushed in a dumbness dumb to me alone.

All of the valley was aloud with brooks;
I walked the morning, breasting up the fells,
Taking again lost childhood from the rooks,
Whose cawing came above the Christmas bells.

I had not walked that glittering world before,
But up the hill a prompting came to me,
"This line of upland runs along the shore:
Beyond the hedgerow I shall see the sea."

And on the instant from beyond away
That long familiar sound, a ship's bell, broke
The hush below me in the unseen bay.
Old memories came: that inner prompting spoke.

And bright above the hedge a seagull's wings
Flashed and were steady upon empty air.

THE "WANDERER"

"A Power unseen," I cried, "prepares these things;
Those are her bells, the *Wanderer* is there."

So, hurrying to the hedge and looking down,
I saw a mighty bay's wind-crinkled blue
Ruffling the image of a tranquil town,
With lapsing waters glittering as they grew.

And near me in the road the shipping swung,
So stately and so still in such great peace
That like to drooping crests their colours hung,
Only their shadows trembled without cease.

I did but glance upon those anchored ships.
Even as my thought had told, I saw her plain;
Tense, like a supple athlete with lean hips,
Swiftness at pause, the *Wanderer* come again—

Come as of old a queen, untouched by Time,
Resting the beauty that no seas could tire,
Sparkling, as though the midnight's rain were rime,
Like a man's thought transfigured into fire.

And as I looked, one of her men began
To sing some simple tune of Christmas day;
Among her crew the song spread, man to man,
Until the singing rang across the bay;

And soon in other anchored ships the men
Joined in the singing with clear throats, until
The farm-boy heard it up the windy glen,
Above the noise of sheep-bells on the hill.

Over the water came the lifted song—
Blind pieces in a mighty game we swing;
Life's battle is a conquest for the strong;
The meaning shows in the defeated thing.

AUGUST, 1914

How still this quiet cornfield is to-night!
By an intenser glow the evening falls,
Bringing, not darkness, but a deeper light;
Among the stooks a partridge covey calls.

The windows glitter on the distant hill;
Beyond the hedge the sheep-bells in the fold
Stumble on sudden music and are still;
The forlorn pinewoods droop above the wold.

An endless quiet valley reaches out
Past the blue hills into the evening sky;
Over the stubble, cawing goes a rout
Of rooks from harvest, flagging as they fly.

So beautiful it is, I never saw
So great a beauty on these English fields,
Touched by the twilight's coming into awe,
Ripe to the soul and rich with summer's yields.

   *   *   *   *   *

These homes, this valley spread below me here,
The rooks, the tilted stacks, the beasts in pen,

Have been the heartfelt things past-speaking dear
To unknown generations of dead men,

Who, century after century, held these farms,
And, looking out to watch the changing sky,
Heard, as we hear, the rumours and alarms
Of war at hand and danger pressing nigh.

And knew, as we know, that the message meant
The breaking off of ties, the loss of friends,
Death, like a miser getting in his rent,
And no new stones laid where the trackway ends.

The harvest not yet won, the empty bin,
The friendly horses taken from the stalls,
The fallow on the hill not yet brought in,
The cracks unplastered in the leaking walls.

Yet heard the news, and went discouraged home,
And brooded by the fire with heavy mind,
With such dumb loving of the Berkshire loam
As breaks the dumb hearts of the English kind,

Then sadly rose and left the well-loved Downs,
And so by ship to sea, and knew no more
The fields of home, the byres, the market towns,
Nor the dear outline of the English shore,

But knew the misery of the soaking trench,
The freezing in the rigging, the despair
In the revolting second of the wrench
When the blind soul is flung upon the air,

And died (uncouthly, most) in foreign lands
For some idea but dimly understood
Of an English city never built by hands
Which love of England prompted and made good.

      *   *   *   *   *

If there be any life beyond the grave,
It must be near the men and things we love,
Some power of quick suggestion how to save,
Touching the living soul as from above.

An influence from the Earth from those dead hearts
So passionate once, so deep, so truly kind,
That in the living child the spirit starts,
Feeling companioned still, not left behind.

Surely above these fields a spirit broods,
A sense of many watchers muttering near
Of the lone Downland with the forlorn woods
Loved to the death, inestimably dear.

A muttering from beyond the veils of Death
From long-dead men, to whom this quiet scene
Came among blinding tears with the last breath,
The dying soldier's vision of his queen.

All the unspoken worship of those lives
Spent in forgotten wars at other calls
Glimmers upon these fields where evening drives
Beauty like breath, so gently darkness falls.

Darkness that makes the meadows holier still,
The elm-trees sadden in the hedge, a sigh
Moves in the beech-clump on the haunted hill,
The rising planets deepen in the sky,

And silence broods like spirit on the brae,
A glimmering moon begins, the moonlight runs
Over the grasses of the ancient way
Rutted this morning by the passing guns.

THE RIVER

All other waters have their time of peace,
Calm, or the turn of tide or summer drought;
But on these bars the tumults never cease,
In violent death this river passes out.

Brimming she goes, a bloody-coloured rush
Hurrying her heaped disorder, rank on rank,
Bubbleless speed so still that in the hush
One hears the mined earth dropping from the bank,

Slipping in little falls whose tingeings drown,
Sunk by the waves for ever pressing on.
Till with a stripping crash the tree goes down,
Its washing branches flounder and are gone.

Then, roaring out aloud, her water spreads,
Making a desolation where her waves

Shriek and give battle, tossing up their heads,
Tearing the shifting sandbanks into graves,

Changing the raddled ruin of her course
So swiftly, that the pilgrim on the shore
Hears the loud whirlpool laughing like a horse
Where the scurfed sand was parched an hour before.

And always underneath that heaving tide
The changing bottom runs, or piles, or quakes
Flinging immense heaps up to wallow wide,
Sucking the surface into whirls like snakes,

If anything should touch that shifting sand,
All the blind bottom sucks it till it sinks;
It takes the clipper ere she comes to land,
It takes the thirsting tiger as he drinks.

And on the river pours—it never tires;
Blind, hungry, screaming, day and night the same
Purposeless hurry of a million ires,
Mad as the wind, as merciless as flame.

*   *   *   *   *

There was a full-rigged ship, the *Travancore*,
Towing to port against that river's rage—
A glittering ship made sparkling for the shore,
Taut to the pins in all her equipage.

Clanging, she topped the tide; her sails were furled,
Her men came loitering downwards from the yards;

THE RIVER

They who had brought her half across the world,
Trampling so many billows into shards,

Now looking up, beheld their duty done,
The ship approaching port, the great masts bare,
Gaunt as three giants striding in the sun,
Proud, with the colours tailing out like hair.

So, having coiled their gear, they left the deck;
Within the fo'c's'le's gloom of banded steel,
Mottled like wood with many a painted speck,
They brought their plates and sat about a meal.

Then pushing back the tins, they lit their pipes,
Or slept, or played at cards, or gently spoke,
Light from the portholes shot in dusty stripes
Tranquilly moving, sometimes blue with smoke.

These sunbeams sidled when the vessel rolled,
Their lazy dust-strips crossed the floor,
Lighting a man-hole leading to the hold,
A man-hole leaded down the day before.

Like gold the solder on the man-hole shone;
A few flies threading in a drowsy dance
Slept in their pattern, darted, and were gone.
The river roared against the ship's advance.

And quietly sleep came upon the crew,
Man by man drooped upon his arms and slept;
Without, the tugboat dragged the vessel through,
The rigging whined, the yelling water leapt,

Till blindly a careering wave's collapse
Rose from beneath her bows and spouted high,
Spirting the fo'c'sle floor with noisy slaps;
A sleeper at the table heaved a sigh,

And lurched, half-drunk with sleep, across the floor,
Muttering and blinking like a man insane,
Cursed at the river's tumult, shut the door,
Blinked, and lurched back and fell asleep again.

Then there was greater silence in the room,
Ship's creakings ran along the beams and died,
The lazy sunbeams loitered up the gloom,
Stretching and touching till they reached the side.

> *   *   *   *   *

Yet something jerking in the vessel's course
Told that the tug was getting her in hand
As, at a fence, one steadies down a horse,
To rush the whirlpool on Magellan Sand;

And in the uneasy water just below
Her Mate inquired "if the men should stir
And come on deck?"   Her Captain answered "No,
Let them alone, the tug can manage her."

Then, as she settled down and gathered speed,
Her Mate inquired again "if they should come
Just to be ready there in case of need,
Since, on such godless bars, there might be some."

But "No," the Captain said, "the men have been
Boxing about since midnight, let them be.
The pilot's able and the ship's a queen,
The hands can rest until we come to quay."

They ceased, they took their stations; right ahead
The whirlpool heaped and sucked; in tenor tone
The steady leadsman chanted at the lead,
The ship crept forward trembling to the bone.

And just above the worst a passing wave
Brought to the line such unexpected stress
That as she tossed her bows her towrope gave,
Snapped at the collar like a stalk of cress.

Then, for a ghastly moment, she was loose,
Blind in the whirlpool, groping for a guide,
Swinging adrift without a moment's truce,
She struck the sand and fell upon her side.

And instantly the sand beneath her gave
So that she righted and again was flung,
Grinding the quicksand open for a grave,
Straining her masts until the steel was sprung.

The foremast broke; its mighty bulk of steel
Fell on the fo'c'sle door and jammed it tight;
The sand-rush heaped her to an even keel,
She settled down, resigned, she made no fight,

But, like an overladen beast, she lay
Dumb in the mud with billows at her lips,

Broken, where she had fallen in the way,
Grinding her grave among the bones of ships.

     *   *   *   *   *

At the first crashing of the mast, the men
Sprang from their sleep to hurry to the deck;
They found that Fate had caught them in a pen,
The door that opened out was jammed with wreck.

Then, as, with shoulders down, their gathered strength
Hove on the door, but could not make it stir,
They felt the vessel tremble through her length;
The tug, made fast again, was plucking her.

Plucking, and causing motion, till it seemed
That she would get her off; they heard her screw
Mumble the bubbled rip-rap as she steamed;
"Please God, the tug will shift her!" said the crew.

"She's off!" the seamen said; they felt her glide,
Scraping the bottom with her bilge, until
Something collapsing clanged along her side;
The scraping stopped, the tugboat's screw was still.

"She's holed!" a voice without cried; "holed and jammed—
Holed on the old *Magellan*, sunk last June.
I lose my ticket and the men are damned;
They'll drown like rats unless we free them soon.

"My God, they shall not!" and the speaker beat
Blows with a crow upon the foremast's wreck;

[454]

Minute steel splinters fell about his feet,
No tremour stirred the ruin on the deck.

And as their natures bade, the seamen learned
That they were doomed within that buried door;
Some cursed, some raved, but one among them turned
Straight to the manhole leaded in the floor,

And sitting down astride it, drew his knife,
And staidly dug to pick away the lead,
While at the ports his fellows cried for life:
"Burst in the door, or we shall all be dead!"

For like a brook the leak below them clucked.
They felt the vessel settling; they could feel
How the blind bog beneath her gripped and sucked.
Their fingers beat their prison walls of steel.

And then the gurgling stopped—the ship was still.
She stayed; she sank no deeper—an arrest
Fothered the pouring leak; she ceased to fill.
She trod the mud, drowned only to the breast.

And probing at the well, the captain found
The leak no longer rising, so he cried:
"She is not sinking— you will not be drowned;
The shifting sand has silted up her side.

"Now there is time. The tug shall put ashore
And fetch explosives to us from the town;
I'll burst the house or blow away the door
(It will not kill you if you all lie down).

"Be easy in your minds, for you'll be free
As soon as we've the blast." The seamen heard
The tug go townwards, butting at the sea;
Some lit their pipes, the youngest of them cheered.

But still the digger bent above the lid,
Gouging the solder from it as at first,
Pecking the lead, intent on what he did;
The other seamen mocked at him or cursed.

And some among them nudged him as he picked.
He cursed them, grinning, but resumed his game;
His knife-point sometimes struck the lid and clicked.
The solder-pellets shone like silver flame.

And still his knife-blade clicked like ticking time
Counting the hour till the tug's return,
And still the ship stood steady on the slime,
While Fate above her fingered with her urn.

*   *   *   *   *

Then from the tug beside them came the hail:
"They have none at the stores, nor at the dock,
Nor at the quarry, so I tried the gaol.
They thought they had, but it was out of stock.

"So then I telephoned to town; they say
They've sent an engine with some to the pier;
I did not leave till it was on its way,
A tug is waiting there to bring it here:

"It can't be here, though, for an hour or more;
I've lost an hour in trying, as it is.

[456]

For want of thought commend me to the shore.
You'd think they'd know their river's ways by this."

"So there is nothing for it but to wait,"
The Captain answered, fuming. "Until then,
We'd better go to dinner, Mr. Mate."
The cook brought dinner forward to the men.

*　　　*　　　*　　　*　　　*

Another hour of prison loitered by;
The strips of sunlight stiffened at the port,
But still the digger made the pellets fly,
Paying no heed to his companions' sport,

While they, about him, spooning at their tins,
Asked if he dug because he found it cold,
Or whether it was penance for his sins,
Or hope of treasure in the forward hold.

He grinned and cursed, but did not cease to pick,
His sweat dropped from him when he bent his head,
His knife-blade quarried down, till with a click
Its grinded thinness snapped against the lead.

Then, dully rising, brushing back his sweat,
He asked his fellows for another knife.
"Never," they said; "man, what d'ye hope to get?"
"Nothing," he said, "except a chance for life."

"Havers," they said, and one among them growled,
"You'll get no knife from any here to break.
You've dug the manhole since the door was fouled,
And now your knife's broke, quit, for Jesus' sake."

But one, who smelt a bargain, changed his tone,
Offering a sheath-knife for the task in hand
At twenty times its value, as a loan
To be repaid him when they reached the land.

And there was jesting at the lender's greed
And mockery at the digger's want of sense,
Closing with such a bargain without need,
Since in an hour the tug would take them thence.

But "Right," the digger said. The deal was made
He took the borrowed knife, and sitting down
Gouged at the channelled solder with the blade,
Saying, "Let be, it's better dig than drown."

And nothing happened for a while; the heat
Grew in the stuffy room, the sunlight slid,
Flies buzzed about and jostled at the meat,
The knife-blade clicked upon the manhole lid:

And one man said, "She takes a hell of time
Bringing the blaster," and another snorted;
One, between pipe-puffs, hummed a smutty rhyme,
One, who was weaving, thudded with his sword.

It was as though the ship were in a dream,
Caught in a magic ocean, calm like death,
Tranced, till a presence should arise and gleam,
Making the waters conscious with her breath

It was so drowsy that the river's cries,
Roaring aloud their ever-changing tune,

Came to those sailors like a drone of flies,
Filling with sleep the summer afternoon.

So that they slept, or, if they spoke, it was
Only to worry lest the tug should come:
Such power upon the body labour has
That prison seemed a blessed rest to some,

Till one man leaning at the port-hole, stared,
Checking his yawning at the widest stretch,
Then blinked and swallowed, while he muttered, scared,
"That blasting-cotton takes an age to fetch."

Then swiftly passing from the port he went
Up and then down the fo'c'sle till he stayed,
Fixed at the port-hole with his eyes intent,
Round-eyed and white, as if he were afraid,

And muttered as he stared, "My God! she is.
She's deeper than she was, she's settling down,
That palm-tree top was steady against this,
And now I see the quay below the town.

"Look here at her. She's sinking in her tracks.
She's going down by inches as she stands;
The water's darker and it stinks like flax,
Her going down is churning up the sands."

And instantly a panic took the crew,
Even the digger blenched; his knife-blade's haste
Cutting the solder witnessed that he knew
Time on the brink with not a breath to waste.

While far away the tugboat at the quay
Under her drooping pennon waited still
For that explosive which would set them free,
Free, with the world a servant to their will.

Then from a boat beside them came a blare,
Urging that tugboat to be quick; and men
Shouted to stir her from her waiting there,
"Hurry the blast, and get us out of pen.

"She's going down. She's going down, man! Quick!"
The tugboat did not stir, no answer came;
They saw her tongue-like pennon idly lick
Clear for an instant, lettered with her name.

Then droop again. The engine had not come,
The blast had not arrived. The prisoned hands
Saw her still waiting though their time had come,
Their ship was going down among the sands,

Going so swiftly now, that they could see
The banks arising as she made her bed;
Full of sick sound she settled deathward, she
Gurgled and shook, the digger picked the lead.

And, as she paused to take a final plunge,
Prone like a half-tide rock, the men on deck
Jumped to their boats and left, ere like a sponge
The river's rotten heart absorbed the wreck;

And on the perilous instant ere Time struck
The digger's work was done, the lead was cleared,

He cast the manhole up; below it muck
Floated, the hold was full, the water leered.

All of his labour had but made a hole
By which to leap to death; he saw black dust
Float on the bubbles of that brimming bowl,
He drew a breath and took his life in trust,

And plunged head foremost into that black pit,
Where floating cargo bumped against the beams.
He groped a choking passage blind with grit,
The roaring in his ears was shot with screams.

So, with a bursting heart and roaring ears
He floundered in that sunk ship's inky womb,
Drowned in deep water for what seemed like years,
Buried alive and groping through the tomb,

Till suddenly the beams against his back
Gave, and the water on his eyes was bright;
He shot up through a hatchway foul with wrack
Into clean air and life and dazzling light,

And striking out, he saw the fo'c'sle gone,
Vanished, below the water, and the mast
Standing columnar from the sea; it shone
Proud, with its colours flying to the last.

And all about, a many-wrinkled tide
Smoothed and erased its eddies, wandering chilled,
Like glutted purpose, trying to decide
If its achievement had been what it willed.

And men in boats were there; they helped him in.
He gulped for breath and watched that patch of smooth,
Shaped like the vessel, wrinkle into grin,
Furrow to waves and bare a yellow tooth.

Then the masts leaned until the shroud-screws gave.
All disappeared—her masts, her colours, all.
He saw the yardarms tilting to the grave;
He heard the siren of a tugboat call,

And saw her speeding, foaming at the bow,
Bringing the blast-charge that had come too late.
He heard one shout, "It isn't wanted now."
Time's minute-hand had been the hand of Fate.

Then the boats turned; they brought him to the shore.
Men crowded round him, touched him, and were kind;
The Mate walked with him, silent, to the store.
He said, "We've left the best of us behind."

Then, as he wrung his sodden clothes, the Mate
Gave him a drink of rum, and talked awhile
Of men and ships and unexpected Fate;
And darkness came and cloaked the river's guile,

So that its huddled hurry was not seen,
Only made louder, till the full moon climbed
Over the forest, floated, and was queen.
Within the town a temple-belfry chimed.

Then, upon silent pads, a tiger crept
Down to the river-brink, and crouching there
Watched it intently, till you thought he slept
But for his ghastly eye and stiffened hair.

Then, trembling at a lust more fell than his,
He roared and bounded back to coverts lone,
Where, among moonlit beauty, slaughter is,
Filling the marvellous night with myriad groan.

WATCHING BY A SICK-BED

I heard the wind all day,
And what it was trying to say.
I heard the wind all night
Rave as it ran to fight;
After the wind the rain,
And then the wind again
Running across the hill
As it runs still.

And all day long the sea
Would not let the land be,
But all night heaped her sand
On to the land;
I saw her glimmer white
All through the night,
Tossing the horrid hair
Still tossing there.

And all day long the stone
Felt how the wind was blown;
And all night long the rock
Stood the sea's shock;
While, from the window, I
Looked out, and wondered why,
Why at such length
Such force should fight such strength.

The River was first published in the *Century Magazine; The Wanderer* in *Harper's Magazine; Watching by a Sick-bed* and *August, 1914,* in *Harper's Weekly.* I thank the editors of these periodicals for permission to reprint them here.

JOHN MASEFIELD.

LOLLINGDON DOWNS AND OTHER POEMS

LOLLINGDON DOWNS

I

So I have known this life,
These beads of coloured days,
This self the string.
What is this thing?

Not beauty; no; not greed,
O, not indeed;
Not all, though much;
Its colour is not such.

It has no eyes to see,
It has no ears,
It is a red hour's war
Followed by tears.

It is an hour of time,
An hour of road,
Flesh is its goad,
Yet, in the sorrowing lands,
Women and men take hands.

O earth, give us the corn,
Come rain, come sun,
We men who have been born
Have tasks undone.
Out of this earth
Comes the thing birth,
The thing unguessed, unwon.

II

O wretched man, that, for a little mile
Crawls beneath heaven for his brother's blood,
Whose days the planets number with their style,
To whom all earth is slave, all living, food;

O withering man, within whose folded shell
Lies yet the seed, the spirit's quickening corn,
That Time and Sun will change out of the cell
Into green meadows, in the world unborn;

If Beauty be a dream, do but resolve
And fire shall come, that in the stubborn clay
Works to make perfect till the rocks dissolve,
The barriers burst and Beauty takes her way,

Beauty herself, within whose blossoming Spring
Even wretched man shall clap his hands and sing.

III

Out of the special cell's most special sense
    Came the suggestion when the light was sweet;
All skill, all beauty, all magnificence
    Are hints so caught, man's glimpse of the complete.

And, though the body rots, that sense survives,
    Being of life's own essence it endures
(Fruit of the spirit's tillage in men's lives)
    Round all this ghost that wandering flesh immures.

That is our friend, who, when the iron brain
  Assails, or the earth clogs, or the sun hides,
Is the good God to whom none calls in vain,
  Man's Achieved Good, which, being Life, abides,

The man-made God, that man in happy breath
Makes in despite of Time and dusty death.

IV

You are the link which binds us each to each.
Passion, or too much thought, alone can end
Beauty, the ghost, the spirit's common speech,
Which man's red longing left us for our friend.

Even in the blinding war I have known this,
That flesh is but the carrier of a ghost
Who, through his longing, touches that which is
Even as the sailor knows the foreign coast.

So, by the bedside of the dying black
I felt our uncouth souls subtly made one,
Forgiven, the meanness of each other's lack,
Forgiven, the petty tale of ill things done.

We were but Man, who for a tale of days
Seeks the one city by a million ways.

V

I could not sleep for thinking of the sky,
The unending sky, with all its million suns
Which turn their planets everlastingly
In nothing, where the fire-haired comet runs.

If I could sail that nothing, I should cross
Silence and emptiness with dark stars passing,
Then, in the darkness, see a point of gloss
Burn to a glow, and glare, and keep amassing,

And rage into a sun with wandering planets
And drop behind, and then, as I proceed,
See his last light upon his last moon's granites
Die to a dark that would be night indeed.

Night where my soul might sail a million years
In nothing, not even Death, not even tears.

VI

How did the nothing come, how did these fires,
These million-leagues of fires, first toss their hair,
Licking the moons from heaven in their ires
Flinging them forth for them to wander there?

What was the Mind? Was it a mind which thought?
Or chance? Or law? Or conscious law? Or Power?
Or a vast balance by vast clashes wrought?
Or Time at trial with Matter for an hour?

Or is it all a body where the cells
Are living things supporting something strange
Whose mighty heart the singing planet swells
As it shoulders nothing in unending change?

Is this green earth of many-peopled pain
Part of a life, a cell within a brain?

[470]

VII

It may be so; but let the unknown be.
We, on this earth, are servants of the sun.
Out of the sun comes all the quick in me,
His golden touch is life to everyone.

His power it is that makes us spin through space,
His youth is April and his manhood bread,
Beauty is but a looking on his face,
He clears the mind, he makes the roses red.

What he may be, who knows? But we are his,
We roll through nothing round him, year by year,
The withering leaves upon a tree which is
Each with his greed, his little power, his fear.

What we may be, who knows? But everyone
Is dust on dust a servant of the sun.

VIII

The Kings go by with jewelled crowns,
Their horses gleam, their banners shake, their spears are many.
The sack of many-peopled towns
Is all their dream:
The way they take
Leaves but a ruin in the break,
And, in the furrow that the ploughmen make,
A stampless penny; a tale, a dream.

The merchants reckon up their gold,
Their letters come, their ships arrive, their freights are glories:

The profits of their treasures sold
They tell and sum;
Their foremen drive
The servants starved to half-alive
Whose labours do not make the earth a hive
Of stinking stories, a tale, a dream.

The priests are singing in their stalls,
Their singing lifts, their incense burns, their praying clamours;
Yet God is as the sparrow falls;
The ivy drifts,
The votive urns
Are all left void when Fortune turns,
The god is but a marble for the kerns
To break with hammers; a tale, a dream.

O Beauty, let me know again
The green earth cold, the April rain, the quiet waters figuring
    sky,
The one star risen.

So shall I pass into the feast
Not touched by King, merchant or priest,
Know the red spirit of the beast,
Be the green grain;
Escape from prison.

IX

What is this life which uses living cells
It knows not how nor why, for no known end,
This soul of man upon whose fragile shells
Of blood and brain his very powers depend?

Pour out its little blood or touch its brain
The thing is helpless, gone, no longer known,
The carrion cells are never man again,
No hand relights the little candle blown.
It comes not from Without, but from the sperm
Fed in the womb, it is a man-made thing,
That takes from man its power to live a term
Served by live cells of which it is the King.
Can it be blood and brain? It is most great,
Through blood and brain alone it wrestles Fate.

X

Can it be blood and brain, this transient force
Which, by an impulse, seizes flesh and grows
To man, the thing less splendid than the horse,
More blind than owls, less lovely than the rose?
O, by a power unknown it works the cells
Of blood and brain; it has the power to see
Beyond the apparent thing the something else
Which it inspires dust to bring to be.
O, blood and brain are its imperfect tools,
Easily wrecked, soon worn, slow to attain,
Only by years of toil the master rules
To lovely ends, those servants blood and brain.
And Death, a touch, a germ, has still the force
To make him ev'n as the rose, the owl, the horse.

XI

Not only blood and brain its servants are,
There is a finer power that needs no slaves

Whose lovely service distance cannot bar
Nor the green sea with all her hell of waves,
Nor snowy mountains, nor the desert sand,
Nor heat, nor storm, it bends to no control,
It is a stretching of the spirit's hand
To touch the brother's or the sister's soul;
So that from darkness in the narrow room
I can step forth and be about her heart,
Needing no star, no lantern in the gloom,
No word from her, no pointing on the chart,
Only red knowledge of a window flung
Wide to the night, and calling without tongue.

XII

Drop me the seed, that I, even in my brain
May be its nourishing earth. No mortal knows
From what immortal granary comes the grain,
Nor how the earth conspires to make the rose;

But from the dust and from the wetted mud
Comes help, given or taken; so with me
Deep in my brain the essence of my blood
Shall give it stature until Beauty be.

It will look down, even as the burning flower
Smiles upon June, long after I am gone.
Dust-footed Time will never tell its hour,
Through dusty Time its rose will draw men on,

Through dusty Time its beauty shall make plain
Man, and, Without, a spirit scattering grain.

XIII

Ah, but Without there is no spirit scattering;
Nothing but Life, most fertile but unwise,
Passing through change in the sun's heat and cloud's watering,
Pregnant with self, unlit by inner eyes.

There is no Sower, nor seed for any tillage;
Nothing but the grey brain's pash, and the tense will
And that poor fool of the Being's little village
Feeling for the truth in the little veins that thrill.

There is no Sowing, but digging, year by year,
In a hill's heart, now one way, now another,
Till the rock breaks and the valley is made clear
And the poor Fool stands, and knows the sun for his brother

And the Soul shakes wings like a bird escaped from cage
And the tribe moves on to camp in its heritage.

XIV

You are too beautiful for mortal eyes,
You the divine unapprehended soul;
The red worm in the marrow of the wise
Stirs as you pass, but never sees you whole.

Even as the watcher in the midnight tower
Knows from a change in heaven an unseen star,
So from your beauty, so from the summer flower,
So from the light, one guesses what you are.

[475]

So in the darkness does the traveller come
To some lit chink, through which he cannot see,
More than a light, nor hear, more than a hum,
Of the great hall where Kings in council be.

So, in the grave, the red and mouthless worm
Knows of the soul that held his body firm.

XV

Is it a sea on which the souls embark
Out of the body, as men put to sea?
Or do we come like candles in the dark
In the rooms in cities in eternity?

Is it a darkness that our powers can light?
Is this, our little lantern of man's love,
A help to find friends wandering in the night
In the unknown country with no star above?

Or is it sleep, unknowing, outlasting clocks
That outlast men, that, though the cockcrow ring,
Is but one peace, of the substance of the rocks,
Is but one space in the now unquickened thing,

Is but one joy, that, though the million tire,
Is one, always the same, one life, one fire?

THE BLACKSMITH

XVI

The blacksmith in his sparky forge
Beat on the white-hot softness there;
Even as he beat he sang an air
To keep the sparks out of his gorge.

So many shoes the blacksmith beat,
So many shares and links for traces,
So many builders' struts and braces,
Such tackling for the chain-fore-sheet,

That, in his pride, big words he spake;
"I am the master of my trade,
What iron is good for I have made,
I make what is in iron to make."

Daily he sang thus by his fire,
Till one day, as he poised his stroke
Above his bar, the iron spoke,
"You boaster, drop your hammer, liar."

The hammer dropped out of his hand,
The iron rose, it gathered shape,
It took the blacksmith by the nape,
It pressed him to the furnace, and

Heaped fire upon him till his form
Was molten, flinging sparks aloft,
Until his bones were melted soft,
His hairs crisped in a fiery storm.

The iron drew him from the blaze
To place him on the anvil, then
It beat him from the shape of men,
Like drugs the apothecary brays;

Beat him to ploughing-coulters, beat
Body and blood to links of chain,
With endless hammerings of pain,
Unending torment of white heat;

And did not stop the work, but still
Beat on him while the furnace roared;
The blacksmith suffered and implored,
With iron bonds upon his will.

And, though he could not die nor shrink,
He felt his being beat by force
To horse shoes stamped on by the horse,
And into troughs whence cattle drink.

He felt his blood, his dear delight,
Beat into shares, he felt it rive
The green earth red; he was alive,
Dragged through the earth by horses' might.

He felt his brain, that once had planned
His daily life, changed to a chain
Which curbed a sail or dragged a wain,
Or hoisted ship-loads to the land.

He felt his heart, that once had thrilled
With love of wife and little ones,
Cut out and mingled with his bones
To pin the bricks where men rebuilt.

THE BLACKSMITH

He felt his very self impelled
To common uses, till he cried,
"There's more within me than is tried,
More than you ever think to weld.

"For all my pain I am only used
To make the props for daily labour;
I burn, I am beaten like a tabor
To make men tools; I am abused.

"Deep in the white heat where I gasp
I see the unmastered finer powers,
Iron by cunning wrought to flowers,
File-worked, not tortured by the rasp.

"Deep in this fire-tortured mind
Thought bends the bar in subtler ways,
It glows into the mass, its rays
Purge, till the iron is refined.

"Then, as the full moon draws the tide
Out of the vague uncaptained sea,
Some moon power there ought to be
To work on ore; it should be tried.

"By this fierce fire in which I ache
I see new fires not yet begun,
A blacksmith smithying with the sun,
At unmade things man ought to make.

"Life is not fire and blows, but thought,
Attention kindling into joy,
Those who make nothing new destroy,
O me, what evil I have wrought.

[479]

"O me," and as he moaned he saw
His iron master shake, he felt
No blow, nor did the fire melt
His flesh, he was released from law.

He sat upon the anvil top
Dazed, as the iron was dazed, he took
Strength, seeing that the iron shook,
He said, "This cruel time must stop."

He seized the iron and held him fast
With pincers, in the midmost blaze,
A million sparks went million ways,
The cowhorn handle plied the blast.

"Burn, then," he cried; the fire was white,
The iron was whiter than the fire.
The fireblast made the embers twire,
The blacksmith's arm began to smite.

First vengeance for old pain, and then
Beginning hope of better things,
Then swordblades for the sides of Kings
And corselets for the breasts of men.

And crowns and such like joys and gems.
And stars of honour for the pure,
Jewels of honour to endure,
Beautiful women's diadems.

And coulters, sevenfold-twinned, to rend,
And girders to uphold the tower,
Harness for unimagined power,
New ships to make the billows bend,

And stores of fire-compelling things
By which men dominate and pierce
The iron-imprisoned universe
Where angels lie with banded wings.

THE FRONTIER

XVII

PERSONS $\left\{\begin{array}{l} \text{COTTA} \\ \text{LUCIUS} \\ \text{THEIR CHIEF} \end{array}\right.$

COTTA

Would God the route would come for home.
My God, this place, day after day,
A month of heavy march from Rome.
This camp, the troopers' huts of clay,
The horses tugging at their pins,
The roaring brook and then the whins
And nothing new to do or say.

LUCIUS

They say the tribes are up.

COTTA

　　　　　Who knows?

[481]

Lucius

Our scouts say that they saw their fires.

Cotta

Well, if we fight it's only blows
And bogging horses in the mires.

Lucius

Their raiders crossed the line last night,
Eastward from this, to raid the stud,
They stole our old chief's stallion, Kite.
He's in pursuit.

Cotta

That looks like blood.

Lucius

Well, better that than dicing here
Beside this everlasting stream.

Cotta

My God, I was in Rome last year,
Under the sun, it seems a dream.

Lucius

Things are not going well in Rome,
This frontier war is wasting men
Like water, and the Tartars come
In hordes.

THE FRONTIER

COTTA

We beat them back again.

LUCIUS

So far we have, and yet I feel
The Empire is too wide a bow
For one land's strength.

COTTA

The stuff's good steel.

LUCIUS

Too great a strain may snap it though.
If we were ordered home. . . .

COTTA

Good Lord . . .

LUCIUS

If . . . Then our friends, the tribesmen there
Would have glad days.

COTTA

This town would flare
To warm old Foxfoot and his horde.

LUCIUS

We have not been forethoughtful here,
Pressing the men to fill the ranks
Centurions sweep the province clear.

COTTA

Rightly.

Lucius

Perhaps.

Cotta

We get no thanks.

Lucius

We strip the men for troops abroad
And leave the women and the slaves
For merchants and their kind. The graves
Of half each province line the road.
These people could not stand a day
Against the tribes, with us away.

Cotta

Rightly.

Lucius

Perhaps.

Cotta

Here comes the Chief.

Lucius

Sir, did your riders catch the thief?

Chief

No, he got clear and keeps the horse
But bad news always comes with worse.
The frontier's fallen, we're recalled,
Our army's broken, Rome's appalled,

My God, the whole world's in a blaze.
So now, we've done with idle days
Fooling on frontiers. Boot and start.
It gives a strange feel in the heart
To think that this, that Rome has made,
Is done with. Yes, the stock's decayed.
We march at once. You mark my words,
We're done, we're crumbled into sherds,
We shall not see this place again
When once we go.

LUCIUS

Do none remain?

CHIEF

No, none, all march. Here ends the play.
March, and burn camp. The order's gone,
Your men have sent your baggage on.

COTTA

My God, hark how the trumpets bray.

CHIEF

They do. You see the end of things.
The power of a thousand kings
Helped us to this, and now the power
Is so much hay that was a flower.

LUCIUS

We have been very great and strong.

[485]

CHIEF

That's over now.

LUCIUS

It will be long
Before the world will see our like.

CHIEF

We've kept these thieves beyond the dyke
A good long time, here on the Wall.

LUCIUS

Colonel, we ought to sound a call
To mark the end of this.

CHIEF

We ought.
Look. There's the hill top where we fought
Old Foxfoot. Look, there in the whin.
Old ruffian knave. Come on. Fall in.

XVIII

Night is on the downland, on the lonely moorland,
On the hills where the wind goes over sheep-bitten turf,
Where the bent grass beats upon the unploughed poorland
And the pine woods roar like the surf.

Here the Roman lived on the wind-barren lonely,
Dark now and haunted by the moorland fowl;
None comes here now but the peewit only,
And moth-like death in the owl.

[486]

MIDNIGHT

Beauty was here, on this beetle-droning downland;
The thought of a Cæsar in the purple came
From the palace by the Tiber in the Roman townland
To this wind-swept hill with no name.

Lonely Beauty came here and was here in sadness,
Brave as a thought on the frontier of the mind,
In the camp of the wild upon the march of madness,
The bright-eyed Queen of the blind.

Now where Beauty was are the wind-withered gorses
Moaning like old men in the hill-wind's blast
The flying sky is dark with running horses
And the night is full of the past.

MIDNIGHT

XIX

The fox came up by Stringer's Pound,
He smelt the south west warm on the ground,
From west to east a feathery smell
Of blood on the wing-quills tasting well.
A buck's hind feet thumped on the sod,
The whip-like grass snake went to clod,
The dog-fox put his nose in the air
To taste what food was wandering there.
Under the clover down the hill
A hare in form that knew his will.
Up the hill, the warren awake
And the badger shewing teeth like a rake.

Down the hill the two twin thorpes
Where the crying night owl waked the corpse,
And the moon on the stilly windows bright
Instead of a dead man's waking light.
The cock on his perch that shook his wing
When the clock struck for the chimes to ring,
A duck that muttered, a rat that ran
And a horse that stamped, remembering man.

XX

Up on the downs the red-eyed kestrels hover
Eyeing the grass.
The field mouse flits like a shadow into cover
As their shadows pass.

Men are burning the gorse on the down's shoulder,
A drift of smoke
Glitters with fire and hangs, and the skies smoulder,
And the lungs choke.

Once the tribe did thus on the downs, on these downs, burning
Men in the frame,
Crying to the gods of the downs till their brains were turning
And the gods came.

And to-day on the downs, in the wind, the hawks, the grasses,
In blood and air,
Something passes me and cries as it passes,
On the chalk downland bare.

XXI

No man takes the farm,
Nothing grows there,
The ivy's arm
Strangles the rose there.

Old Farmer Kyrle
Farmed there the last;
He beat his girl;
(It's seven years past).

After market it was
He beat his girl;
He liked his glass,
Old Farmer Kyrle.

Old Kyrle's son
Said to his father,
"Now, dad, you ha' done,
I'll kill you rather.

"Stop beating sister
Or by God I'll kill you."
Kyrle was full of liquor.
Old Kyrle said, "Will you?"

Kyrle took his cobb'd stick
And beat his daughter.
He said, "I'll teach my chick
As a father oughter."

Young Will, the son,
Heard his sister shriek,
He took his gun
Quick as a streak.

He said, "Now, dad,
Stop, once for all."
He was a good lad,
Good at kicking the ball.

His father clubbed
The girl on the head.
Young Will upped
And shot him dead.

"Now, sister," said Will,
"I've a-killed father,
As I said I'd kill.
O my love, I'd rather

"A kill him again
Than see you suffer.
O my little Jane,
Kiss goodbye to your brother.

I won't see you again,
Nor the cows homing,
Nor the mice in the grain,
Nor the primrose coming,

Nor the fair, nor folk,
Nor the summer flowers
Growing on the wold
Nor aught that's ours.

MIDNIGHT

Not Tib the cat,
Not Stub the mare,
Nor old dog Pat
Never anywhere.

For I'll be hung
In Gloucester prison
When the bell's rung
And the sun's risen.

*   *   *

They hanged Will
As Will said,
With one thrill
They choked him dead.

Jane walked the wold
Like a grey gander;
All grown old
She would wander.

She died soon.
At high tide
At full moon
Jane died.

The brook chatters
As at first,
The farm it waters
Is accurst;

No man takes it,
Nothing grows there,
Blood straiks it,
A ghost goes there.

XXII

A hundred years ago, they quarried for the stone here;
The carts came through the wood by the track still plain;
The drills shew in the rock where the blasts were blown here,
They shew up dark after rain.

Then the last cart of stone went away through the wood,
To build the great house for some April of a woman,
Till her beauty stood in stone, as her man's thought made it
      good,
And the dumb rock was made human.

The house still stands, but the April of its glory
Is gone, long since, with the beauty that has gone,
She wandered away west, it is an old sad story,
It is best not talked upon.

And the man has gone, too, but the quarry that he made,
Whenever April comes as it came in old time,
Is a dear delight to the man who loves a maid,
For the primrose comes from the lime. . . .

And the blackbird builds below the catkin shaking
And the sweet white violets are beauty in the blood,
And daffodils are there, and the blackthorn blossom breaking
Is a wild white beauty in bud.

XXIII

Here the legion halted, here the ranks were broken,
And the men fell out to gather wood,
And the green wood smoked, and bitter words were spoken,
And the trumpets called to food.

And the sentry on the rampart saw the distance dying
In the smoke of distance blue and far,
And heard the curlew calling and the owl replying
As the night came cold with one star;

And thought of home beyond, over moorland, over marshes,
Over hills, over the sea, across the plains, across the pass,
By a bright sea trodden by the ships of Tarshis,
The farm, with cicadæ in the grass.

And thought, as I, "Perhaps I may be done with living
To-morrow, when we fight. I shall see those souls no more.
O, beloved souls, be beloved in forgiving
The deeds and the words that make me sore."

XXIV

We danced away care till the fiddler's eyes blinked,
And at supper, at midnight, our wine-glasses chinked,
Then we danced till the roses that hung round the wall
Were broken red petals that did rise and did fall
To the ever-turning couples of the bright-eyed and gay,
Singing in the midnight to dance care away.

Then the dancing died out and the carriages came,
And the beauties took their cloaks and the men did the same,
And the wheels crunched the gravel and the lights were turned
    down,
And the tired beauties dozed through the cold drive to town.

Nan was the belle and she married her beau,
Who drank, and then beat her, and she died long ago,
And Mary, her sister, is married and gone
To a tea planter's lodge, in the plains, in Ceylon.

And Dorothy's sons have been killed out in France,
And Mary lost her man in the August advance,
And Em, the man jilted, and she lives all alone
In the house of this dance which seems burnt in my bone.

Margaret and Susan and Marian and Phyllis
With red lips laughing and the beauty of lilies
And the grace of wild swans and a wonder of bright hair,
Dancing among roses with petals in the air.

All, all are gone, and Hetty's little maid
Is so like her mother that it makes me afraid.
And Rosalind's son, whom I passed in the street,
Clinked on the pavement with the spurs on his feet.

ROSAS

ROSAS.

ROSAS

There was an old lord in the Argentine,
Named Rosas, of the oldest blood in Spain;
His wife was the proud last of a proud line,
She ruled his house for him and farmed his plain:
They had one child, a tameless boy called John,
Who was a little lad a century gone.

This little boy, the Rosas' only child,
Was not like other children of his age,
His body seemed a trap to something wild
That bit the trap-bars bloody in his rage.
He had mad eyes which glittered and were grim;
Even as a child men were afraid of him.

And once, when old Lord Rosas at a Fair
Talked with his friends, this little boy being by,
An old man called the child and touched his hair,
And watched the wild thing trapping in his eye,
Then bade the child "Go play," and being gone
Wept bitter tears in sight of everyone.

And when Lord Rosas asked him, why he cried,
He said "Because I see, round that child's head,
A sign of evil things that will betide
Through him, being man. There is a blur of red,
A blur of blood, a devil, at his side;
I see his future. That was why I cried.

ROSAS

I am an old, old man limping to death,
And many a wicked thing have I seen done.
Bloody and evil as the Preacher saith
Are ill men's dealings underneath the sun.
But this bright child is fated to such crime
As will make mark a bloody smear on Time."

So he went weeping, while the gossips bade
Lord Rosas not to heed the poor old loon.
Lord Rosas died soon after and was laid
Deep in the pit where all lie late or soon.
Under the flagstone in the chancel dim
Evil and happy fate were one to him.

After his death, his widow ruled the son
Some few short years; some bitter bouts they had;
That old hot proud un-understanding one
Roused night and day the devil in the lad,
She with her plans, and he with all his dreams
Of the great world washed by the ocean streams.

*   *   *   *   *

It was the custom in the outland plain,
That young men, nobly born, should serve awhile
Under some merchant, keeping store for gain,
So to learn commerce, and by service vile,
Sweeping the floors, to sense (with gritted teeth)
Man and this world of his from underneath,

And seeing life, because those merchants' stores
Were clubs and markets used by everyone
For plots and bargains and the test of ores.

ROSAS

Señora Rosas ordered that her son
Should like his father, enter, being of age,
A country storehouse as the merchant's page.

"I do as father did?" he answered, "I?
Sweep out a cheater's office with a broom,
And peddle sardines? I had rather die.
While there's a cow to brand or horse to groom
I'll be a man. So let your merchant find
Some priest or eunuch with my father's mind."

She spoke again. He said, "I will not go."
"Then," she replied, "My son, you shall not eat,
Nor drink, until you do. You tell me, No.
A resty calf that quarrels with the teat
Shall starve, for me. Men, lock this braggart lad
Into his room." They did as they were bade.

They left him in his room all through the day,
With neither food nor drink; they asked him thrice,
"John, here is dinner; will you not obey?"
They brought him raisin biscuits to entice
Him to obey. His friend the horse-herd came.
But John would neither answer nor be tame.

When twilight fell, his mother asked again,
"John, be advised, be wise and do my will.
Why be so headstrong, giving me such pain?
Are you not hungry? There is dinner still.
Say you will go, then come and eat with me."
"I won't," he said. "Then you may starve," said she.

So when the night was dark, the mother said,
"Leave him to-night, to-morrow we shall find
His fal-lals cured and I shall be obeyed.
No cure like hunger to a stubborn mind."
Then through the keyhole to her son she cried
"Goodnight, my son." None answered from inside.

Then, when the morning came, they knocked the door,
"John, will you go?", they asked. No answer came.
One said, "I see him lying on the floor.
He is asleep or playing at some game,
Come, Master John, don't treat our lady so.
Look, here are eggs, be good and say you'll go."

No answer came, so then they craned, and peered
Into the keyhole at the room beyond.
"Pray God," said one, "It be not as I feared,
A lad so proud should never be in bond.
He had his Indian lance-head on the shelf.
John, Master John. He may have killed himself.

John, God, he has. He's lying on the floor,
Look, there's his body. Fetch the crowbars here.
Yes, he is dead, God help us; burst the door,
Run for a doctor, one. A dear, a dear,
He was the likeliest lad there ever was.
Now, Ramon, heave. Now Martin, now Tomás.

Heave." So they hove and entered with the heave;
What they had thought was John was but a pile
Of clothing, rolled to man's shape to deceive.
John was not there, he had been gone awhile.

ROSAS

His bed was cold, a pencilled letter lay
There on his clothes, but John had run away.

"Dear Mother," said the letter, "You and I,
With different souls must live by different laws.
I give back all you gave me, now goodbye.
If I go naked hence, you know the cause.
I keep my father's name. When I am gone
I shall be gone forever. I am, John."

He had gone naked into the night air.
He and his Mother never met again.
He wandered southwards, many leagues from there,
Past the last ranches to the Indian plain,
South to the ranges where the spirits brood,
To daunt wild horses for his livelihood.

* * * *

There on the ranges with a half-wild crew
Of Gauchos, cut-throats, thieves, and broken rakes
He caught and broke wild horses. There he knew
Death as the bloody pay of all mistakes.
There, in the Indian forays he was bred
To capture colts and squaws and scalp the dead.

There he got strength and skill, till all men there,
Even the Indians, spoke of him as fey.
He beat the unbacked stallion from his mare,
And mounted him, and made the beast obey.
And bitted him and broke, and rode him home
Tame as a gelding, staring, white with foam.

There was no horse so wild he could not break him
By hands and one small thong; no Gaucho brave
Wrestling him naked, knee to knee, could shake him,
Or in the knife game give him what he gave,
Or in the midnight's thundering cattle hunt
Pass the mad herd, like him, to turn their front.

But most of all, men saw him take the lead
In war time, when the Indian tribes were out;
Then he paid bloody threat by bloody deed,
And many a painted Indian in his clout
Swung from the oak-tree branches at his order.
The forays ended while he kept the Border.

Then, when the March was quiet, he became
A rancher there, and wed, and gat a child,
A little girl, (Manuela was her name).
Then, as the darling of that frontier wild,
He moved and ruled and glittered and was grim
Among the Gaucho troops who worshipped him.

There was a little child (an old man now)
Who saw him pass once in those Indian days,
"Lean, quick and cruel, with a panther-brow
And wandering eyes that glittered to a blaze,
Eyes of a madman, yet you knew him then
The one man there, a natural king of men."

And cantering with him rode the frontier band
Whooping and swearing as they plied the quirt,
The thousand rake-hells of the South Command
With tossing bit-cups bright and flying dirt

ROSAS

And Rosas far in front; his long red cloak
Streaming like flame before the thunder stroke.

*　　　*　　　*　　　*　　　*

There were two parties in that distant state,
The Whites and Reds, who, for long years, had filled
The lives of all the country with their hate,
The graves of all their churchyards with their killed.
There was no White or Red with hands not brued
Or smutched in blood in that old party feud.

This feud made havoc in the land; yet still
Stopped at the ranges where Lord Rosas rode,
There the wild Indians were enough to kill,
Christians were friends, men held the common code,
"Death to the Indians"; but within the pale
Red against White made murder an old tale.

And in the city where the Senate sat
So violent this bloody quarrel was
That men stole to their business like the cat
By silent streets where pavements sprouted grass,
And at the corners crouched with stealthy eyes,
Peered, and drew back, or flashed upon their prize.

This state of daily murder, nightly plot,
Killing and burning of the White and Red,
Lasted three years, till in the land was not
One home of man without some victim dead;
Then, in the guilty Senate, someone sane
Cried, "Whites and Reds, let us have peace again.

ROSAS

This quarrel makes us beasts in the world's eyes,
Anarchs and worse. O let this murder end,
Before God smites us down to make us wise,
Let us forget our pride and condescend;
Forget the past, and let some leader make
Order among us for the great God's sake."

Then someone said, "What leader? What man here
Could both sides trust? All here are Red or White.
This bloodshed will go on another year,
Or ten more years, until we Reds requite
Some of our wrongs, until the Whites restore
Their bloodied spoils; then peace comes; not before."

Then there was tumult; but the first took heart,
And spoke again, "We are all sick with blood.
Let be old sins and spoilings. Let us start
Another page. Have done with flinging mud.
Bury the wicked past. Let both sides strive,
Since both sides care, to save this land alive."

Then an old White began: "We Whites have striven
Against injustice; not for lust of gain.
You Reds no less. Now in the name of Heaven
Let not our fellow sufferer plead in vain.
Life makes us neither Red nor White, but men
Self-bound in hell. Let wisdom free us then?"

Then the first speaker answered, "It is clear,
Since this great city is so racked with feud,
And we so stained with blood, that no one here
Can bring back quiet to the multitude.

All here have taken part.   Peace cannot come
But by pure hands, into this devildom.

What I propose is, that we straightway call
Young General Rosas and the South Command
(Men of no clique, but trusted soldiers all)
Here to make peace, that so this groaning land
May, with the help of one whom all can trust,
Finish with feud and rise up from the dust."

There was much talking, but since all were tired
Of murder in the streets, and no way shewed
Save this, to bring the quiet long-desired,
It was decreed; and so a horseman rode
To summon Rosas north.   It was not long
Ere Rosas came, with troops, a thousand strong.

Then Rosas wrote to tell them: "I have come,
I and my men, obeying your request;
I shall remain until the morning drum,
Then I go back, unless your House invest
Me with the absolute command, to deal
As I think fit to save the Commonweal."

Much as they longed for peace, this bid for power
Startled the House; they cavilled; they demurred.
At dawn Lord Rosas wrote: "In one more hour
I return South, so send me instant word."
"It makes him King," they thought, yet in their lust
For party vengeance, all agreed they must.

ROSAS

So, with both parties hoping for the lives
Of all their foes, through Rosas, there was calm,
And Reds and Whites both went to whet their knives,
Licking their lips for blood. Without a qualm
The Señate voted, "Let it be agreed
That Rosas come"; and so it was decreed.

So Rosas entered in and took command
  And ruled the city to a Roman peace.
For three long days the cut-throats in his band
Killed at his nod, and when he bade them cease
The town was tame, for those who could not flee
Were killed or crushed. "I rule henceforth," said he.

    *   *   *   *   *

So Rosas came to power. Soon his hold
Gripped the whole land as though it were a horse.
Church, Money, Law, all yielded. He controlled
That land's wild passions with his wilder force.
And through their tears men heard from time to time
His slaves at worship of his clever crime.

And if the city, terrified to awe,
Loathed him, as slaves their masters, he was still
The Gaucho's darling captain; he could draw
Their hearts at pleasure with his horseman's skill.
None ever rode like Rosas; none but he
Could speak their slang or knew their mystery.

So that, in all his bloodiest days, a crowd
Of Gauchos hung about his palace-gate,
And when he went or came they shouted loud
"Long life to Captain Rosas." They would wait

For hours to catch his nod. Their patient rags
Were brighter to his soul than flowers or flags.

And with this Gaucho power he ruled his slaves
By death alone; within his audience halls
Stretched end to end on Indian lances' staves,
Were long red streamers propped against the walls
Crowned by these words "Death to the Whites"; but he
Dealt death to Reds and Whites impartially.

Death was his god, his sword, his creed of power,
Death was his pleasure, for he took delight
To make his wife and daughter shrink and cower
By tales of murder wreaked on Red or White,
And while these women trembled and turned pale,
He shrieked with laughter at the witty tale.

Those two alone could counter Rosas' will;
His wife and daughter; they could bend his mind
To mercy (sometimes) from a purposed ill;
So, when his heart some bloody deed designed,
With merry cunning he would order one
To jail those women till the deed was done.

He had one jest, which was, to bid to feast
Someone most staid, some bishop without speck.
Some city-lord, some widow-soothing priest.
And then to drop red fire-ants down his neck;
Then, as his victim flinched and tried to hide
His pains, Lord Rosas laughed until he cried.

ROSAS

He held no Council; but a Gaucho fool,
Dressed like a British general, played the clown
About the palace, and was used to rule,
Vice-regent for him, when he left the town.
No other colleague had he, but at hand
He kept some twelve, his chosen murder-band.

These twelve were picked young nobles, choicely bred,
Sworn in a gang, the Thugs or Gallowsbirds,
A club of Death, of which he was the head,
That saved the State great cost in lawyer's words;
Writs, prosecutions, bails, defences, pleas,
Were over-ruled by judges such as these.

For, if he wished a person killed, he bade
The victim and the chosen murderer dine
In palace with him, while the minstrels played,
And he was host and joked and passed the wine,
And at the midnight he would see them start
Like friends for home, and all the time the cart

Stood waiting for the corpse at the street-end.
And then the murderer, warming to his man
In the dark alley's chill, would say, "My friend,
I love this talk," and then would jerk a span
Of knife into his throat and leave him dead;
Then tell the dead-cart-gang and go to bed.

Thus Rosas ruled; yet still, he feared the Church
That outlasts men, so, on a day, he cried
"Martin, our patron Saint, shall quit his perch;
No dirty foreign saint shall be our guide.

[508]

Priests of those churches which have Martin's head
Over their altars, shall put mine instead."

This the priests did, with many a pious phrase
About obedience. When the deed was done
His haters gave up hope. They could not raise
Any rebellion against such an one.
He was like god, a prying god, who saw
Even in their souls the breakers of his law.

The terror of his rule hung like a ghost
Thirsty for blood, about men's haunted minds,
Those who dared whisper what they felt were lost;
He ground their fortunes as the miller grinds;
And in their hate men heard the Gauchos sing
"God-given Rosas is indeed a king."

*   *   *   *

There was a soldier in the city there,
Colonel O'Gorman, with an only child,
A girl, Camilla, worshipped everywhere
For merry sweet young beauty dear and wild.
So dear and merry she was like the sun
Shining and bringing life to everyone.

And in the Bishop's house, there lived a priest,
The Chaplain Laurence, who was sick with shame
At all his Church's sitting at the feast
With bloody-handed men who went and came
Unchecked, unbraved, condoned; he longed to break
With such a Church, for his religion's sake.

But, being bent, by training, to obey,
And having hope and an appointed task,
He held his tongue, and wrought, and went his way,
And hid his weary heart behind a mask,
Though it was hard. As City Chaplain he
Was widely known throughout the Bishop's see.

And being fond of music, it so fell
That he and that Camilla sometimes met
In quires and singing places; ah, too well
For those two souls their red and white was set.
For love went winging through their hearts, and then
What else could matter in this world of men?

They became lovers, but by secret ways,
With single words, with looks, in public rooms,
Among a world of spies, in a great blaze,
They hid this splendid secret of their dooms.
Often a week of longing had to end
Without one word or look from friend to friend.

So months of passionate trouble passed them by
Making them happy with intensest pain
That brought them down all heaven from the sky
And by sharp travail made them born again.
Could they but speak, their passionate souls made blind
Trod the high stars in the eternal mind.

Till, in the Spring, Camilla's father planned
To take Camilla to the country, there
(So he informed her) he would plight her hand
To young Lord Charles, his neighbour's son and heir;

"For it is time, my dear, that you should wed
One like Don Charles, a friend and lord," he said.

Yet, seeing white dismay upon her face,
He said, "Be calm; the wedding cannot be
For some weeks more; you have a little grace,
But still, to-morrow you must start with me,
For you must meet Lord Charles, and come to know
Your luck, dear child, that you should marry so."

All through that day she entertained the guests;
All through the evening, as her father's slave,
She sang and played; but when men sought their rests,
Even as the thin ghost treads the church's nave,
She crept out of the house to tell her man,
Laurence, her loved one, of her father's plan.

She reached the Bishop's house in the dead night.
Far off, the dogs barked; then a noise of bells
Chimed, and the abbey quire shewed a light
Where sleepy monk to monk the office tells.
Lorenzo's lamp still burned; he paced his room;
His shadow like a great bat flitted gloom.

There she stood crouched. Two drunken friends went by
Singing, "I feel inclined." She drew her breath.
All the bright stars were merry in the sky.
She called to Laurence, then, as white as death,
She yearned and prayed. His feet upon the stair
Creaked, a bolt clocked and then her man was there.

She told her tale (a bitter tale to both),
Then Laurence said, "Since it has come to this,
This must decide me, and my priestly oath
Must now be broken. I have done amiss
Loving you thus in secret; now our sin
Must front the world; a new time must begin.

I have long known that such a break would come.
I cannot longer serve this Church of ours,
That sees red crime committed and is dumb,
And strows an atheist's path with holy flowers.
We two will fly, to start another life
Far from this wicked town, as man and wife.

And if the life be hard, it still will be
A life together, and our own, and all
That life can offer me is you with me.
If you are with me, let what may befall."
"I, too, say that," Camilla said, "Where two
Love to the depths, what evil can men do?"

They looked a long look in each other's eyes;
Then hand in hand they put aside the past,
Father, and priestly vows; for love is wise,
Love plays for life, love stakes upon the cast,
Love is both blind and brave, love only knows
Beauty in the night a little flame that blows.

When the great gates were opened, and the carts
Set out upon the road, those two were there
Bound for the West with quiet in their hearts.
The beauty on them made the carters stare.

ROSAS

For any error now, if you and I
Help them in this their trouble. Shall we try?"

The Bishop said, that he was deeply touched
To hear such Christian words, that he would strive
To reach these children whom mistakes had smutched,
"To bring them peace and save their souls alive."
"I, too, will strive," said Rosas; "let us learn
First, where they are, and urge them to return.

Now that their first hour's madness must be over
They must a little crave for what was life
Before their fall, and hunger to recover
Comrade or friend, even as man and wife.
Who were your chaplain's friends before the fall?"
"A priest," the Bishop said, "from Donegal.

The priest Concannon was Lorenzo's friend;
He may have heard where they have pitched their tent;
He lodges in the parish: shall I send?"
"No, I will write," said Rosas; so he went
Home to his palace, and in little space
Concannon was before him face to face.

And what with wine and flattery and deceit
He turned Concannon's head and made him tell
The name of those young runaways' retreat
Where they taught school beneath the Mission bell.
Lord Rosas said, "When they return to town
We two will back them till they live it down."

So thinking that the pair were now forgiven,
But for some penance and a reprimand,
Concannon left him, giving thanks to heaven
That mercy's spirit governed in the land.
"They will return," he said, "and wed, and make
Amends for all this passion of mistake."

But when he left, Lord Rosas called his guard
To gaol his daughter; then, when she was fast,
He sent a troop of lancers riding hard
To seize those lovers; ere the night was past
Those two poor souls on whom the world had risen
Were chained like thieves and carted to a prison.

But there their guardian, seeing their estate,
Two gently nurtured souls of no proved crime,
Knocked off their irons, and let women wait
On poor Camilla who was near her time.
He lent her music, and with fruit and flowers
And pleasant talk amused some bitter hours.

But in the midnight, as he slept, there came
A man from Rosas, with a sealed command
Which ran, "Take out those lovers without shame,
Before the dawn, and shoot them out of hand.
This is your warrant. Rosas." This he read
Shocked to the heart, but tumbling from his bed

He called his men to change the courier's horse,
Then risking place and life, he wrote to say
"I have your Lordship's order, but perforce
Wait confirmation, ere I can obey.

These two are boy and girl: You cannot mean
To kill these two, whatever they have been."

He sent this letter to his lord, and then
Took horse himself, because he hoped to plead
With Rosas' daughter, for full many men
Had wrought that gentle soul to intercede
For them, in trouble; but he rode in vain;
She was imprisoned and he lost his pain.

But writing down his news, he bribed her guard
To carry it to her; they took the bribe,
Then tore his note and flung it in the yard
Under his eyes, and mocked him with a gibe.
"No messages will go to her," they said,
"Until your friend, the dirty White, is dead."

When this had failed, he bribed a man to bear
A letter to Lord Rosas in his room,
Pleading Camilla's state. To his despair
The answer came, "Baptise the woman's womb;
Let her drink holy water and then die.
Shoot them at dawn, or hang for mutiny."

One of the Stranglers Gang, who once had known
Camilla's father, brought this final word,
Adding, "Be wise; let sleeping dogs alone.
Do as he bids, for it would be absurd
To disobey, it could not save the two,
Even for a day, and he would murder you."

So, giving up all hope, he took his horse;
But, as he rode, another scheme seemed fair,
"Even now," he said, "things need not take their course;
Her father may appeal," but coming there
He found her father gone, two days before,
To France (they told him) to return no more.

He turned away, but then, one other chance
Remained, to beg the Bishop to appeal;
But some great suit of church inheritance
Had taken him from town. The whetted steel
Wanted its blood. "So they must die," he cried.
And as he rode he felt death run beside.

So, in the dawn, the drummers beat the call,
And those poor children, wakened to be killed,
Were taken out and placed against a wall
Facing the soldiers; then the bell was stilled
That had been tolling, and a minute's space
Was given for their farewells and last embrace.

And Laurence said, "Camilla, we shall be
In death together. In some other life,
If not in this, dear, you will be with me.
O my sweet soul, O my beloved wife,
You come to this through me. O my sweet friend,
My love has brought you to this shameful end."

"Not shameful," said Camilla, "All I did
I have done proudly. As I have begun,
So let me end. What human laws forbid
By love's intenser canon we have done.

ROSAS

Let love's intenser purpose heal the smart
At having done with this poor timorous heart.

I would have loved this little child in me
To suck my breast and clap its little hands,
And rest its little body on my knee,
And be like you; but now the running sands
Come to an end, and we must die, my own.
So be it; we have loved unto the bone."

Then hand in hand they faced the firing squad
Who shot them dead into their waiting graves,
Love for each other was all the wealth they had,
Love that atones, the steady star that saves,
Love that, when shattering bullets broke them blind,
Lit them a path and linked them mind to mind.

* * * * *

When the dog's pity of their death was told,
Lord Rosas straight proclaimed, "I have upheld
This country's morals, as I shall uphold.
There they lie dead, those wicked who rebelled.
I have made pure the country's spotted fame."
The country read the story and was tame.

But man by man, they crept out of the land
Day after day, till there were thousands fled
Who in their exile, swore them to a band
Not to return save over Rosas dead.
Though they lodged earthen like the naked worm
This tale of those poor lovers kept them firm.

[519]

ROSAS

Thousands they were and daily they increased
With arms and faith, until their multitude
Fell on Lord Rosas as the supping east
Falls on the barrens where the spirits brood.
They came resolved to kill him or to die,
"Remember those poor lovers," was their cry.

When Rosas heard their clamour he prepared
His Gaucho lancers. From a rolling hill
Outside the city, all the plain lies bared,
Cornfields, and waters turning many a mill,
Cities and woodlands, and a distance dim;
There Rosas watched his Gauchos fight for him.

But from the sworn attackers came a shout
"Remember those poor lovers," and their charge
Scattered the Gaucho lancers in a rout,
And chased their remnants to the river marge.
Then Rosas turned his horse and rode alone
To some mean dockyard where he was not known.

There, casting loose his horse, he bought a coat
Fit for a sailor, and in this new dress
Shipped as a seaman in a cargo-boat
Then leaving port, for England, as I guess.
There on her deck that night he took his stand
And looked his last upon his native land.

He died in England many a year ago;
His daughter, too; both lie in English soil.
They say that great moon-daisies love to grow
Over Camilla, and with loving toil

ROSAS

Soldiers who drill there train the rose-tree boughs
Over the daisies on their narrow house.

A white rose on Camilla and a red
Over Don Laurence, and the branches meet
Mingling their many blossoms overhead
Drawing the bees, and when the sun is sweet
In April there, the little children lay
"Gifts for the pretty lovers" on the clay.

Printed in the United States of America